"It's not often you get a how-to book at th... but that's exactly what REO Boom is. It's a step-by-step guide to the techniques and strategies that a few people in the know are using to make millions in real estate right now! There's a small window of opportunity and only a select few are taking advantage of it. Read REO Boom to find out how you can be one of them!"

—DIANE KENNEDY, CPA, *New York Times*–bestselling author
of *Loopholes of the Rich*, *Real Estate Loopholes*, and other tax and financial books

"REO Boom is an amazing how-to manual that vividly displays encyclopedic, A-Z knowledge of the REO goldmine that exists in today's market. This book's prodigious amount of useful and instructive detail provides savvy agents an incisive, step-by-step guide to earning a six-figure (or even seven-figure) annual income. But beyond REO listings and sales, when put into action, REO Boom's counsel will lift agents to a new plane of excellence with all of their clients and customers."

—GARY W. ELDRED, PhD, bestselling author of *Investing in Real Estate*

The Shah brothers have made it simple and easy for real estate professionals who want to be successful in the REO game! REOs will be a part of our industry for years to come, and every agent should use the exhaustive resources presented in this book to create his or her individual strategy for success!

—MIKE PAPPAS, CEO/President of The Keyes Company

"If you're interested in making money in the REO boom, this book must find a place on your bookshelf."

—MATTHEW MARTINEZ, author of *How to Make Money in
Real Estate in the New Economy*, *Investing in Apartment Buildings*,
and *Two Years to a Million in Real Estate*

"This book will open your eyes and expand your horizons with regard to real estate opportunity."

—VINCE POSCENTE, *New York Times*–bestselling author of *The Age of Speed*

"Boom Bang Boom! *REO Boom* is the best insiders' guide for real estate agents that we've ever seen. Every agent in our office is getting a copy to use on a daily basis."

—Bestselling authors PETER CONTI and JERRY NORTON, FlipGuys.com

"If you want to take serious money to the bank with REO success, read this book! I'm all about knowing your market, and this book is your key to demystifying the REO process."

—SUSIE HALE, Founder and CEO of eFrogPond, Inc.

"For both the big picture and a detailed, comprehensive guide through the REO maze, look no further than *REO Boom*, written by two experts who live and breathe in this space every day."

—CRAIG CHEATHAM, President and CEO of the Realty Alliance

"Today's real estate environment is constantly changing and competitive. You must have a competitive edge to succeed. *REO Boom* is the blueprint that will give you that edge! A must-read for anyone in real estate."

—GINNY SHIPE, CAE,
Chief Executive Officer of the Council of Real Estate Brokerage Managers

"The REO Brothers have hit the ball out of the park with this book! Not only does it follow an easy step-by-step process on how to own the REO market, the myriad 'Insider Tips' are fantastic! *REO Boom* is required reading for any real estate professional who wants to compete and win in the current market."

—JULIE GARTON-GOOD, DREI, C-CREC, Founder of the International Association of Real Estate Consultants® and author of *All About Mortgages*

"This book is an absolute eye-opener. The REO opportunities that exist for real estate entrepreneurs are incredible. Read this book and run to implement Aram and Tim's easy-to-follow strategies. Then just cash the checks!"

—CLIFF PEROTTI, CRB, GRI, CDPE, International Speaker, Coach, and Consultant, and author of *The Real Estate Entrepreneur*

"*REO Boom* is powerful material. REO properties are an important sector of the Real Estate Market, and this book is the blueprint to help you get your share!"

—MERLE L. WHITEHEAD, President/CEO of RealtyUSA

"Having been in real estate for over twenty years, I know how technical and involved REOs are. After reading *REO Boom* I just wished I had this Book in my arsenal years ago. If you think you can just wing REOs like some do with short sales—think again. You need to make *REO Boom* your real estate bible. To be successful in REOs it takes mastery, and this is the only book you will need to be an REO Master."

—KB COLLINS III, Esq., short sale attorney and real estate instructor

"I've interviewed many who are in the REO business, but the Shah Brothers stand head and shoulders above the crowd. No one has the systems, tools, and mapped-out strategies like those presented in *REO Boom*. This book should be required reading for real estate brokers!"

—JONATHAN D. NICHOLAS, CRB, co-host of the Property Beat Radio Show

AN INSIDERS' GUIDE FOR REA

REO BOOM

HOW TO MANAGE, LIST, AND CASH IN ON BANK-OWNED PROPERTIES

ARAM SHAH AND TIM SHAH

BenBella

BENBELLA BOOKS, INC.
DALLAS, TEXAS

BenBella Books, Inc.
10300 N. Central Expressway, Suite 400
Dallas, TX 75231
www.benbellabooks.com
Send feedback to feedback@benbellabooks.com

Printed in the United States of America
10 9 8 7 6 5 4 3 2 1

REO BROTHERS and REO FARM are the trademarks of REO BROS INC

 is a registered trademark of REO BROS INC

Library of Congress Cataloging-in-Publication Data is available for this title.
ISBN 978-1-936661-56-5

Copyediting by Erica Lovett
Proofreading by Alice Sullivan
Cover design by Michael Fusco, M+E Design
Text design and composition by Maria E. Mendez, Neuwirth & Associates, Inc.
Printed by Berryville Graphics

Distributed by Perseus Distribution
http://www.perseusdistribution.com/

REO Boom
*is dedicated to the tens of thousands
of real estate agents across the country who kept their faith in
the real estate business. Stay strong, follow the systems,
and seize the opportunity.
This book is for you—the real entrepreneurs.*

Contents

[PART FOUR]

MILKING THE REO GAME • 295

"Change is the law of life. And those who look only to the past or present are certain to miss the future."

—John F. Kennedy

ACKNOWLEDGMENTS

THIS BOOK IS a collection of years of experience. What you are reading is our refined trial and error methods that helped us create systems that produced us millions of dollars of gross commission income a year in the REO business.

We would like to thank everyone we have worked with and come across in our day-to-day business operations: all the real estate agents, title companies, finance companies, vendors, banks, sales representatives, and asset managers. Unfortunately we can't name you all because of the confidential nature of the business but you know who you are.

We'd like to specifically thank our REO team for being with us from day one and contributing to our success and your success. Also, to all those agents and brokers we coached one-on-one; every day is a learning experience and a new battle that truly makes you stronger. Keep your eye on the prize and remember persistence wears resistance.

Next, we would like to thank our publisher, Glenn Yeffeth; our editor, Leah Wilson; and the entire publishing team at BenBella Books, Inc. You have a remarkable organization and an entrepreneurial spirit. You have done a whole lot to make *REO Boom* such a huge success. Also, we would like to thank Jonathan D. Nicholas for his diligent marketing and PR work; you put great quality information in the hands of great people; that's explosive!

In addition, we would like to thank the National Association of Realtors, the members of all the local Boards of Realtors, and the Council of Real Estate Brokerage Managers for their visionary thinking in bringing REO education to the forefront. Also, we would like to thank all the REO organizations for continuous education, support, and the up-to-date market stats in the business.

Both of us want to thank our families and our significant others, including Aram's wife Melissa Arias Shah, for their love and support. You mean so much to us and we love you. We also want to particularly thank our parents, Mukesh and Daksha Shah. You taught us the most important values—education, love, perseverance, and faith—that carried us through all the ups and downs in our lives. We are truly a product of your environment.

Finally, we'd like to thank all the real estate agents in the world who know how to face adversity and are not afraid to adapt to change. We hope this book can touch the lives of hundreds of thousands of agents like you, while helping you achieve financial success in your REO business.

We wish we could have had a step-by-step guide when we started. Thus, the value you will receive after reading this book is priceless, as it is our "blood, sweat, and tears." We challenge you to finish this book cover-to-cover within the next thirty days and begin implementing the systems immediately. Our goal is to input seeds into your garden and help you grow them through our trials and tribulations.

Introduction

THERE HAS NEVER been a better time to get into the real estate business. Or maybe we should say, *back* into the business. Like many other types of agents in the marketplace, a lot of real estate professionals have lost their zest, zeal, and "oomph" and have decided to focus their interests elsewhere. Some are on the fence, and some are giving it one last shot.

Well, we're here to tell you real estate is far from over. The real money is now, and what you are about to discover in this book will guide you step-by-step through how to become successful in the new and improved real estate business, real estate bank-owned properties (REOs).

The old days of aggressive prospecting and marketing campaigns with high fixed costs are over. Look around you. Depending on what city you are in, foreclosures, or the REO boom, as we like to say, are all around you.

Some proponents or "experts" say that to make a million dollars in the real estate business, you need to budget approximately 10 percent of your gross commission income (GCI) toward lead generating activities (i.e., marketing and advertising). Who has over $100,000 in this market? While this model might have worked in an "up market," it definitely will face resistance in a "down market" such as the one we are facing today.

Why? Although the game might remain the same, the players have changed. No longer can you list your neighbor's house, because the equity in that home is wiped out or upside down. The pot of gold has shifted from the consumer back to the bank. Thus, the key to success in the real estate world is shifting your focus and energy to the direct source: banks! This requires landing a bank contract and then properly managing the contract to create a pipeline of income by selling bank-owned properties (REOs).

Imagine earning a million dollars without doing print ads, newspaper ads, magnets, calendars, radio, car signs, etc. No more aggressive marketing and prospecting campaigns.

What we will show you in this book is how to convert REOs into your own personal ATM, all on a "shoe-string" budget. It's simple. It's a science. But it's not rocket science. All you will need to follow the system is tenacity and discipline.

Real estate is cyclical, and so the secret formula for success is timing. What separates the top 10 percent of successful agents from the bottom 90 percent is the ability to get in and out of a market at the right time. Remember the housing and condo craze? Practically anyone could have listed a customer's home between 2000 and 2005 and subsequently have sold it for that same customer, making a double dip of commission within a six-month period. Those days are gone. The good news is, something better is here, but the window of opportunity is short. The time to get in is now.

This book is designed for two groups of agents. The first is the real estate agent, team, or broker who is not in REOs but wants to get in. They are tired of attempting "short sales," new construction, or rentals. If you fall into that category, we will show you how to break in the REO game and land a bank contract. You will learn how to build a team, set up systems, and use other vendors' money (OVM) in the interim to bankroll your operations. As an added bonus, we have provided a free detailed asset management list of the various direct banks and outsourcers in the marketplace for you to apply to (see Appendix B).

The second group is those who have dabbled with broker price options (BPOs) or may have been lucky enough to have been assigned an REO property or two through an outsourcer or asset management company but who want to grow their business. If you're a member of this category, we will teach you how to grow and build an automated cash flowing business by obtaining "direct" bank contracts so you can earn over a million dollars within twenty-four months. We will provide you with an REO blueprint: a step-by-step, easy guide to follow.

You will also learn how to implement the "REO Plus Model" to perfect everything from initial occupancy check reports (OCRs), to the BPO, to managing evictions, to issuing your bid-scopes, to inputting listings, to performing monthly marketing reports (MMRs), to managing multiple offers, to managing closings, to the most tedious of it all—reimbursements.

As you will see later, dealing with banks is tricky. Once you are in, you have an unlimited opportunity to create wealth—unless you do not perform. Some banks will not give you a second chance. They do not have the time or patience for error, as they expect to work with only the best.

Finally, this book serves as an added bonus for consumers, both home buyers and investors, who are looking to purchase their own REO property. We will uncover the inside secrets on how things work from a real estate agent's perspective. For example, you will learn why your offer never gets accepted or why a home listing shows "pending sale" the same day it comes out on the market. By the end of this book, you will learn exactly who to contact to purchase your dream home or investment property.

Are you ready to cash in on the REO boom? If so, the material you are about to read will take your real estate business to the next level. No matter where you are in your real estate career, we challenge you to finish this book within thirty days and implement the system by putting bank-owned properties on your priority list.

The work here is a collection of almost a decade of real estate experience, tried and tested in some of the most depressed real estate markets across the country. Our vision—although the voice you'll hear throughout the book is Arams's—is to share this easy step-by-step manual with all the real estate entrepreneurs in the country who step up to adversity and know how to spearhead change with action.

If that sounds like you, turn the page now—let's gets started.

FREE $295 VALUE REO BONUS PACK

As a thank you for reading this book, we have included a FREE bonus pack filled with updated REO bank lists, tips, forms, newsletters, audio, and video interviews. Please log on and register today:

www.reoboom.com/bonus

[PART ONE]

LAUNCHING YOUR REO BUSINESS

Inside the REO Game

*"You cannot teach a person anything;
you can only help him find it within himself."*

—GALILEO

I REMEMBER WHEN no one wanted to learn about REOs.* When
I used to mention REO, agents thought it was some type of company I
was trying to recruit for. It was uncommon knowledge that REO stood
for "Real Estate Owned." Everyone used to say, "REO, what's that?"
Agents used to give me the cold shoulder when I offered to coach them
on obtaining REO listings. Maybe it was because REOs weren't as popular back then as they are now. Or maybe it was because the concept
of REOs was too new to be fully understood. Whatever the reason, one
thing is true: all those naysayers came back.

It's quite obvious that *now* is the perfect time to get into the REO
game. However, there are still many agents out there who don't completely understand the potential of REOs. Some agents think that
REOs are too much trouble, and others think that because they have
one REO account they are set. Because there is so much speculation
on the nature and business of REOs, everyone has a different opinion.

This book isn't for everyone. For those of you who don't want to
learn the insider secrets of REOs, there is no need to continue reading. For those of you who don't want to capitalize on the lucrative
real estate–owned market, perhaps you will be better off taking your

* Whenever we use "I" throughout, we mean Aram.

chances with rentals or short-sales. But for those who want to get into REOs, keep reading. REOs may seem "new," but the fact is that they have been a gold mine ever since the late 1980s.

A HISTORY LESSON FROM THE RTC

In good times or bad, foreclosures have always symbolized savings, value, and deals. If you look at history, we faced a similar REO explosion during the late 1980s when the savings and loan (S&L) banks went belly up, partly because of the underperforming assets such as residential mortgages, mortgage backed securities, construction loans, and other investment securities. Some loans back in the day actually allowed you to assume a mortgage without qualifying. Can you believe that?

To remedy the crisis, Congress passed the Financial Institutions Reform, Recovery, and Enforcement Act of 1989 (FIRREA), an act that created the Resolution Trust Corporation (RTC) to bail out S&Ls, also called "thrifts." The RTC used three techniques to dispose of these toxic assets: direct bulk sales, auction bulk sales, and mortgage securitization (similar to what is going on today). These three services made a lot of people a lot of money; in a very short time span, from 1989 to 1995, many even became millionaires.

FIRREA guided RTC by giving it a very important rule (a rule you will see throughout this book in today's time): Maximize the return from the sale and disposition of troubled assets. Basically, help! Stop the bleeding fast and get government money back! If you have not done so already, please highlight this rule now. It is the backbone of success in your REO career and is the dominant theme throughout this book.

MAXIMIZE THE RETURN OF TROUBLED ASSETS IN THE SHORTEST AMOUNT OF TIME

The RTC followed the rule in three ways. First, it made the S&Ls merge, consolidate, or reorganize. Next, it liquidated their assets and sold them to get the invested money out. Finally, it sold off or shut down the S&L entirely.

Recognize any similarities with today? Do you recall Bank of America merging with Merrill Lynch? Or how about when Washington Mutual was seized and its assets were stripped and sold to J.P. Morgan Chase & Co? The RTC stepped in, placed the thrifts in conservatorship or receivership to supervise and control the S&Ls, and then managed their assets.

However, the RTC couldn't do it alone. It needed a partner: the private sector. The RTC would jumpstart the program, oversee it, and get funding for it, but it couldn't execute the program by itself. Instead, it set the policy and let someone else to do the dirty work. Since the RTC didn't have the expertise or the time to run all the programs itself, it did something better: gave an opportunity to others. With the RTC's initiatives, a door opened up for all the private companies in the marketplace, including auction companies, asset valuation companies, and asset management companies, to handle these opportunities.

Does history repeat itself? Absolutely. Congress created the Troubled Asset Relief Program (TARP) modeling it after the RTC, under the Emergency Economic Stabilization Act of 2008 (EESA). TARP allowed the United States Department of Treasury to purchase or insure up to $700 billion (a.k.a. "bail out money") of distressed assets as a remedy to our subprime mortgage meltdown. Congress's mantra then and now is insure, supervise, and receive.

And here we go again. Except this time it's bigger and stronger than ever. RTC ended up costing the American tax payer approximately $132 billion, which was nowhere close to the massive $700 billion dollar mark we face today. What is the lesson?

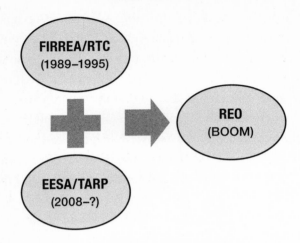

REOs are in abundance and they are here to stay. If RTC lasted six years (1989 to 1995) and resulted in costs adding up to less than half of the damage of today's crisis, then we can reasonably assume TARP (signed into law in 2008) will last at least six years, if not more. My assumption is REOs will last until late 2017, approximately a time and a half longer than RTC.

BIG PICTURE ON REOS

So, why is a bank-owned property called an REO? About a year ago, I was sitting in a "certified REO expert" seminar. It was a three-day "intensive training" on how to become a certified REO specialist and get thousands of REO listings and pretty much retire in three years. Being in the business for quite some time, I had never heard of a so-called "certification," so naturally I was intrigued. As the guest speaker was concluding and "pitching" the audience into purchasing additional software, CDs, DVDs, and other promotional materials—or, as we like to call it, "upselling"—a young attractive lady with curly hair raised her hand with a confused look and asked, "I'm sorry, but what does REO stand for?" Not once throughout the seminar did the guest speaker define REO. I couldn't believe it.

REO stands for real estate–owned property. I've also referred to it sometimes as bank-owned property, because it's actually the bank's or mortgage lender's (or trustees') real estate–owned properties that were acquired by foreclosure. They couldn't sell prior to foreclosure at a short sale, they couldn't sell it at the court house or trustee auction, and now they are forced to take the property back in inventory. Remember, foreclosure is the legal process of forcing the sale of a home so that an individual or a bank can get the money they loaned back.

The timeline of receiving an REO back into inventory varies depending on whether the property is in a judicial state or non-judicial state. Judicial foreclosure procedures are used by states that use "mortgages" as the security instrument for property loans. Non-judicial foreclosure procedures are followed by states that use "deeds of trust" as the security instrument to secure their loan to a borrower. The main difference between the two is court involvement.

Generally, foreclosure in a non-judicial state is a faster method because there is no court intervention. However, in today's real estate market, both processes are taking double the customary time due to the influx of foreclosures, lack of staff, and various court provisions that must be met before the procedure can move forward.

For instance, according to an article written in *The Palm Beach Post* on May 12, 2011, entitled "Painful Stretch: Florida Foreclosures Grow Lengthier," Florida takes approximately 619 days from the time the foreclosure is filed to the time the bank repossesses the home. This is much higher than the national average of four hundred days that was reported in the first quarter of 2011.

A good rule of thumb is to expect at least a year regardless of the foreclosing procedure. An easy way to discern a judicial state from a non-judicial state is whether there is judge involvement.

JUDICIAL—JUDGE REQUIRED (COURTS)
NON-JUDICIAL—NO JUDGE REQUIRED (TRUSTEES)

In a non-judicial state, deeds of trust allow a trustee to commence a foreclosure sale without the use of a court because of the loan contract's "power of sale" clause. This clause states that the borrowers agree to the sale of their property to pay off the balance of the loan in the event of a default. A major difference between deed of trusts and mortgages is that the lender cannot go after a "deficiency judgment" against the borrower if what they eventually sell the property for is less than what was owed on the loan.

NON-JUDICIAL (DEED OF TRUST) STATES

Alabama, Alaska, Arizona, Arkansas, California, Colorado, District of Columbia, Georgia, Hawaii, Idaho, Iowa, Michigan, Minnesota, Mississippi, Missouri, Montana, Nevada, New Hampshire, North Carolina, Oklahoma, Oregon, Rhode Island, South Dakota, Tennessee, Texas, Virginia, Washington, West Virginia, Wisconsin, and Wyoming

---

In a non-judicial state, there are three parties involved:

1. Borrower (Trustor)
2. Third-party bank chooses to look after its interest (Trustee)
3. Bank/Lender (Beneficiary)

The foreclosure process begins with the borrower missing his or her first payment. Once payments fall thirty to ninety days behind, the lender will file a "Notice of Default" with the local county recorder. Once notice is recorded and a copy is given to the borrower, the reinstatement period (depending on the state) begins where the borrower can bring the mortgage current.

Approximately three months after the Notice of Default, a "Notice of Trustee's Sale" is prepared and published in an adjudicated newspaper that runs once a week for approximately three consecutive weeks. In addition, the Notice of Trustee's Sale is recorded in the local County's Recorder's office. If the borrower cannot reinstate the mortgage, the property is sold to the highest bidder at the Trustee Auction on the sale date or the property reverts back to the beneficiary (bank).

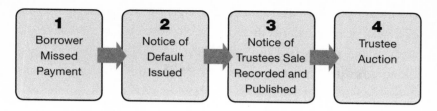

In contrast to non-judicial deeds of trust, a mortgage is a judicial process, because the lender (mortgagee) proceeds with the foreclosure through the courtroom in front of a judge without the use of a third-party trustee. The actual lender must sue the borrower and obtain an order from a judge to foreclose. Thus, there are only two parties involved:

1. Person who borrows money (Mortgagor)
2. Bank/Lender (Mortgagee)

Once a borrower misses payments the lender sends a "Notice of Default" in approximately ninety days. This notifies a borrower that they are in default of their mortgage and that the lender will start the foreclosure proceedings. About a month later, the lender will file a "Lis Pendens," which is Latin for "pending lawsuit." The Clerk of Court for the county will record the Lis Pendens and make it public.

If no "Answer" is filed by the borrower within twenty days stating that they dispute the lawsuit, the lender will begin the filings to obtain a Final Judgment. This is usually done in steps. First, the lender will file a motion for a "Default Judgment" forfeiting the right of the borrower to contest the foreclosure. Next, approximately forty-five days later, the lender will file a motion for "Summary Judgment," wherein the lender will present the case against the borrower to foreclose on the mortgage and grant the lender the right to sell the property at the court house steps via auction.

Upon receiving the Final Judgment, the court will set a foreclosure sale date or "Court Auction" within approximately thirty to forty-five days, and the highest bidder will be awarded the property. Overall, the customary time frame takes anywhere between six months to one year or longer, depending on if the borrower has retained an attorney to file answers and seeks adjournments of hearings to dispute the validity of the foreclosure. With the amount of foreclosures flooding the court house steps, there is just not enough time in a day to schedule cases.

JUDICIAL (MORTGAGE) STATES
Alabama, Alaska, Arizona, Arkansas, California, Colorado, Connecticut, Delaware, Florida, Georgia, Hawaii, Illinois, Indiana, Iowa, Kansas, Kentucky, Louisiana, Maine, Maryland, Massachusetts, Minnesota, Mississippi, Missouri, Montana, Nebraska, Nevada, New Jersey, New Mexico, New York, North Carolina, North Dakota, Ohio, Oklahoma, Oregon, Pennsylvania, Rhode Island, South Carolina, South Dakota, Texas, Vermont, Virginia, Washington, Wisconsin, and Wyoming

Some states allow both a non-judicial and a judicial foreclosure sale, but some types of foreclosure are more common than others. For example, in Alabama, although both types of foreclosure sales are allowed, judicial foreclosure is not common. Therefore, a lender may decide to proceed with a judicial foreclosure and seek a deficiency judgment in court if the defaulted borrower has good income and valuable assets.

However, if the lender does obtain the deficiency judgment, borrowers may act by filing bankruptcy, which again delays the entire process before the bank receives the inventory into its hands. Because laws are always changing, it is important to keep up with your state law, as changes in statute may impact the timeline of receiving an REO property.

NON-JUDICIAL & JUDICIAL STATES
Alabama, Alaska, Arizona, Arkansas, California, Colorado, Georgia, Hawaii, Idaho, Iowa, Minnesota, Mississippi, Missouri, Montana, Nevada, North Carolina, Oklahoma, Oregon, Rhode Island, South Dakota, Texas, Virginia, Washington, Wisconsin, and Wyoming

Regardless of the process, at the end of approximately six months to a year (maybe longer), if the property is not purchased by the highest bidder at auction (court house or trustee) or through pre-foreclosure (i.e., via short sale), the property reverts back to the bank. Also, because the banks are in the business of making loans and not building and selling homes, they need to move these homes as quickly as possible so they can get the tied-up money out and eventually make a loan to someone else.

 **INSIDER TIP**

The sole objective of a bank's sale of an REO is to stop the bleeding. The bank is trying to sell the REO in the shortest amount of time for the most money possible.

The million dollar question is, who gets the bank listing after it reverts back to the banks? You do! That's right, local real estate agents in local markets. Banks have a centralized office somewhere—let's say in Dallas, Texas, or Los Angeles, California—and they have hundreds of thousands of properties they manage. It is nearly impossible for them to assign their entire inventories to one or two "powerhouse" agents, so the market is open and the time to enter is now!

THE REAL ESTATE ENTREPRENEURIAL TIMING

Now is the perfect time to enter the business. If you are already in—congrats! I believe great opportunities come only once or twice in a lifetime, and this is one of those great opportunities that you absolutely cannot miss. All across the United States, foreclosure rates are rising. Chances are, within a five-mile radius of your home, you will see a foreclosure or bank-owned sign outside. With personal bankruptcy rates rising, consumer debt skyrocketing, and the use and abuse of defaulting toxic mortgages such as subprime mortgages and option adjustable rate mortgages (ARMS), our housing market is crashing.

This is excellent news for real estate agents! I know that sounds crazy, but in the scope of things for our business, there is an inverse correlation between the health of our economy and your success in the REO business. The worse our economy gets, the better you do.

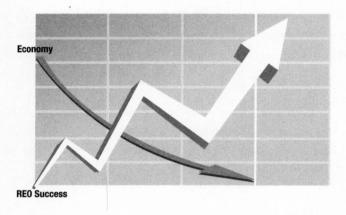

This is the only business where unemployment, bankruptcy rates, mortgage defaults, etc., actually contribute to REO success. It is unfortunate, but as real estate entrepreneurs our job is to step in front of opportunities.

Peter F. Drucker, in his book *Innovation and Entrepreneurship*, defines entrepreneurs as individuals who exploit opportunities created by change and who create something new or different. It is those who step in front of change, embrace it, and act upon it who will succeed.

CHANGE IS GOOD. CHANGE IS REOS.

The market has shifted. Conventional sales are going by the wayside. The wave of the future is REOs. The more foreclosure bank-owned properties there are in the marketplace, the more homes will be listed from the banks, and the faster they can sell. Sure, if everyone goes into foreclosure in the country then there will be no buyers, but because the free market always corrects itself, that will not be the case. If the deal is good enough, there will always be a cash buyer ready to buy.

In DSNEWS.com, a publication tailored to the mortgage default servicing industry, an article revealed that Auction.com, a real estate marketing and disposition services site, offered 35,350 foreclosures, or $2.4 billion dollars of troubled assets, in 2010.

According to RealtyTrac.com, an online marketplace for foreclosure properties, their year-end foreclosure report for 2010 stated a record 2,871,891 U.S. properties received foreclosure filings, up 2 percent from the 2009 stats and up 23 percent from the 2008 report. Basically, one in forty-five homes in 2010 received a foreclosure filing, with five states making up 51 percent of the nation's foreclosure activity: California, Florida, Arizona, Illinois, and Michigan.

Whether you work in these "hot bed" markets or not, foreclosures and bank-owned repossessions are everywhere. Remember the days of listing properties and qualifying buyers with zero percent down? How about the "Ninja or Liar Loans" that the mortgage industry used to quickly approve someone with absolutely no income, assets, or means but who they still deemed had a decent enough credit score to "qualify"? At one point in time, it was almost easier to buy a home than to get approved for a car.

NINJA—NO INCOME, NO JOB/ASSETS

The NINJA, combined with option ARMS, was the formula for self-destruction in the housing market. Remember, option ARM offered the borrower several options to pay every month, including a "minimum payment" option that was even less than the interest-only payment. Because this option was less than the cost of interest, the difference was added to the actual loan balance, leaving the loan to explode and the borrower to lose hope. Imagine watching your loan balance grow every month. What would you do?

This, when combined with the expired government moratoriums (suspension/freeze) on foreclosures, has now resumed the progress of foreclosure activity as banks try to clear out their backlog of properties. What this means is opportunity. A shift in the real estate market has happened. It has gone from conventional listings to REOs, and now is the time to step in front of this boom.

NINJA + DEFAULTS + MORATORIUMS = OPPORTUNITY

THE REO GAME

The REO business is a game. It's easy. It's really like riding a bike. Once you learn, you never forget. If you are one of the one million–plus members of the National Association of Realtors® (NAR), you know the difficulties and intricacies of getting a correctional listing. There are countless hours spent preparing listing presentations, rehearsing, pitching, selling, etc. Each listing is different. Each situation is different. You do not know when or where your next listing is coming from. Sure, over time you will have a sustainable business, but that takes years of building a referral network, good will, and cash flow.

Unlike conventional real estate, the REO business is constant. It's almost guaranteed money! I say "almost" because with a few exceptions, which we will cover later in this book, every listing sells. Don't you wish you could say that about all your other listings? Why do they sell? It is a foreclosed REO, and in the mind of a buyer:

REO = DEAL

Analyze your local multiple listing service (MLS) or county courthouse statistics and you will see foreclosure REO days on market (DOM) are usually less in amount than those on conventional listings. Notice how fast REOs get scooped up. This happens because foreclosure REO listings are predictable sales. I think of each REO listing as an ATM.

REO = ATM

What do an REO listing and an ATM have in common? Your money. Your job is to cash in on the listing as fast as possible and pull out your money, just like with an ATM. Therefore, the key to mastering the REO game is this: the faster you can turn out an REO from the beginning of the process to the end, the faster you will get another property in inventory and the faster you can make your commission.

THE SIX STEPS OF THE REO CYCLE

Once the bank takes possession of a property back in inventory, its main objective is nothing more than to sell it at the highest possible price to minimize its loss on the original loan. So, the bank wants two things from you. First, a decent market price sale, and second, a lightning-fast turnaround time. What do they not want? They do not want to see a fire sale or slash-and-burn mentality. Let's take a look at the six steps of the REO cycle.

1
Occupancy Check Reports
(Cash for keys, clean out, utilities, bank appraisal ordered)

2
BPO Order
(Property visited, broker price opinion submitted)

3
Repairs Bids
(As-is vs. repaired analysis, scope of work, weekly inspections, contractor management)

4
Listing & Marketing Updates
(REO listed, MMRs, LPRs, Magnet marketing plan implemented)

5
Offers & Extensions
(MOM, extensions, negotiations handled)

6
Closings & Reimbursements
(Title management, reimbursements, fall throughs, auctions management)

REO BOOM!

The REO cycle is simple. The faster you can master these six steps, the more REO properties you will earn.

> **Step 1:** Occupancy Check Reports (OCRs)
> **Step 2:** Broker Price Opinions (BPOs)
> **Step 3:** Repair Bids
> **Step 4:** Listing & Marketing Updates
> **Step 5:** Offers & Extensions
> **Step 6:** Closings & Reimbursements

 **INSIDER TIP**

Asset managers that work for banks give listings to agents who can close within ninety days for them. The faster you can master the REO cycle with minimum error, the more business you will receive.

The main difference between the conventional real estate business and the REO business is that in the REO game, approximately 80 percent of your business (i.e., listings) will come from one to three clients. That's all it takes to become a multi-million dollar producer in this business.

When I first started in the REO business, I had absolutely no idea what the potential or outcome was going to be. I thought, great— a bank listing. It will probably take months to sell, I have to do a ton of marketing, spend hundreds of dollars, etc. My first REO listing was a single family home for $288,500. It was a gorgeous home on a lake, five bedrooms, and was built fairly new. The day I got the listing price from the bank I listed it on the multiple listing services and had over thirty showing requests and seven offers within three days. I couldn't believe it. I sold it within four-teen days after the contract being accepted and got my next REO assignment the day after.

—Daniel Brown
Los Angeles, CA
REO listing agent

THE FIVE BIGGEST REO BENEFITS

REO Benefit #1: Consistent Cash Flow (CF)

Imagine saving three to five years of conventional marketing, advertising, prospecting, etc., and developing the same pipeline of income immediately. The main difference between the old-school way of doing real estate and the new frontier of REOs is that now you are actually running a business. You will be transitioning from sales to management. It's actually the best of both worlds. You have a constant pipeline of "hot" deals coming in without the overhead or the hassle of being a home builder. About 60 percent of your time will be dedicated to management, and 40 percent will be focused on sales, managing your contract with the bank, and selling your own REO listings to end customers who are craving deals.

- Time (28%)
- Money (72%)

You can count on a consistent stream of cash flow: pending transactions, closed transactions, and new property "assignments" coming in. You can cut your costs, as well as expand, contract out, budget, etc., because you know exactly how much money you will be making and when you will be making it. Remember, every property sells; it's just a matter of when. Therefore, REOs provide a predictable, quantifiable income.

REO Benefit #2: Banker's Hours

Another benefit to selling REOs is that you will work banker's hours. That's right; once you set up your dream team and systems and master the REO cycle, you work when the banks work: Monday through Friday, 9:30 A.M. to 4:00 P.M. Can you work more? Sure. You can always try to find more customers for your exclusive listings, but it's an option you have, not an obligation.

No more driving around like a taxi-cab driver, no more presenting countless offers that all seem to get rejected or seem to be presented too late, as the property happens already to be "under contract." As an REO agent, you now hold the power. Every REO is a deal, a hot buy that everyone wants. There is an old adage that says "cash is king." I will add to that by saying that in this business:

$$REO = KING$$

Remember what else REO is?

$$REO = ATM = CASH$$

Therefore, back to the old adage:

$$CASH = KING$$

REO Benefit #3: Less Hassle

REOs are a clean transaction. Unlike a short sale, where you wait six to eight months, going back and forth negotiating with the borrower's mortgage lenders (and sometimes two or three lenders) to accept the offer, you have a property that has reverted back to the bank with no mortgages or tons of paperwork to deal with.

Also, because REOs offer "free and clear title" (no liens or encumbrances), it eliminates the chances of your transaction not closing. REOs also require less disclosures since the banks have never seen the property, never lived in it, and do not know the previous owner. Thus, REOs are truly "as-is."

REO Benefit #4: Instant Referral Base

The intangible benefits of an REO are long lasting. Because bank-owned properties drive buyers like magnets, you will build an instant database of buyers. Think about this. In an average year using the REO Plus model (see Chapter 3), you will close 250-plus REOs per bank contract. That's about 250 buyers who will eventually need to sell their home one day.

You have just built an instant pool of customers who have already done business with you. You have an instant referral base waiting. Send them a reminder every year (e.g., Christmas card, etc.), and guess who will be the first person they call when they are ready to sell? You!

REO Benefit #5: Fast Brand Name

Within six months of your start in the REO business, everyone will know who you are without the need of fancy advertising campaigns. You will instantly be recognized as a leading REO agent in your market, and your phone will not stop ringing. Each phone call is a warm lead. Each lead is one step closer to putting a hungry buyer into a vacant REO.

Agents will want to take you out to lunch. Title companies will solicit you. Mortgage professionals will be your best friends and invite you to dinner parties. You will even be invited to mention a few words as a "keynote" speaker at real estate seminars. Buyers and sellers will call the numbers on your signs because they know you are the "direct source" for good deals. This last benefit is a less tangible one that feels great!

THREE BIGGEST REO MYTHS

"It is your decisions, and not your conditions,
that determine your destiny."
—ANTHONY ROBBINS

There are certain moments in our lives that shape us. There are forks and crossroads where we must choose a direction to take. Choices are complex and difficult on the road to success. However, without taking action, we are saying to ourselves that we are content with being discontent. Many people have misunderstandings and pre-conceived notions of why things won't work or why they shouldn't do things. This is fear and pain speaking. These are myths.

The only way of being successful is fighting fear with faith, and pain with passion. You have a choice. You set your own destiny. Take action now. Opportunity is waiting. When you focus on the end result, the middle and the beginning appear. Only you can create your own destiny.

Myth #1: It's Too Late to Get In

Did you know the average foreclosure cost for a single property is approximately $50,000, or as much as 30 to 60 percent of the outstanding loan balances? This was reported in a policy paper by the Mortgage Bankers Association on May 28, 2008, according to several independent studies.

Multiply $50,000 by 2,871,891 (the number of U.S. properties receiving foreclosure filings in 2010) and what do you get? A whole lot of money the lenders are losing. Think about it. Banks have to fix up the homes, pay real estate commission, keep up the taxes, pay insurance, do maintenance, pay attorney fees, etc. They are bankrolling all of these expenses while the property is decreasing in value every month.

BANKS NEED REO AGENTS

Banks need you. They need your expertise. Only you are the expert in your market. They do not have the capacity or money to manage the sales process, and they are hungry for good agents. Now is the most opportune time to get in. After completing this book you will know everything about the REO business and you will be equipped to approach any asset manager in the country. Remember, fight fear with faith and action; you create your own destiny.

Myth #2: It Takes a Ton of Money to Manage the Properties

So you heard through the grapevine that you need over $50,000 to manage a contract for a bank. Maybe you heard you have to pay for each property's electricity and water bill, change locks, clean pools, etc., which can break your bank account. Well, if you heard that, I want you to know it is completely FALSE. Sure you have to change locks and turn on utilities, but you will do this by using other vendor's money (OVM), which you will learn about in Chapter 3.

You will learn exactly how to use OVM with little to nothing out of your own pocket. Actually, the magic number to get started in the REO business is approximately $1,000. That's all it takes to get your contract off the ground. Each agent I consulted with spent approximately $1,000 to go from their first BPO assignment to a closed transaction. The timeline per each property is approximately ninety days:

NEW BPO➡ LISTED➡ OFFER ACCEPTED➡ CLOSED DEAL = 90 DAYS
(7–10 DAYS) + (21 DAYS) + (14 DAYS) + (30–45 DAYS)

After receiving your first property assignment and listing it on the market, the bulk of your time is spent managing the closing process. This time period will depend upon your skills and the speed of your internal network (bank, title-company, mortgage partners, etc.). So within ninety days of receiving your first assignment, you will be able to successfully close your first transaction.

With that closing commission you will be able to invest more BPO assignments (Step 1 of the REO cycle). Sometimes you may receive five or ten new assignments at the same time from one bank or different banks. The more the better; the more visits to the ATM, the better for you.

You usually have either money or time on your side when you first start. If you are low on money, you are high on time. So, if you don't have the money to hire staff, you will be putting in a lot of time in the beginning. Once you have successfully closed about ten REO properties, you will be ready to bring in your dream team and leverage your money to get you more time, and to get you more money!

We call this the 90/10 REO rule. For the first ninety days after you receive your first assignment, you're putting in a lot of time (fifty to sixty hour weeks). You continue to put in a lot of time until you reach your first ten closings, which then allow you to bankroll the growth of your business.

Once your cash flow kicks in, you cut back on your time. You then leverage your time by recruiting your dream team (see Chapter 3). With more free time and a support team, you are ready to domino the effect in generating more cash.

THE 90/10 REO RULE

FIRST 90 DAYS

■ Time (28%)
■ Money (72%)

FIRST 10 CLOSINGS

■ Leverage
■ Money
■ Time

"I can still remember to this day. We spent about $40 dollars on a lockbox, about $120 on changing the locks, $40 dollars on yard signs. Within 30 days we got our first REO listing under contract. I couldn't believe it. My wife and I closed that transaction in 55 days and cleared $3,500. It was so easy, and profitable. We turned our first $3,500 into over $300,000 our first year in the business."

—Rob Smith
Detroit, MI
REO listing agent

Myth #3: You Need Experience to Be Successful

Experience is overrated. What matters more are preparation, diligent work, and opportunity. You can have fifteen years of experience and be complacent. Or, you can have six months experience but work twice as hard and fast as someone with decades of experience.

When I first started early in my career, I was scared. After filling out my contract and submitting back the signed master listing agreement (MLA) to the banks, I almost did not want a property. I was scared because I had never listed, managed, and sold a bank-owned property. I was petrified.

After having several internal conversations with myself, and using some Anthony Robbins self-help techniques, I got over the fear factor and leaned on what I knew best: my work ethic, passion for real estate, and ambition. After closing my first REO transaction, I felt like I had accelerated my learning curve by five years. I had all the experience I needed from managing the REO cycle.

 **INSIDER TIP**

Six months in the REO business is equivalent to eighteen months in conventional real estate. You learn so much, and so quickly, that your learning curve accelerates three times as fast.

If you have a real estate license, feel a passion for real estate, know how to enter a listing in the multiple listing service (MLS), and have the discipline to follow the different models in this book, you will have more than enough experience and confidence to speak to any asset manager in the country.

Experience is a mindset. Set your mind to be disciplined and hardworking, and ignore the three biggest REO myths. If you follow the systems outlined in this book with the correct mindset, we guarantee you can and will be successful in the REO business.

POINTS TO REMEMBER

- Hard work, passion, and discipline outweigh experience.
- It takes less than $1,000 to start.
- 90/10 REO Rule: Your first ninety days is time intensive and cash poor until your first ten closings. Then you will have more cash to leverage and hire your dream team so you can invest less time to produce more cash.
- REO = ATM = CASH.
- REO Cycle = six steps. The faster you can master it, the more listings you will receive.

- REOs are 60 percent management and 40 percent sales.
- Five Biggest REO benefits: consistent cash flow, banker hours, less hassle, instant referral base, and fast brand name.
- REO contracts are a million dollar business. Eighty percent of your business will come from one to three clients.
- The faster you can close within ninety days, the more listings you will receive from asset managers.
- REOs are here to stay. Expect a window to about year 2017.
- Banks want you to maximize the return of their troubled assets in the shortest amount of time.
- REOs are easy, predictable, and constant. They are a great opportunity that comes only once or twice in a lifetime. The window is short. The time to act is now.

Getting in with Asset Managers

THE MILLION-DOLLAR REO CONTRACT

Dealing with banks is like dealing with a first-time home buyer. They want everything for nothing, they want it fast, they want it now, and they think they are always right. Is it worth it? Absolutely. One direct bank contract will make you a million in gross commission income (GCI) within a year or two. Two direct bank contracts will make you two million. Three to five will net you $1 million in your pocket. Assuming, of course, you follow Chapter 4 through Chapter 9 and manage your bank contracts right.

Here are the breakdowns from what you can expect. Each company I coached achieved $1 million in GCI within the first twenty-four months. Here is the formula to gross $1 million dollars per direct bank contract:

Inputs (What you need flowing in)
- 3 new BPO assignments/properties a week minimum
- 30 "active" listings a month (i.e., active on the MLS)
- 100 or more total properties in inventory at any given time
- 35 percent or greater "in-house buyer" ratio (i.e., you find your own buyers and make both sides of the commission)

Outputs (What you will get flowing out)
- 250-plus closed REO transactions in a year
- $1 million-plus in gross commission income (GCI)

This assumes the average sales price (SP) is over $120,000, the average listing commission (LC) received is greater than 2.5 percent, and you are making 3 percent as the selling agent (SC) representing the buyer at least 35 percent of the time. Remember that with REOs, unlike with short sales, the listing agent is able to keep both sides of the commission from the listing and selling side. Therefore, if you as a listing agent procure a buyer for the property, you will obtain the commission from both the listing side and the selling side.

In fact, for each company I coached, they averaged approximately $120,000 to $150,000 in their selling price and a 35 to 40 percent in-house buyer ratio. They found their own buyers and made both sides of the commission (listing + selling) without spending any additional monies on promotions, advertising, or marketing.

$$\$120,000 \text{ SP} \times 2.5\% \text{ LC} \times 250 \text{ CLOSINGS} = \$750,000$$
$$\$120,000 \text{ SP} \times 3.0\% \text{ SC} \times 87 \text{ CLOSINGS} = \$313,200$$

$$
\begin{array}{lr}
\text{LISTING SIDE:} & \$750,000 \\
+ \text{ SELLING SIDE:} & \$313,200 \\
\hline
\text{TOTAL GCI} = & \$1,063,200
\end{array}
$$

This is in line with the National Association of Realtors®, which stated the national median home sales price on existing homes for January 2011 in the United States is approximately $158,800. Do the numbers using these figures, and your GCI comes out to approximately $1.4 million.

 **INSIDER TIP**

Some banks offer you 2.5 percent to list, some offer 3 percent. Also, the majority of them always offer the co-operating agent 3 percent plus bonuses for finding the buyer. So the minimum you can get is 2.5 percent, and the maximum is up to you!

Also, remember that only 35 percent (approximately 87 closings out of 250) have to come from you finding your own buyer. Anything above this percentage will require you to invest money into marketing and advertising which will be eating away from your bottom line profits.

In the REO business, you will make approximately 35 to 50 percent net profits before taxes (after all expenses) depending on how well you can control and adjust your expenses. Adjusting is sometimes more important than controlling, because as you are looking at your "pending sales" waiting to be closed on, you need to know when to staff up (i.e., bring on more assistants) or cut down in the upcoming months to offset your pending sales. Therefore, using a conservative figure per direct bank contract, you are looking to gross $1,063,200 and net $372,120:

$$\begin{array}{r} \text{TOTAL GCI} = \$1,063,200 \\ \times \quad 35\% \\ \hline \$372,120 \text{ NET} \end{array}$$

Once you master one direct bank contract, you can replicate this and add on until you can achieve a goal of three direct bank contracts to net you a million dollars.

3 DIRECT BANK CONTRACTS = $1 MILLION NET

THE MASTER LISTING AGREEMENT (MLA)

Landing a master listing agreement (MLA) is like getting drafted to play major league baseball without throwing a 98 mile-per-hour fastball. With hard work, passion, and focus both can make you a millionaire. An MLA is your exclusive right to manage, market, and list bank properties for a specific time period (usually ninety days).

This means whichever property the bank assigns you is yours exclusively until you sell it or they remove it. What it doesn't mean is that you are the only one who will receive properties in your area. You receive new property assignments based on performance. So as long as you are doing your job correctly and adhering to your MLA, the bank will not remove the property from you. However, the minute you underperform or violate your MLA, you're warming up the bench or being demoted to the minors.

YOU RECEIVE NEW PROPERTY ASSIGNMENTS BASED ON PERFORMANCE

When I first started I made a brutal misstep: I repeated the same mistake twice. I was completing a BPO and forgot to make the adjustments for the living area of the comparable properties, as theirs were greater than the subject's. About a month later, after doing twenty-five flawless BPOs, I made the same mistake and the asset manager chewed me out. He remembered the exact mistake I had made the first time. He even recalled the REO ID of the property and address. Maybe the second time triggered his annoyance over the first, but he told me one more mistake would mean a "performance issue." I never repeated that mistake again.

In fact, what I tell my team and agents that I coach now is: never make the same mistake twice. If you can heed one piece of advice, make it this one: write down when the asset manager says you did something wrong (whether you agree or disagree) and never repeat that mistake again.

NEVER MAKE THE SAME MISTAKE TWICE

 **INSIDER TIP**

Each asset manager at a bank has a different style and tolerance. You will get three different answers from three different asset managers even if they work in the same company. The best thing you can do is write down their likes and dislikes so you don't repeat the same errors twice.

It is necessary for you to read the master listing agreement (MLA) you have with your bank. Read it twice. When I first started, I did not pay any attention to the MLA because I was so happy to have "gotten in" with a bank. However, what I later came to realize was that asset managers are held responsible for agents adhering to the MLA. Make sure you do not put your asset manager's job on the line. Read the MLA and follow each section of it carefully.

After landing your first contract with a bank, execute! Go above and beyond every time. I always tell my agents or mentees to exceed expectations of asset managers each time you communicate with them. Think of it like this: each time you are able to speak with them on the phone, or send an email to them, you are given the opportunity to sell yourself even more, an opportunity that other agents are begging to have.

Consider your asset manager as your boss. Ultimately, you want that person to depend on you to follow the MLA and guidelines, maximize performance measures, and help the asset manager maximize his own goals. When an asset manager is assigning a property, you want him to assign it to you without a moment of hesitation.

To ensure this positive relationship, use every opportunity you have to sell yourself, your performance, and your results to your asset manager. Every phone call, email, and conversation with an asset manager is like gold. You must take advantage of the opportunity and always exceed his expectations. If you are on a conference call with five other REO agents, make sure you speak up and show off. Ask important questions but never ask something that you can look up in your MLA. Get him to confirm that you are doing a good job. Make him aware of your performance, and then go above and beyond his expectations.

Once you have impressed an asset manager, you need them to write a letter of recommendation for you. Don't be afraid to ask. When I was coaching an agent back in the summer of 2010, I remember the agent telling me, "But I'm happy with only this bank. I don't need any more banks, so why should I ask for the letter of recommendation?" Here was my response:

There are many reasons behind asking for a letter of recommendation besides the obvious opportunity of acquiring new accounts with other banks. First, you are getting the asset manager to put in writing his recommendation for you. Having him simply write this reassures new banks of the fact that they can trust you; it serves as reinforcement to them that they can count on you.

Second, you are getting your foot in the door to get a letter of recommendation from the director of the asset manager (his boss). It is much more effective to start with a letter from an asset manager than to go directly to the top for a letter of recommendation. Once you have the letter from the asset manager, you can request a meeting with the director and have the asset manager's letter as a selling point for the director to write his own letter of recommendation.

Third, if at any point you get stuck in the mud with an asset manager, the effect will be somewhat mitigated by him having written a letter of recommendation in the past. Think of it as if he is endorsing you. It's very tough for an asset manager to go from the point of writing a letter of recommendation for you to completely disliking your performance.

After your performance is above par and you are able to obtain letters of recommendation from the top management or at least an asset manager, you can go out and market yourself to other banks. Very few agents are confident enough to ask for a letter of recommendation because they do not possess the know-how to execute 100 percent of the time.

Unlike them, and unlike those who haven't read this book, you will know exactly what banks want, exactly how to give them what they want, and exactly how to earn $1 million net within twenty-four months as an REO agent. Keep on reading!

ASSET MANAGERS EXPOSED

If there is one thing that you need to master from this book, it is to know what asset managers want and then deliver it to them. This one element will make or break you. Asset managers are simple. They only want three things from you: experience, on-time closings, and bonuses. Are you knowledgeable about REOs? Do you have systems in place? Can you follow through and close on schedule? Can you help them meet their monthly quotas and bonuses?

If you can master these three things and perform well, you will get your three (or more) new BPO assignments a week. If not, you may get a second chance, and maybe even a third, but rarely have I ever seen someone get more than three strikes against them before they get all their properties re-assigned (removed and given to another agent) or receive the dreaded "termination" notice.

Asset managers hate re-doing your work. They are not getting paid to babysit you. It is your responsibility to know what to do and how to handle each situation. If you have a three-hundred page sales guide manual (a rule book addendum to your MLA) that you are expected to read cover-to-cover before you receive your first BPO, then you better have read it. If you don't perform well, they have to press the reset button. This is the button that re-assigns your property to another agent, getting a "second opinion BPO," and essentially re-starting from scratch.

Every time you speak, email, or chat with an asset manager, do not spend the time ineffectively. Do not ask a question that can be looked up in your MLA. Do not ask a question that can be answered via an internet search.

 **INSIDER TIP**

Before you email or ask a question on the phone, make sure the answer is not already stated in the sales guideline manual. This is one of an asset manager's biggest pet peeves.

Imagine being an asset manager and having hundreds of agents asking remedial questions. How would you be able to get any work done? Asset managers receive over 250 emails on any given day. Now imagine this: the emails they get from you as an agent are not to ask silly questions, not to ask for guidance, not to ask situational questions, but to show off your performance. You will impress them, rather than annoy them, and stand out from the crowd!

From the initial occupancy check and BPO assignment to closing, minimize your communication to an asset manager until it's time for you to show off. Let them know that you are working 24/7, that you know what you are doing, and that they can count on you to close.

When I first started, I made the mistake of emailing an asset manager questions that were somewhat contradicted by the MLA. I immaturely thought that by pointing out a gap in the master listing agreement, I would seem smart. I remember that day perfectly. Here is what I wrote to the asset manager:

> Dear X, I am completing this BPO on a duplex; however, the master listing agreement states that duplexes are considered multi-family homes while the tax record on this property indicates a single family zoned residence. Please advise.

The response:

> Please do not email me questions that can be answered by looking at the FAQ section.

The take-away: Asset managers simply do not want to be bothered with simple questions such as the above. Do not try to impress your asset managers by pointing out inconsistencies with policies and procedures. They don't care.

The Three Biggest Asset Manager Pet Peeves

While speaking to several hundred asset managers across the country, I listed the top three asset manager pet peeves about doing business with REO agents (new or seasoned):

1. **Forced to Babysit.** They hate babysitting work. They want someone confident who understands the local market. If they give you a task, they want it done on or before the deadline. They do not want to ask you more than once for the deliverable. Asset managers look at fifty to sixty BPOs a day, which gives them approximately two or three minutes to review each one. The last thing they want to do is ask, "Where is xyz agent's BPO?"

2. **Left Blind.** They hate the dark. They want to know every detail of every transaction for each property. Whether they look at it or not, they need it. First, it gives them the ability to make a decision on pricing or repair, and second, they need to cover their assets (CTA) from their manager in case something goes sour in the transaction. They feed off of information; information is light. Because each bank usually has its own web-based log-in portal to communicate, make sure you update that every day on each property. If a repair wasn't done correctly, update that. If you had only one showing request from other sales agents this week, update their system. Always cover your assets (CYA) as well. It makes you look sharp and shows you are detailed. Always keep the asset managers informed.

3. **No Results.** They hate non-performers. They want results, not efforts. They can't stand excuses and the "we tried our best" mentality. They want results. They have their goals and numbers to meet, and they want an REO agent who can meet and exceed their goals. Communication is crucial, especially with numbers. Since asset managers usually have spread sheets and financial data they are looking at all day, you want to communicate with them in their language. Quantify everything, including the number of days on the market, the list price versus the

sold price, the number of showings, etc. The last thing an asset manager wants to see is an agent who is non-responsive and who can't get results. The ultimate outcome of being results-driven is closings. You must close every transaction in time, at worst—the earlier the better.

Below is an email from an asset manager. Although we changed the name for confidentiality purposes, pay close attention the tone and notice the annoyance this asset manager felt. This is the type of email you do not want to have waiting for you in your inbox:

Time is of the essence. [Being timely] is something that I would like to see more of. February was an extremely disappointing month for me and I wanted to express this issue. I did not make my goal and could have with a little more help and determination from my agents. Every day I put effort into these closings: calling buyer's title, HOA, and even lenders. Unfortunately, I have not seen the same dedication from my agents. Going forward, I need you to take ownership over these deals and closings. I need realistic dates, extensions, and updates. I need fast responses to my emails. I need the attached form **COMPLETELY** filled out with every offer.

The minute the deal is accepted, I need **contracts back in five days**. Management will be canceling deals on day six going forward. When contracts are signed, I need you on top of the buyers for condo approval and I need you on the HOA to send the updated estoppels. I understand title companies are slow, non-responsive, and hard to work with, but if we can get all our ducks in a row and give them everything they need there is no excuse. If buyers are dragging their feet there will be no more extensions; we have a date and everyone needs to commit to it. We cannot make a game of it with the attitude "it will close when it closes." I have monthly goals that I need to meet and I need agents who want to help me reach them and go beyond those numbers. I want to know that I can depend and trust in these deals that you are bringing me. Spring is coming, which means more properties. Your closing performance is what reflects more inventory going forward.

—Mary Brown,
Asset Manager

ASSET MANAGERS PROFILED

Overall, bank asset managers tend to be reserved. They are not the typical real estate person. I believe they adopt such personas intentionally to stay in the shadows of the business. They do not announce they are asset managers (they do not want to be bombarded with inquiries), they do not have business cards, and they do not give out free information.

Therefore, if you are in a real estate meeting, chances are you will not know who is an asset manager. They want privacy so they can get their job done, meet their quotas and deadlines, and go home just like the rest of us. They are employees who work for banks or outsourcers with required to-do lists for each property they manage.

When I was first getting started in the business, I went to a real estate conference in Las Vegas. There were hundreds of booths and personnel all over. Each booth had about fifty real estate agents all looking for and waiting to talk to an asset manager. I knew my chances of squeezing in there was slim to none, so I decided to go the lounge area and grab some food. After ordering, I met a very nice lady and naturally started up a conversation. I told her that I was in the REO business and was an agent in Florida and shared with her some of my experiences with properties.

Within fifteen minutes she opened up and that told me she was an asset manager who worked for a national bank. I couldn't believe it. I quickly handed her my business card and even offered to buy her a drink (pretty risky move). About a month later I got an email with an invitation to apply as an agent for her bank to handle the REOs. I got in!

DIRECT VERSUS OUTSOURCER ACCOUNTS

One of my agents once asked me, "What is the difference between an asset manager and a sales rep?" I answered back, "Nothing, from your perspective." You must treat whoever feeds you properties like gold, whether their title says "asset manager" or "sales representative." Generally, however, the difference between the two positions depends on whether they are working for a bank directly or working with an outsourcer.

After a bank gets the foreclosed property back in inventory, it has to make a choice. It can either sell the property directly through its in-house "sales representatives" (bank employees) by assigning properties to direct REO listing agents (you), or give it to a wholesaler or "outsourcer" who hires "asset managers" (employees of outsourcers), who handle thousands of properties on a flat fee base for the banks.

These asset managers will then allocate properties to different REO listing agents throughout their local markets. We use sales rep and asset manager interchangeably throughout this book because regardless of who it is, you will treat both of them equally as your boss. The breakdown looks something like this:

BANK INVENTORY REO

DIRECT	OUTSOURCERS
■ Uses direct REO agents	■ Employed by banks to manage large volumes of properties
■ Pays high commission	
■ Gives high volume to their "IN-NETWORK" direct REO agents	■ Payed "per file" fee (e.g., $800–$1,500)
	■ Gives less volume/ commission to REO agents but employs more agents

A bank's main objective is to get the highest price for its REO asset in the shortest amount of time. It also believes in using both channels (both direct and outsourcers) so one side doesn't have too much power. Typically, when banks have a lot of volume, they bring on outsourcers to help them manage the workflow; otherwise they would have to incur a lot of time and money in hiring and firing staff (i.e., their sales representatives).

On average, each sales representative has up to five hundred REO assets to manage at one time in their territory. During slow inventory levels, they can drop down to about one hundred REO assets.

Conversely, when times are slow and the inventory level is low, banks reduce the volume of REOs given to outsourcers, keeping the inventory internally and assigning it to direct REO listing agents.

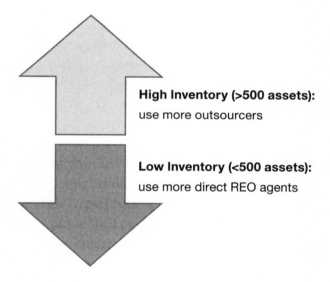

High Inventory (>500 assets):
use more outsourcers

Low Inventory (<500 assets):
use more direct REO agents

 **INSIDER TIP**

Typically banks keep 60 percent of the REO inventory internally and outsource 40 percent. During slow times, banks keep 80 percent and outsource 20 percent so they can avoid employee cutbacks.

A typical direct REO bank structure team would look something like this:

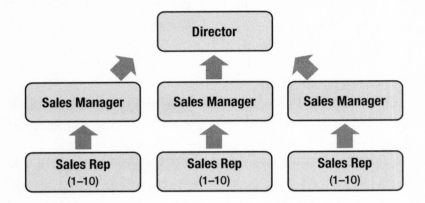

On average, an REO division at a bank that works with direct REO agents usually has a team of thirty per territory, which starts off with a director (for instance, "Director of REO Dispositions"). Each team will cover large grounds of territory with centralized staffing and support at their headquarters (e.g., Dallas, Texas). So a team may set up a remote office somewhere in California and cover the West Coast. Another team may be in Florida and cover the Southeast.

Under the director will be about three sales managers who supervise the sales representatives (your boss). Each sales rep, approximately ten per sales manager, will have territories throughout each state or even multiple states. Their work load is managed by an inventory level ranging from one hundred to five hundred REOs.

Similarly, instead of you dealing directly with the sales rep, you would deal directly with an asset manager who works for an outsourcer. Think four to five big real estate brokerage offices combined. They have enough liquid money to manage thousands of properties at once. Usually they have about $5,000 per property in working capital. They, in turn, would assign you properties depending on the zip codes you service.

The question is, which contracts do you want to obtain? Both! Your job as an REO agent is to get into all the direct accounts. If you're starting from scratch, you will most likely get an outsourcer account before a direct account. This is good. You want to build a track record of performance before stepping up to the big volume. Regardless, your goal is to get both. Remember, to net a million dollars, you need three direct accounts. Any additional outsourcer accounts are just gravy!

THE FIVE BIGGEST DIRECT ACCOUNT BENEFITS

1. **Working with Decision Makers.** You are working directly with the bank's employees. You know what they want, when they want it, and what it takes for you to help them meet their numbers. You have power to express your opinion. Plus, there are no middle men involved as there would be if you were working with an outsourcer. You have control in marketing, listing, and selecting certain vendors—from locksmiths to repair specialists.

2. **Earning Full Commission.** As a direct REO listing agent, you will always make your listing commission (e.g., 2.5 percent or 3.0 percent). However, you also can get the selling agent or cooperating agent's side if you find your own buyer. Plus, many times banks will offer you incentives to close deals by certain months (e.g., $5,000 bonus if closed by July 31, 2012).

3. **Earning Guaranteed Commissions.** You will always make your listing side commission. Unlike working with outsourcers who sometimes pay you to complete one or two steps of the REO cycle (e.g., $50 for a BPO), your listing commission is locked in.

4. **Obtaining High Volume.** Generally, working direct with the banks means you receive a higher volume of properties than if you work with outsourcers. Obviously, this depends on your performance, but the better you do the more properties you get.

5. **Using Leverage.** Once you excel and perform with one direct account, you have the power to approach other direct accounts. When you work with a direct account you become a "mini outsourcer." This takes skills and talent. If you perform well, other banks pay attention. In this business, knowledge is scarce. If you can manage the account, perform well, and produce stats, you can take that reputation and go after other large institutions.

 **INSIDER TIP**

> The biggest asset in the REO business for a bank is an agent who can
> perform. Because the learning curve is so steep, once you get a good
> handle, you will be what every bank is looking for—a seasoned agent.

Unlike with a direct account, when you work with an outsourcer
they may not give you the high level of volume you need. For example,
my direct accounts make up 70 percent of the REO listings that come in,
and my outsourcer accounts make up 30 percent. So, if you are receiving twenty new BPO assignments a month from a direct account,
expect to receive six new BPO assignments from an outsourcer.

Another thing to watch for with an outsourcer is that they may
not hire you for the actual management or listing of the property.
Remember, there are six steps in the REO cycle. Many times, you may
register and get set up with an outsourcer account, but your asset manager will simply pay you a flat fee to just do steps one and two for
them—the initial occupancy check and BPO.

For example, some outsourcers pay as little as $25 for a completed
BPO, while others may pay as much as $250. Sometimes, if they like
your work, they may come back to you and ask you to manage and list
the property. Therefore even though you want both types of accounts,
your goal should be to go after direct accounts as they will get you to a
million dollars faster.

HOW TO LAND YOUR FIRST BANK CONTRACT

If you think doing BPOs for $50 or submitting your résumé to hun-
dreds of banks will land you a contract—think again. This alone does
not work. I have heard many stories from asset managers, some so
shocking you wouldn't believe it. One of the best stories I heard was
about when an asset manager was approached during a local conference by a female stripper. The asset manager told me, "All I could
remember was high heels and a business card." She was literally hired
by an agency to pose as an "employee" of a real estate firm and seduce

asset managers, in the hopes of that real estate firm being awarded a bank contract.

Real estate agents have tried everything under the sun to get a contract, from begging to bribes. None of those things work. And the absolute worst thing you can do is go to an asset manager and "product puke" on them. Before you get their names or even shake their hands you are sixty seconds in to why your company is the biggest, best, strongest, fastest, etc. You have to understand that if you find an asset manager (they are very covert), the last thing they want to talk about is business.

Instead of trying to sell yourself and your skills, try talking to an asset manager as if they were any new acquaintance. We know that sounds counter-productive, but it is the truth. Think about the last time someone walked into your office or called you on your cell phone cold turkey. What was the first thing that went through your mind? Your defense walls went up and you automatically thought "NO" or "NOT INTERESTED" before the person said one word. Same goes with asset managers.

I went to a yearly training in Florida once for a national bank. They had invited both outsourcers and their own direct REO listing agents. The outsourcers internally invited local REO agents so they could get trained as well. The event was hosted at a five-star hotel and was attended by well over five hundred people; it started each morning at 8:30.

As I grabbed my Starbucks Skinny Vanilla Latte and walked to my seat, I heard the following from the director of the bank: "After I get off this stage, do not approach me with your business card and do not ask me about becoming a direct REO listing agent." He had given us his upfront expectation for peace within fifteen minutes of the two-day live training event. Imagine, five hundred hungry REO agents rushing him every opportunity they see: in the bathroom, at the coffee stand, at lunch, at his car, etc. It would have been a nightmare.

Getting in with asset managers is all about building relationships. Get to know them. Let them get to know you. Be sincere. Talk about your kids, weather, basketball, a recent move—anything other than business. I always coach my agents to use The REO FARM™ Play when meeting an asset manager in person (or over the phone) for the first time.

THE REO FARM™ PLAY: TALK ABOUT THE FARM

F—Family   R—Recreation
A—Association   M—Motivation

The REO FARM Play can be mixed and matched depending on the situation you are in. You do not have to start talking about family if you notice an opportunity to jump into recreation. The goal is to build rapport and a relationship before discussing business.

The first topic is "F" or **Family**. Talk about yours first, and then let them talk about theirs. This discussion can range from kids, to spouses, to family values. For example, you can ask about where the asset manager is originally from, if they have kids, if their kids are grown, how they started in this career, etc. Remember, get the asset managers talking. The more they talk and the less you do, the better.

In the back of their mind they will think you will be great to deal with on a day-to-day basis (great listener) and you will rack up some subconscious mental points in your favor. I use this topic all the time; it works great.

Next is "A" or **Association**: Who are you associated with? Were you referred by anyone? How about any associations you both belong to?

Any clubs or memberships you belong to that are interesting and relevant? For example, you may be part of REO 4 Kids, which gives $100 of each REO closing to the Make-a-Wish-Foundation, helping children across the country that are in need.

This topic can encompass both real estate related and non–real estate related matters as long as they keep the conversation flowing.

"R" or **Recreation** is what the asset manager likes to do for fun: Golfing, skiing, running, fishing? Ask them. Find out if they have any particular hobbies. Are there any photographs you can swap from some exciting recent adventures?

The last topic is "M" or **Motivation**. We refer to this as the money or the business part. The first three REO FARM Plays are designed to connect with the asset manager and build rapport. The final step is to tune into their emotions; the kinesthetic, touchy-feely kind of stuff.

When you notice an asset manager leaning forward or the pitch of their voice rising when you are on the phone, you have pressed their hot button. Now you want to build the seller's motivation by making them think of their current needs or wants in their REO business.

Remember the bank's ultimate goal? To maximize return and minimize disposition time; now is the time to drill their needs. We want you to play piano on their emotions. Bring out that motivation. The best way to do this is by asking motivation questions (i.e., asking about their business needs). However, the key in asking is not being too direct. I often phrase the motivation questions in reverse to transition to the motivation topic: "So I heard you have incredible REO agents in your market," or "Your REOs are probably all disposed within 60 days or less in your market, huh?"

Phrase questions as if you know what the responses will be. Most of the time the person you're speaking to will automatically say something like "I wish" or "There is always room for improvement." Very rarely do I find an asset manager that states their business is perfect, especially after the first three steps of The REO FARM Play. As soon as they give you one opening (no matter how small) we want you to go in for the kill and squeeze their pain points. For example, let them start telling you about how they can't find a good agent in their area. Or let them tell you how they have to continuously repeat information to agents who make the same mistakes over and over again.

ASK MOTIVATION QUESTIONS IN REVERSE TO TRANSITION TO THE "MOTIVATION" TOPIC

When they start to open up and discuss their current business, volume, days on market, properties, etc., urge them to tell you more about it. Your goal is to show (not tell) them how you could be a great fit for their goals. Asset managers have families to feed and goals to meet. Draw out their motivation by discussing what they are lacking in their territory and what they are looking for so you can connect emotionally with them. Remember, they need you to help stop the bleeding. You should run through The REO FARM Play in five minutes or less. Do not spend any longer.

However, never mention anything about your business or what you can do for them until they ask you. This is the biggest mistake I see new REO agents make when they try to get business from asset managers. If you product puke on them about why you are the best, you will have lost them. Instead, always think Motivation over Business (MOB). Let the first three steps of The REO FARM Play warm them up and build some motivation. They will naturally ask you about yourself. The agents I coach have told me that, when they use the FARM method, they usually get asked to share information about themselves in under five minutes—questions such as "How many transactions did you close?" or "What's the name of your company?" These are "closing questions" and are a very good signs.

ALWAYS THINK MOTIVATION OVER BUSINESS (MOB)

Remember, your overall goal is to make a friend, build relationships, and connect with the asset manager emotionally. Get them to start talking about themselves and watch how easy it is to get their business card. Most of the time they will ask you for your business card, which is when you can reciprocate the request.

As mentioned before, many asset managers do not have business cards. The ones who do carry only two or three at a time and only give them out to real prospects they can envision themselves working with.

TRICKS OF THE TRADE

So you now feel comfortable talking to asset managers, but where do you find them and how do you get in front of them? Also, what are the tools and systems you need to provide them with? In order to land your first account you must know both what is necessary and what is good to have.

Necessary (Prerequisites)
1. A strong application
2. A vast buyer network

Good to Have
1. Networking and referrals
2. Automated systems

A Strong Application

You might have heard the phrase "location, location, location" in reference to about real estate. Well, I like to say getting your first bank contract or account is all about applying, applying, applying. We want you to apply to every single bank and asset management company in the market (see Appendix B). The first thing an asset manager does when looking for an agent is to see if they are in their pool of applications. If you don't apply, you will be left out. However, before you do, there are three things you need to have perfected:

1. Polished Résumé
2. Polished Proposal
3. Application Questions

The Ten Tools for a Polished Résumé

Your résumé is your lifeline. It summarizes your entire work history into one page (yes—please keep it only one page). If you have ever hired someone, you probably spent no more than thirty to sixty seconds glancing through their résumé before deciding whether to call that person in for an interview or not. This is exactly what asset managers do when hiring. Your goal with your résumé is to hook the asset managers. You want them to pay attention fast.

To catch the attention of asset managers, you need the following ten items or tools on your résumé (see Appendix O):

1. Your Contact Info
2. Your Mission Statement
3. Your Resources
4. Your Team
5. Your Experience
6. Your Education, Certifications, Affiliations
7. Your Platforms
8. References
9. Logos (company and affiliations)
10. Charities

First is your **contact information**. If you have any personal email accounts (Gmail, Hotmail, Yahoo, BellSouth), lose them now. You must have a company email account (e.g. janedoe@xyzrealty.com) and your own website. Many applications ask for your own website because they want to make sure you are capable of marketing all their listings. Therefore, talk about how you will effectively market bank-owned properties. A website also looks professional and shows you are willing to make an investment in your business.

Be sure to include any designations that you have after your name (e.g., Jane Doe, ABR, CRS, GRI). Finally, include your real estate license number and direct cell phone number. Your entire contact information should be at the header on the very top.

Second, start off with your **mission statement**. I use something like this: "To assist homeowners in purchasing affordable homes in XYZ State by partnering with neighborhood stabilization vendors." You want a quick, one-sentence statement that aligns your goals with your bank's goals. Find out what your bank's values are and create something similar for your résumé. Hopefully you will already have something consistent.

Third step is to discuss your **resources**. You will need the following resources from your broker. If you are with a broker who does not have the following, you must find another broker fast:

1. $1,000,000 coverage of error and omission insurance
2. $2,000,000 coverage of general liability insurance (general aggregate and not less than $1,000,000 per occurrence)
3. $1,000,000 coverage of workers compensation (bodily injury by accident, bodily injury by disease, and disease aggregate)

Remember, each state has specific laws on what is the appropriate amount of insurance. Check with your state laws or broker. Some may actually require less.

Also with the insurance information, as part of the resources section, is any **special guarantee** you may promise. For example, you can state something like: "Our promise is to return missed calls and emails within one hour," or "Our team all possess bachelor's degree or xyz certifications. We guarantee satisfaction or we will manage your REO listing for free."

 **INSIDER TIP**

Always include your unique value proposition in the résumé (in bold) with a guarantee or claim you make that will separate you from the competition.

One thing that I put on my résumé as a resource is any special technology I am using—for example, a QR Reader for Barcodes or a special custom iPhone application that I provide to my home buyers.

Anything, that stands out, especially with technology, needs to be highlighted in this section.

Finally, discuss how much money you or your broker has allocated per property. If your broker has deep pockets, now is the time to showcase this. Asset managers know that when an agent is being backed by a broker that has $15,000 per property or north of $1,000,000 in liquid assets, they are serious.

The biggest misconception agents have is when they think they do not have enough resources to get into the REO business. This is a big fat myth. You do not need any of these resources; your broker does. Find a broker who has these resources and join their umbrella. Ask them specifically about meeting these thresholds. Also, ask them how much money they have liquid. Tell them you are building a team, you have a business plan (this book), and you are ready to go after all the direct and outsourcer accounts in the market.

Your broker is your business partner. You bring in the clients, and they bank roll your operations. Your team will do the work and they will fund the operations. You should be receiving nothing less than an 80 percent commission split. When your volume picks up, you need to be on a 100 percent plan. If you can't find a broker who can meet the minimum thresholds or who is willing to do put you on a 100 percent commission plan, contact me and I'll guide you in the right direction. Failure is not an option.

The fourth item mentioned on your résumé is **your team**. We go into this in Chapter 3, where we discuss the two different REO business models on which to operate your business efficiently. Basically, on your résumé you want to highlight your team and its strengths. For example, include the number of agents in your team or in the company, the number of support staff, and the number of offices your broker has, along with the zip codes you service.

The fifth section is your track record or **experience**. How many REOs have you closed? How many BPOs have you done per month? What percentage of your cash for keys was successful? This can also include conventional sales. Talk about your closing ratio. What other clients are you servicing? Maybe you have done a couple of BPOs for some outsourcers or your broker has a bank contract with a major bank. Put it on your résumé.

List out all the different banks you or your broker have done REOs for in bullet points. Let them know you are seasoned. A great way to show this is by creating a landing page, a separate single web page that talks about all your REO experience, and including it as a separate link under the comments section of the application.

 **INSIDER TIP**

If you have never done a BPO before, then do mock BPOs. Start with your house. Reverse engineer the process. Do mock BPOs with your family's or friends' homes. They will love to get a free valuation. Remember, there is no "NO"; only "How can I?"

Also, do you have a big buyer's pool? Remember, asset managers need (not want) agents who have a large following. Now is the time to highlight it. If you are brand new and your answer is zero, then you must find a broker who has some experience and leverage their stats. The real estate business is a team sport. You are only as good as your weakest link.

The sixth section is your **education**. Asset managers need REO agents who are educated on the subject. They have zero room for error. Your first step is reading this book from cover to cover twice. Next, you want to get some credentials behind your name.

There are various professional certifications and designations that are affiliated with the National Association of Realtors®. For example, the accredited buyer representative (ABR), certified residential specialist (CRB), Graduate Realtor® Institute (GRI), and the Short Sales and Foreclosure Resource (SFR) are some of the most common.

You also have platform certifications, such as Equator.com and Res.net. In addition, you have choices of many training programs, such as thefivestarinstitute.com and the certified distressed property expert (CDPE). Finally, you have your REO affiliations, such as REOMAC and National REO Brokers Associations (NRBA).

My rule of thumb is to work backward. Find out what accreditation or education the specific bank is looking for and then make sure you have it. There are a lot to choose from. Don't break your neck trying to figure out which one is right. At the end of the day, banks want to make sure you know what you are doing and you have a large customer base to close deals.

 **INSIDER TIP**

Find a certification that your competition doesn't have. For example, I am a member of the Better Business Bureau (BBB), one of the most trusted and respected organizations around. Be different. Be unique.

Finally, if you are classified as a minority-owned business enterprise (MBE), small disadvantaged business, small business, veteran-owned business, service-disabled veteran-owned business enterprise (DVE), woman-owned business enterprise (WBE), or disabled business enterprise (DBE), then you may have an advantage. Make sure you obtain the necessary certifications validating your status and have it ready to submit to the bank.

Some diversity memberships you can belong to (and put on your résumé) are the National Association of Hispanic Realtors (NAHREP), the Asian Real Estate Association of America (AREAA), and the National Association of Real Estate Brokers (NAREB).

Seventh on your résumé is **platform usage**. Platforms are online websites that connect banks and real estate agents. Many banks communicate and assign properties through a common platform such as Equator.com. Therefore, knowing and mastering a bank's platform is critical. Which platforms have you used before? List out all the platforms you or your broker have used. Many platforms offer a free membership (see resources in Appendix A).

You must log in and obtain every single free membership so you can put on your résumé that you have experience using the platform. Also, because asset managers find agents based on zip codes, you'll also have the availability in purchasing extra zip codes to broaden your visibility on the platforms.

 **INSIDER TIP**

If it's allowed, try signing up with two accounts on each platform. On your second account, put a zero in front of your license number and an "A" in front of your name. This way, when asset managers search in your specific zip code, you come up first alphabetically.

Therefore, knowing various platforms and mastering them is critical. The last thing you want to do is get a new BPO assignment and not know how to upload pictures or your report.

Eighth on your résumé are **references**; the more the better. If you are just starting out, you may not have references from asset managers. That is OK. Remember, just because you don't have any doesn't mean anyone in your office or your broker doesn't. Find an office or broker who has worked with some type of asset manager so you can possibly list their name and phone number as a reference.

Alternatively, you can list references from suppliers, customers, contractors, or other agents. Asset managers are looking for anyone who can validate your work ethic and experience. For now, if you're starting out, just put on your résumé "available upon request."

The second to last requirement of a polished résumé are the **logos**. This, along with the charities, is the aesthesis part of the résumé. Place your company logo at the top in the header and all of the platform certification logos throughout the right side of the résumé (see Appendix O).

Last but not least is the **charity** aspect. Identify a charity that you want to be a part of and place its logo and name at the very bottom of the résumé. REO 4 Kids or United Way are two. You can donate a portion of every closed REO toward these foundations and make a difference in peoples' lives. It's a great feeling for you, and asset managers love it.

I have seen hundreds of résumés in all different orders. I find that keeping it in this template is the most efficient use of space and the most appealing for asset managers. However, because banks' policies are constantly changing, feel free to mix and match this information based on any specific preferences you discover. We have included a sample template in Appendix O for you to see. Please feel free to download a copy at reoboom.com as well.

The Polished Proposal

If your goal with your résumé is to hook the asset managers, then the goal of your polished proposal is to reel them in. Once they see your résumé they will reach out to you by either emailing you asking you for some more information or calling you on your cell phone. It is imperative that your voice mail greeting is clean and professional. No music in the background. Don't have an assistant record a message for you. Remember, it's a cell phone, meaning it's a private line to you. Make sure the recording is yours and be ready to answer the phone.

The proposal is the second part to a strong application. Think of it as an extension of your initial résumé. It consists of some more deliverables that you will need to provide with your application:

1. Copy of your state real estate license
2. Copy of your broker's real estate license
3. Copy of all your insurances (error and omissions, general liability, workers' compensation)
4. Copy of certifications or accreditations (platform, diversity, etc.)
5. W-9 (request for taxpayer ID number and certification)
6. Your coverage areas (all zip codes you cover)
7. Your list of references (phone numbers, names, emails) or actual letters
8. A list of clients served (direct or outsourcer accounts)
9. Statistics about your track record (e.g., sales volume in past three years)
10. A business plan (your team, capabilities, technology, etc.)

I have seen proposals as short as five pages and as long as five pages. The length of your proposal will depend on how detailed and polished you want it to be. If you want a sample of a proposal, please log on to reoboom.com and download a free template.

Make sure you include a cover letter, and combine all ten items above into one PDF file (see Chapter 3). Also include a table of contents similar to this:

Table of Contents
- Introduction
- Clients Served
- Past Track Record
- Our Coverage Areas
- Our Team
- Our Technology
- Our Financial Capabilities
- Our Designations and Credentials
- Our Memberships
- Client References
- Licenses and Insurances

The proposal is the opportunity to put on the sizzle. Include a lot of charts and graphs highlighting historical data and sales trends in your market. Make it sexy. Wine and dine them with the "bells and whistles." Also, make sure you have good quality photos (visit istockphoto.com) and your contact information as the header or footer of every page. Chances are they will glance through one-third of it before making a decision to interview you for a direct REO listing position.

The Application Questions

Finally, the applications; many of my young fresh real estate graduates tell me it's almost as nerve wrecking as applying for colleges. I can see why. Let's take a look at a real questionnaire from a direct bank:

SAMPLE DIRECT BANK APPLICATION

Real Estate Agent Application

1. Agent Name
2. Company Name
3. Franchise Name
4. Email
5. Broker Name

Real Estate License Info

1. License Number
2. Number of years License Active
3. Licensed in more than one state (y/n)
4. Member of local MLS (y/n)
5. Coverage amounts of e/o insurance

REO Experience

1. How many years managing and selling?
2. How many REO closings do you average a month?
3. Total REO closed sales volume for last year?
4. Total REO closings in last twelve months?
5. Average sold price in last twelve months?
6. Your percentage of final sales price to initial BPO?
7. Total number of REO listings in last twelve months?
8. Total of REO listings that have been assigned to you from other agents in last twelve months?
9. Average list price?
10. Average days on market?
11. Average days from initial assignment to listing?
12. Company names and number of assignments in last twelve months?

Office Capabilities

1. Do you have an operating manual (y/n)?
2. Number of successful cash for keys in last twelve months?
3. Overall cash for keys success ratio?

4. Years of experience?
5. Describe your Initial Occupancy Check Process (time frames and best practices used by your office).
6. Describe how you manage utilities.
7. Describe how you manage the rekey process.
8. How do you obtain accurate information for HOAs?
9. How do you handle code violations, fines, and liens?
10. Describe your accounting process.
11. How much available capital do you have?

General Information

1. Describe your certifications.
2. Are you certified by Federal, State, or Municipal Government as a minority-owned enterprise, a small disadvantaged business, or a female-owned business? (y/n)
3. List all the organizations you belong to.
4. Where do you do your business banking?
5. Where do you do your personal banking?

If you are thinking there is no way you can answer these questions— don't worry. By the time you finish this book you will be able to answer every question. When you get questions like these, it's best to type all of your responses and email them, along with the application, in PDF form. Usually, the boxes they give you are short and you will not be able to answer the "REO Experience and Office Capabilities" questions fully. By sending a separate attachment, it shows you gave time and dedication to filling out the responses.

Building a Buyer Network

Asset managers do not care too much about degrees, pedigrees, and certifications. Are they nice to have? Sure. However, don't get hung up on getting the newest and greatest certification. Also, just like any-thing else in life, there are credible and non-credible certifications. I have seen many people create a weekend $300 "REO course" and print out a loose-leaf paper "certification" just to get your money. There are reputable companies out there with weight behind their names who give bonafide classes, and then there are the "gurus" online who are selling you on magic.

I am a big believer in education. I attend almost every seminar and course I can when I have time from the National Association of Realtors® or similar trade organizations. Educating yourself is the best investment. For example, it took me years of hard-knock experience and time to write this book that you can absorb within a day or two. Education is wonderful. Learning from others is the ultimate leverage.

Once you become knowledgeable about a subject and understand the modus operandi of it, you need to develop a pool of buyers into your network. Asset managers want or need an REO agent who can sell homes and who have access to large pools of buyers. The bigger your network is of home buyers and investors, the more likely you will get the banks to notice you. Remember what asset managers want—closings.

Therefore, the first thing you need to do is develop your website and online social media presence (see Appendix A). You will need:

1. A Retail Website
2. A Landing Page
3. A Squeeze Page
4. Search Engine Optimization
5. Press Releases
6. Google Ad Words
7. Social Media Marketing
8. Drip Campaigns

What is going to separate you from the thousands of agents who want to get their feet wet with REOs? Your brand. Many MLS systems allow you to advertise other agent's listings as long as you credit their brokerage company. Your first goal is to have a pipeline of buyers logging into your website or a database. I want you to start blogging about

REOs, writing articles, and synching via syndication all the REOs in your local market to your website (see Chapter 6). Become the "REO expert" online. When people think of REOs in your market, they should think about you.

Banks want to know if you have a large portal of buyers and that you can service those buyers with the properties on your website. You need a landing page that is separate from your website. A landing page is a lead capture page that is a single web page that is either transaction-based (you're trying to sell something) or reference-based (you're simply providing information). You will be using the reference-based landing page to obtain bank contracts.

You can direct your followers on Facebook, Twitter, etc., to your landing page or from your email marketing campaign. The landing page can also be used on your application to sign up for different bank contracts, which we will discuss later. Landing pages are faster, cleaner, and only one simple page, versus a website with many links. When conducting email marketing campaigns always remember to comply with the federal CAN-SPAM Act of 2003 (e.g. have a clear opt-out feature, etc.).

Another application technique I teach my REO agents is to hit the pavement—literally. For the brand newbies who just received their real estate license, I tell them to think creatively. I have them put up local signs throughout their farm area (their target marketing area) with a message similar to this:

FREE
BANK-OWNED LIST
888-XXX-XXXX,
X 100 24-Hr. Rec. Msg.

🏠 **INSIDER TIP**

When installing signs throughout your farm area, use attention-grab-
bing headlines and a toll-free twenty-four-hour recorded message so
the potential customer can call at any time and not feel pressured to
talk to someone live. Finally, use a hand-written or "freestyle" cursive
font as if you actually wrote it yourself with a black bold magic marker.

I remember during the late '90s and the early part of the year 2000,
back when there was equity left in homes, I used to see signs everywhere that said "WE BUY HOUSES" or something similar. Investors
would pick up "deals," repair the homes, and then put them out in the
market to sell to homeowners. Everyone was happy as the market was
appreciating.

Now the opposite has happened. There are a ton of foreclosures and
an incredible opportunity for homeowners and investors to purchase
homes. They are desperate for a good deal as the market heads back
toward 1990 pricing. Think about it. If you can buy a home at full retail
price today and rent it out, and your rent covers your mortgage, taxes,
and insurance and gives you a nominal cash flow a month, it's a good
time to buy.

Alternatively, if the price of building a home from scratch is greater
than purchasing a fairly new REO, it's a good time to buy. My general rule of thumb is, when your mortgage amount (with a 10 percent
down payment) and the market rent amount are about equal—it's a
good time to enter the market.

GOOD TIME TO BUY:
MORTGAGE AMOUNT = MARKET RENT AMOUNT

Therefore, to build a large home buyers list, instead of "WE BUY
HOUSES" you need to flood your farm area with signs reading "WE
SELL HOUSES CHEAP." We would put out about one hundred signs

every weekend in different busy intersections on Friday afternoon and then pick them up on Sunday night. With a toll free number, you can have technology screen out calls by recording your automatic voice message (see Appendix A).

Make sure before you put out signs you are not violating local, state, or real estate laws. We would recommend getting one hundred 18" x 24" plastic signs on a yellow background with black hand-written font (only one color, but double sided). You want to maximize exposure on both sides of the street. Also order one hundred wire stands (either 6" × 18" or 6" × 24") so you can stake your signs into the ground.

Another alternative is to make smaller signs with your squeeze page site address on them. A squeeze page is like a landing page in that it's only one page, but the goal is to capture email addresses. When someone clicks on the squeeze page, there are no links going out to another website (i.e., no hyperlinks or navigations).

Keep content on the squeeze page to a minimum. You do not want your buyers to click away. Remember, your goal is to get your prospective buyers' email address so you can begin sending them bank-owned listings or other messages to build a relationship. The bigger your network, the more value you provide, both to your buyers and to the banks.

 **INSIDER TIP**

Combine a squeeze page with an auto-responder so you can put communicating to your buyers on autopilot. As soon as they opt-in and give you their email address, your auto responder will begin sending them follow-up emails. You can buy a software program or hire someone relatively inexpensive from odesk.com or elance.com to set up both.

The next thing you want to do is identify where all the first time buyers hang out. Where do they go to learn about buying homes? The best place to find them is to partner with a local mortgage professional. What I advise my agents to do is find a mortgage pro that specializes in local county grants and down payment assistance programs for first-time home buyers.

These lenders are always putting on free seminars to educate consumers on how they can get free money, help with their down payment, or closing costs assistance when they purchase their first home. This is an excellent opportunity for you to get your fifteen-minute plug in discussing REOs in the market. Make sure you bring food or something of value to your mortgage partner and the home buyers. Don't forget to pass around a signup sheet so you can gather emails and contact information for your database.

INSIDER TIP

Another alternative is to contact your local county's housing assistance department and find out when they are hosting their next free seminar. Tell them you are an expert in REOs and you would like to speak for five to ten minutes discussing the ins and outs of REOs and how easy it is for first time home buyers to buy one.

Starting an REO Bus Tour

One thing that I love doing is conducting weekend REO bus tours. This is a great "co-op" project to do with a housing inspector, a mortgage professional, a title expert or attorney, and a couple of agents in your office. First, you want to identify a team of people who are complementary to your business and are willing to share the costs of expenses (renting a bus, hiring a driver, gas, food, website, etc.).

Next, you pre-market to consumers with the goal of gaining thirty passengers, charging around $50 to $75 per passenger or couple for a four-to-six hour tour on Saturday morning that includes free food (the price will depend on your costs). Finally, you schedule appointments to view different bank-owned homes in different parts of your city.

One of the co-op partners can be on the loud speaker announcing the agenda for the day ("We will see REOs ranging from $85,000 to $135,000") and the other co-op partners can talk about their specific expertise or prequalify the homebuyers individually. Expect to knock out around seven to ten homes in a day. It's a lot of work but a lot of fun as well. Remember, the goal is to build a large buyer network. From my experience, only about 10 percent or fewer of the people who go on the tour end up placing offers on homes.

Your next large pool of buyers will be investors, and your next step is to build up a large investor list. You will be faced with properties that will not be eligible for financing, and you need investors with all cash to purchase them. The best place to find investors is real estate investor meetings.

To find a local association, visit nationalreia.com. Attend each investor monthly meeting and introduce yourself as the REO expert. Capture as many emails as you can from each investor and put them in a Microsoft Excel spreadsheet or a database program such as top-producer.com or act.com.

Once you have your large buyer network of both home buyers and investors, you want to continuously stay in front of them and create a "drip campaign." Just like a faucet that drips, you want to drip your messages to them continuously via email and social media.

Send them a series of emails or newsletters, "friend" them on Facebook, give updates about what's going on in the REO world on Twitter. You can use a social media dashboard such as hootsuite.com to automate the entire process for you. Some things to consider when using a drip campaign:

1. Space out your messages. Don't drip too fast; otherwise it can be information overload. Once a week is good.
2. Provide value. Teach them and don't sell.
3. Have a clean list. Don't have duplicate emails in your list; otherwise your buyers will be annoyed.
4. Personalize your list. Use the buyer's first name on emails ("Dear James").
5. Play fair. Have an opt-out feature. Quality is more important than quantity.

After you build a strong buyer network, you will be ready to start mingling and networking!

Networking and Referrals

Landing your first bank account is a science. However, it's not rocket science. It's a step-by-step process. You build a strong résumé and proposal, you apply to every bank in the market, you brand yourself as an expert, and you build a large buyer database. These are the necessities. You must crawl before you walk.

PREPERATION + PLUG = FIRST BANK CONTRACT

The next phase is what is good to have. We call it the plug. Many people say luck is nothing more than when preparation meets opportunity. You are already prepared. Now you need the opportunity or the plug. You get plugged in by mastering the two proven methods in gaining bank accounts: the reach around and the REO lunch method.

The Reach-Around Method

I have many friends. My single friends always seem to be on the prowl looking to meet other people to date. They go to lounges, clubs, bars, always looking to meet the perfect soul mate. I have friends who have been single for a long time. They may date here and there, but it usually phases out within a year or so. I also have many married friends.

Out of all my friends who are married, about eight out of ten of them met their significant other through a friend. It was a referral.

Can you go out and meet people at nightclubs, bars, and sporting events, and end up married and living happily ever after? Sure. However, sometimes it's easier if you can get a subtle introduction from someone else. This is the Reach-Around Method. You are getting a referral or introduction from someone you know who can vouch for you. Instead of attacking the asset manager at a conference as everyone else does, you are reaching around their wall of defense and obtaining an easy entry point by gaining a recommendation from another REO agent.

Befriend your competition. Yes! You heard me correctly. Your goal is to find other REO agents in the market place and obtain a referral. You may think it's hard to do, but that is how the pros get in and multiply their business. Think about it—would an asset manager rather be bombarded with fifty hungry sharks attacking them at REO events, or by someone they already work with on a day-to-day basis?

The first step is to find the players of the game and get to know them. Find a map online and identify the players of the REO game in your area within a ten mile radius. Go through their MLS listings. Visit their REO properties. Call their offices and meet them. If they happen to be brokers, say you are looking for a broker who has experience doing REOs. If they are agents, say you wanted to pick their brain because you noticed how successful they are. Stroke their ego. Take them out to lunch. Your goal is to reverse engineer their success.

Another tactic is to find areas that are out of your target market (fifty-plus miles) and identify some REO agents. Tell them you are willing to do work for them in your specific area if they ever have any properties. Work out a commission split. No one turns down business. If an REO agent gets an assignment seventy-five miles away from them, it would behoove them to find someone in that local market to handle the listing and work out a commission split versus driving up and down every day servicing the property. Many agents list zip codes out of their farm area and get many listings that may be too cumbersome for them to handle—but not for you.

Finally, you can reach around asset managers by identifying the common contractors that are part of the "in-network." Many banks have a certain number of contractors that REO listing agents are forced to use (see Chapter 6). You can ask the REO agents on the MLS listing who the in-network contractors are or drive to some of the listings they are doing work on (e.g., rehab) to find them.

Tell them you are going to be an REO listing agent for XYZ bank and you want to introduce yourself. Take them out to lunch. Sometimes the contractors are the ones who can really pack a powerful punch with their letters of recommendations. Whether you have your first account or not you need to think, believe, and act like you do. It's the power of the self-fulfilling prophecy. If your mind believes, acts, and thinks positively, then the stars will align to make your beliefs and behaviors come true. Always think positive. This is a secret that will take your business from good to great.

 **INSIDER TIP**

Befriend your competition and common "in-network" contractors that asset managers use to obtain referrals and letter of recommendations.

The next place to meet REO agents is through networking. You need to go to as many conferences, expositions, and events as possible. Attend all the REO meetings you find. You need to associate with the right people, primarily agents who can give you a plug. Trade contacts with them. Find someone who has a bank that you want and offer to switch contacts. Maybe someone in your office or your broker has a bank contract and knows an asset manager; trade them your asset manager's information for theirs.

There is nothing better than getting an REO agent to send a subtle email to an asset manager stating, "In case you are looking for good quality agents in your area, I know and recommend XYZ." Soon you will be receiving an email from an asset manager asking for your résumé and proposal, followed by a phone interview.

The Five REO Conference Rules

Alternatively, you can sign up for REO conferences that are targeted toward asset managers. This is what all the bigwig (decision making) asset managers, their managers, and their directors attend. These conferences are a double-edged sword because usually they're expensive, you may have to be invited or be an existing member, and you may have a lot of competition trying to play the exact same game you are.

If you decide to go, follow these five conference rules:

1. Never attack
2. Get an introduction
3. Sit at the bigwig table
4. Talk about the FARM
5. Snail mail a thank-you card

First, never attack asset managers by running up to them and saying, "Hi, my name is XYZ, and here is my business card." Remember, they will be looking for the exit sign as soon as they see you coming if you're attempting only to product puke.

Second, try to get an introduction from someone you see. Maybe through your networking you find an REO agent in the room that you know. Maybe that person knows an asset manager who works in your specific territory. It's that easy.

Third, sit at the asset manager table. Act like you were assigned to sit there and play dumb by saying, "Oh my gosh, this is the asset manager table . . . maybe I should leave." Someone next to you will say, "Don't worry about it," and you're on the right track to making introductions. It's always better to ask for forgiveness later versus asking for permission upfront.

Fourth, remember use The REO FARM Play and do not discuss business until you build motivation. Remember MOB. Talk about everything else other than business, and let them lead you to that topic. Be their friend first.

Fifth, the same day when you are in your hotel or when you come back home, write a hand-written thank you card and mail it to the asset manager via snail mail (good old-fashioned postage) because it takes thought and shows effort on your part.

Following up at this point is critical. Never seem desperate by asking for properties. In the REO business, properties are earned, not expected. Therefore, have patience and be subtle. Never pester them; asset managers hate that. Patience is a virtue. Put the asset manager on a hand-written drip campaign so you can stay fresh in their mind. As soon as there is a need in their area, you will be the first person they think of. Remember, you need to be prepared and you need a plug to land a bank contract. Your chance to get the plug is at conferences, when you're face-to-face with asset managers. By attending conferences and following the 5 REO conference rules you have a chance to increase your network.

The REO Lunch Method

This is a strategy I developed when noticing how many REO agents in the marketplace were not performing to asset manager expectations. As you would take someone out to lunch in exchange for earning their business or learning something from them, you want to offer asset managers free BPOs. Say to them, "I will do a second opinion BPO absolutely free, as many as you need."

By doing an alternative BPO, you can demonstrate both your dedication and the quality of your work. Delayed gratification is the name of the game. You must invest in your business. Either you have time to invest or money. Invest your time by doing BPOs, and then teach other agents on how to do BPOs (see Chapter 5) to gain experience. Remember, asset managers want experts in their area; become their REO expert.

Build a team of BPO specialists and approach asset managers by saying you have a BPO team ready at their disposal absolutely free. It's the principal of reciprocity. Sooner or later, the asset manager will return the favor from your free REO lunch and award you your first property.

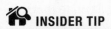 **INSIDER TIP**

Send a hand-written thank you card from a buyer you represented in an REO transaction. Find out who the asset manager was on the file and tell them thanks for their hard work, mention how fast the closing was, and offer to do a free second-opinion BPO on another property.

Automated System

The final method that's good (but not necessary) to use to land your first account is an automated system. You must systemize the application process and keep the contents fresh. A system is nothing more than an organized process that helps your team produce consistent results over and over again. The trick is to make it automated.

50 percent of becoming a successful REO listing agent is landing your first contract, and the other fifty percent is executing properly. Both must be systematized. We go into that in Chapter 11. For now, your goal is to create scripts, worksheets, and step-by-step instructions that you can use to automate your application process.

Many bank applications are the same. They ask pretty much the same questions. Therefore, you can create a simple checklist or FAQ and outsource your application process to someone else. The cheapest and easiest way to do this is by putting up a bid for data entry on odesk.com.

There are many people hungry and desperate for work who would love to fill out applications all day long for less than $3 an hour. Yes! That was not a misprint. It's incredible how cheap labor is overseas and how impressive the quality is. As a real estate entrepreneur you need to minimize your costs as much as possible and maximize your results. Plus, you're providing work to someone less fortunate. It's an ultimate win-win.

Once you get your first property, you will be tested. You will have one shot. If you blow it, you will never receive another property again.

HOW TO MULTIPLY YOUR BUSINESS

Once you land your first account, everything else becomes easy. You may have a couple of outsourcer accounts or a direct bank account. In Chapter 3, we will discuss which REO models to implement to manage your accounts. You can boot strap and use as little as cash as possible or you can frontload your cash, invest in your business, and create an assembly line.

After you receive your first bank contract, you want to quickly leverage that and go after more. If you applied to every bank in the marketplace, it will only be a matter of time before everything falls into place like a puzzle. Meanwhile, you can recruit REO agents from other companies and bring them to work with you. Synergize together. You may have one contract, and they may have another. Join forces.

I have an REO agent who managed to put together a syndicate of different REO agents and created an umbrella under his broker, and now they have almost every REO account in the market. They worked as a team. Sometimes the whole is greater than the sum of the individual parts. They all pool their funds together and share expenses. Creativity is key.

An alternative strategy is to expand by partnering up with a broker who is willing to open multiple branch offices in different areas. Let's say you have a direct bank contract in one area but you find out they need agents in other areas. Talk to your broker and have them bankroll the other offices as branch offices subject to you obtaining more business. You can grow both vertically and horizontally.

In the REO business, you can build crazy momentum. Everything happens in layers. It's nothing more than a science. All you need is passion, dedication, and a vision and you will succeed.

THE ASSET MANAGER VISIT

After you land your first contract and have some active listings, an asset manager may want to visit your facilities. Asset managers sometimes get assigned a day in the field to visit their REO agents. They want to see agents' faces and know who they are doing business with on a more personal level. If you think talking on the phone was nerve-wrecking, this is borderline panic attack.

The first thing you want to do for an asset manager's visit is plan. Make sure your team is dressed professionally, the office is clean, and everyone is at the office. It's always better to over-dress than under-dress; even if it's ninety-eight degrees outside, wear a suit (both ladies and gents).

Next, be a good host. If the asset manager comes in early in the morning, buy some coffee and bagels. Likewise, buy some sandwiches if they come in the afternoon. Most likely you will be going on a field visit to some of your listed REOs with your asset manager. Many times banks like to send out rookie asset managers to all their REO agents in the field so those new asset managers can learn. It's imperative you make a great impression. Remember, you are the expert in your market. You are the expert, not them. Therefore, have confidence (but not arrogance).

If you do drive to see properties, take them in your car. Have the day pre-planned by asking them which properties they want to see. Use mapquest.com or have an up-to-date navigation system ready in your car. I have seen many REO agents blow their first asset manager visit by not updating their navigation software.

Sometimes you will visit your competing agent's properties as well. Do not talk bad about their properties when you are there. Give constructive criticism and honest feedback. If you are feeling nervous, remember The REO FARM play. It has put me at ease many times.

A usual field trip lasts half a day. Be prepared. I like to have some water in the car in a cooler, or I stop at gas stations in between property visits. I usually do not play music in the car because I already have a pre-planned agenda on what I want to discuss. Always be prepared. Have three to five key points memorized that you want to highlight. Why you are the best? What makes you different? What's your competitive advantage?

Also, if they come in the morning you will be starving by the time you visit three or four properties. Take them out to lunch. Some bank's policies will not allow you to pay, but always offer. If they say no, then at least you tried. When you drop them off, make sure you plan to avoid any rush-hour traffic. Thank them and invite them again. This is crucial.

You must invite them back with a time and date. They will say "I'll let you know" or "I'll get back to you," which is good. Always keep the doors open. Finally, mail them a hand-written thank you card. Thank them for their time and tell them you look forward to helping them achieve their goals. After the day is done, it will feel as if a heavy weight has dropped from your shoulders because you will have built great rapport, established trust, and made an impression.

LANDING BANK CONTRACTS IS A SCIENCE, BUT IT'S NOT ROCKET SCIENCE. FOLLOW THE FORMULA FOR SUCCESS.

FIVE HOT TIPS FROM SEASONED REO AGENTS

After speaking to hundreds of seasoned REO agents in the field who deal with asset managers and sales reps, we have collected these five most common responses as some HOT tips to guide you in communicating with asset managers.

HOT TIP #1: Know Your Real Customer

In the REO business, your primary customer is your asset manager. Pick up every phone call and return every email the same day; don't forget about them. No matter how busy you are, even if it's after hours or on weekends, answer your cell phone. They have about two to three minutes to tell you what they need from you. Be ready. Jot down their likes and dislikes and respect their time. Some will like for you to call, while others will find it annoying. Earn their respect.

Even if you have a contract with an asset management company, if your asset manager does not like you, you will not get any properties. Your asset manager is your number one customer, your number one supplier, your number one everything. Never forget that, and you will never forget about them.

HOT TIP #2: Be Meticulous

Details. Details. Details. When communicating with asset managers, buyers, title companies, lenders, and everyone else, make sure you are extra-detailed so there is no ambiguity in what you say. Write each REO ID in the subject line of the email or property address. Keep each email separate; don't talk about three properties in one email. Provide extra communications by updating both the bank online platform and sending an email to your asset manager. Make an impression that you are capable, willing, and trustworthy with your communications.

HOT TIP #3: Learn from Your Competition

Be on good terms with competing agents and network with other REO listing agents. Save months of time, energy, and effort by learning from your peers what works and what doesn't work in the business. Learn from others' mistakes; don't implement something without checking to see if your competition has tried it and been successful.

HOT TIP #4: Over Deliver Customer Service

Do the asset manager's job. Over deliver customer service by going the extra mile. For example, do bi-weekly inspections on your properties versus weekly. Identify any iota of a liability issue and report it immediately to your asset manager. If you see an edge cap on a stair rail or a green pool with mold, report it and arrange to remedy the situation immediately.

Another great example of over delivering on customer service is to close your transaction early. Close it seven to ten days early and watch how thrilled everyone becomes. This is the ultimate proof of high-quality customer service. Your buyers will most likely compliment the bank, which will trickle down to your asset manager, who then will compliment you. Talk about a win-win-win.

Finally, spend quality time with selling agents and buyers. Give them high quality customer service. Don't be terse on the phone. Remember, a good reputation takes time to build, but a bad reputation spreads like wildfire.

HOT TIP #5: Manage Your Time Effectively

Your asset manager is your business partner. If they lose their job, you lose yours. Therefore, you must do everything in your power to follow the rules and get your assignments in on time. Each asset management company and bank has different timelines when they need tasks delivered by. Print out each one and put them on a pin board in your office. One bank might want a BPO turned in within twenty-four hours, and another one may allow you seventy-two hours. Effective time management is critical in the time-sensitive REO business.

SHARE YOUR STORY

Do you have a success story you would like to share on how you implemented these strategies and landed your first account? Please log on
and submit it for your chance to be featured in the next revised edition
of REO BOOM:

www.reoboom.com/story

POINTS TO REMEMBER

- Plan and prepare for the asset manager's visit. It can make or break your business.
- Use the REO Lunch Method and do free second opinion BPOs for asset managers. Eventually they will pay back the favor by giving you properties to manage.
- Remember the five REO conference rules: never attack, get an introduction, sit at the bigwig table, talk about the FARM, and snail mail a thank-you card.
- Never discuss business before building motivation. Ask motivation questions in reverse to transition into the motivation topic of the FARM. Remember MOB—Motivation Over Business.
- Use the Reach-Around Method to gain a plug with asset managers by befriending your competition and common contractors.
- A large buyer network is what banks want. Use yard signs combined with landing pages and drip campaigns to build a large buyer network.
- A polished résumé hooks the asset manager, while the polished proposal reels them in. Always include a unique value proposition with a guarantee in your résumé that separates you from your competition.
- Use The REO FARM Play to build relationships with asset managers. "F" stands for Family, "A" stands for Assocations, "R" stands for Recreation, and "M" stands for Motivation. Always talk about the farm.

- With times of high inventory (greater than five hundred assets), banks shift inventory to outsourcers more than direct REO agents.
- The five benefits of working with direct banks are: working with the decision maker, earning a full commission, earning a guaranteed commission, obtaining a high volume of properties, and using leverage.
- The three biggest pet peeves of asset managers are agents who have to be babysat, agents who keep asset managers in the dark, and agents who cannot produce results. There is no E for effort. Only R for results.
- The REO business is a million dollar business: 1 direct bank account = $1MM gross and 3 direct bank accounts = $1MM net.

Setting Up a Lean REO Machine

BUILDING YOUR DREAM TEAM

You are about to be the type of REO agent asset managers love. Your secret weapon? Your dream team. Early in my career I quickly learned that asset managers gave a lot of volume and the right kind of volume to the agents they loved. I remember this local agent who was just starting off. He wasn't big. As a matter of fact, he didn't have a fancy website and still had an old AOL email account (by the way, if you have any email account other than one attached to your website name, turn to Chapter 7 immediately). However, for some reason this agent would get the highest-priced REO listings in the best neighborhoods.

I'm talking about four bedroom, 3,000 square feet, water front, single family homes that were so hot, they would get under contract within one hour of being listed on the MLS (before the three-day bank rule was in effect—see Chapter 8). He got on the bank's "A" list and he did it by mastering only one thing—performance. He had a lean, mean, fighting machine system. Not one phone call would be missed, nor would any offers fall through the cracks. He had his system down to a science. We call this "building your dream team."

In Chapter 2 we discussed the main goals of banks: to sell their REOs for the highest price possible in the shortest amount of time. This is also known as asset recovery. Remember what asset manager's goals are? To close! They care about one thing and one thing only: closings. This means closing fast, closing early, and closing at their targeted list price or above. If you have ever seen the famous scene in the movie *Glengarry Glen Ross*, you know the saying: ABC. That is what they base their motto on.

A-LWAYS
B-E
C-LOSING

Remember, asset managers or sales representatives for banks are employees who get a salary and have a bonus structure based on the amount of closings they do. If you can help them perform and make them look good so they can achieve their sales numbers, they are going to love you.

The only way this can happen is by creating a lean REO system with a stellar dream team. When I say lean I am talking about being financially fit; in other words, profitable. There are two models that will help you accomplish this: the "REO Bootstrapping Model" and the "REO Plus Model."

THE REO FOOTPRINT

Before we get into the two systems, let's go over the big picture of how you fit into the basic REO footprint:

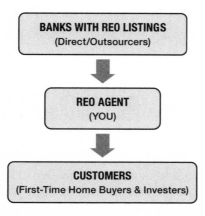

You (or your brokerage company) act as an intermediary between banks and customers. Think of it as operating in a network. It's a network that provides value to all parties because the more properties you can list and sell for the banks, the more properties you will receive back. Also, the more REO properties you receive, the more you can offer and sell to your customers.

As an REO agent your job is to grow your network by connecting hungry home buyers and investors looking for great deals with distressed banks looking to unload their properties. The bigger you can make this footprint or network, the more value you can add to all parties and the faster you will reach a million dollars net.

LARGE NETWORK IS KEY!

REO banks want an REO agent who has the ability to handle volume. They want to feel confident, comfortable, and secure that the listings they give out will close in time and the property will be taken care of. The more properties you handle and turn within ninety days, the more you receive. Success breeds success.

—Mark Miller
Atlanta, GA
REO listing agent

As an REO agent, your specialty or niche market is bank-owned properties. The more customers you can reach out to, the bigger the network of clients you will have to present to the different banks. Once the banks know you have a big following, they will feel confident about giving you properties to manage and list. It's a full circle.

AGENT NICHE:
BANK-OWED PROPERTIES

The REO Boot Strap Model footprint will cost you less than $1,000 to get started and should be used after the 90/10 REO Rule (i.e., after you have successfully closed approximately ten REO transactions). You can technically use it from the start, but the goal is to preserve your cash as much as possible to bankroll your operations.

After you have scaled your footprint to a certain threshold, you will start using the REO Plus Model. The great news is both models are easy to start, and are duplicable; both models have been tested throughout different states in the United States with various REO agents.

REO CUSTOMERS

In order to successfully grow your footprint, you have to provide value to your customers. The first question you must ask yourself is, what is your value proposition (VP)? What is the exact problem or need you are solving for your customers? In order to answer this, you also need to figure out the identity of your customers.

 **INSIDER TIP**

The biggest mistake you can make is to not realize who your primary customer is. In the REO business, your primary customer is not the home buyer. It is the bank!

In the REO business, you have two sets of customers. First are the primary customers, which are your suppliers. These are the banks and outsourcers that feed you the properties or "new BPO assignments" to manage. Your number one priority is to take care of your bank and outsourcer contracts (also called "MLA" or "Master Listing Agreements"). When you see in your caller ID that an asset manager is calling, I don't care if you are on the phone with an in-house (no co-operating agent) cash customer for a $400,000 listing that is at the closing table ready to sign. You tell that customer you will call them back and hang up so you can speak to the asset manager.

In Chapter 1, we mentioned how every REO property sells. Remember, REO symbolizes a free and clear property for a customer at a discounted price that the seller needs (not wants) to get off their books.

The question then becomes not *if* the property will sell, but *when* it will sell. Therefore, you must take care of your primary customers—the banks who have given you the guaranteed sale of an REO property.

Next are your secondary customers—home owners and investors. Your main focus is to convert each lead who contacts your office and put them into your current upcoming REOs. For example, you may have sixty properties in inventory but only twelve that are active and ready to be sold on the market. The rest of the properties may have a tenant inside, need repairs, etc. Therefore, your job is to pre-sell the remaining inventory.

The easiest way to do this is to pre-qualify your secondary customers through a mortgage partner (Chapter 9) and pre-sell your up and coming inventory. Usually homeowners are first-time buyers who have sufficient income or credit to qualify for their first home. They meet the minimum standards to qualify for a home loan, and usually have a down payment less than 10 percent.

Investors are customers who have usually purchased more than one home before and are looking to either rent out the property or resell the property after three or four months for a profit (this is commonly called "flipping"). They usually purchase with all cash or have a large chunk of money to use as a down payment (i.e., 20% percent or greater).

INSIDER TIP

Investors are looking for an REO home that has been on the market for over ninety days that has substantial repair issues so they can buy it, fix it up, make it financeable through FHA or a conventional loan, and sell to a home buyer.

Regardless of whether the secondary customer is a home owner or an investor, they are looking for a great deal. Sometimes, they are looking for a steal. There is no better deal than you pre-showing your exclusive inventory (since it's not on the MLS yet), so they have a head start over the competition.

Your job is to provide them with what they need: REOs. You are the direct source of REOs or "deals" in your local market. Never forget this. The value proposition for your customers is exclusive REOs at an incredible price, delivered to them free of charge.

CUSTOMER VP:
EXCLUSIVE REO DEALS FREE

While you are providing your customers a direct list of properties delivered daily or weekly, you are also solving your supplier needs by offering them a large pool of qualified buyers in your local market. By qualifying and screening (via your mortgage partners) your influx of leads, you can match-make buyers and REOs more quickly.

Remember, banks are bleeding; you are an expert in your local market and they need your help. They need to minimize their loss by achieving a fast turn-around time. Therefore, the value propositions for your suppliers are a large qualified network of buyers and faster closings.

SUPPLIER VP:
LARGE POOL OF BUYERS; FAST CLOSINGS

REO BOOTSTRAP MODEL

In the book *The Art of the Start*, author Guy Kawasaki talks about the art of bootstrapping or growing your business from the inside, using the cash you have in your bank account as opposed to borrowing money or raising venture capital. Sometimes you're just forced to bootstrap.

Before I received my first assignment I had about $1,000, a strong will, and a desire. As the "housing bubble" was bursting, money was very tight. I had no choice. I had to tread water very carefully. I couldn't afford to hire staff, I had to count every penny, and I outsourced everything to odesk.com. My tradeoff was time. So it took me a little longer to get up and running. That was OK. Rome wasn't built in a day.

In Chapter 1, you learned about the 90/10 rule. The first ninety days after you receive your first assignment you will be working long hours and doing everything yourself until you successfully close your first deal. You will then take that commission check and bankroll it or invest it into more BPO assignments until you successfully close ten REOs. You will then have enough cash saved up in your bank account to bring on your dream team.

The great thing about REOs is that you get new assignments based on performance. Therefore, you perform well (i.e., without mistakes and close on time) and you will be rewarded with another assignment. If you close all ten, you will get ten more. REOs are predictable sales. They are predictable closings because every REO closes; it's just a matter of when.

Therefore, you can use the REO Bootstrap Model to stay financially lean in the business and offer a value proposition to your customers. Here is how it works.

REO BOOTSTRAP MODEL

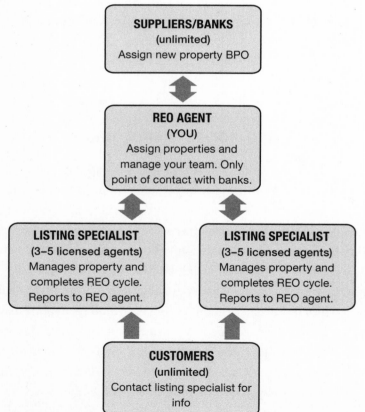

When you have less than thirty active REO listings on the MLS, you will assign properties to your listing specialists (licensed real estate agents) and they will be responsible for the entire REO cycle, from occupancy checks to making sure the transaction closes. You will act as their asset manager. Everything will funnel through you for review, and have your name on it, and then you will submit the tasks to the bank.

Why thirty? From trial and error, through different parts of the United States, I have found as you continue to build your business north of thirty active REO listings, your quality of work using this model begins to head south. Your listing specialists have a hard time managing the workflow and, more importantly, deadlines.

However, the work load is manageable under thirty active listings. Therefore, as you receive a new property or "BPO assignment" from a bank, you will internally assign each property to a listing specialist in your team. A listing agent has to be a licensed real estate agent, because they will be showing and selling homes.

I have approximately three to five listing specialists in my team per each direct bank contract. This allows me to manage the workflow more easily, as well as maintain proper accountability. These specialists will be responsible for handling every step of the REO cycle until the property closes. This includes changing lockboxes, adding yard signs, driving expenses, posting notices, marketing, updating websites, maintaining utilities, and paying for minor repairs until the bank reimburses them for those expenses. In exchange, you will share 40 percent of your listing commission with them.

If the listing specialist finds their own buyer for the property, you will share the sales commission equally.

Commission Split to Listing Specialist
- 40 percent from listing side
- 50 percent from selling side (if they procure their own buyer)

Example: A $200,000 home closes, and your listing commission (LC) is 2.5 percent (your total commission is $5,000). From the 2.5 percent you are giving up 40 percent to your listing specialist. Also, let's say your listing specialist finds their own buyer and earned you 3 percent as a selling commission (SC). Remember, selling commission is usually a full 3 percent, as the banks want an incentive for agents to bring in buyer offers. Therefore, the payout to your listing specialist would be as follows:

$200,000 × 2.5% (LC) × 40% = $2,000.00 (to listing specialist)
$200,000 × 3% (SC) × 50% = $3,000.00 (to listing specialist)

By sharing your listing commissions, you will make less, but you're saving cash. Instead of putting your own money in the business, you are sharing expenses with your listing specialist.

When starting off in the business, it is very important to keep your fixed costs low. Watch every penny. I coach my REO agents to set up free bi-weekly conference calls on skype.com or freeconferencecall. com to talk about the weekly tasks. That way, you can save the cost of travel, hourly office space, and time.

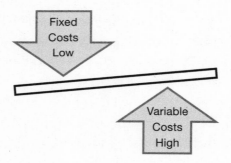

Variable costs are costs that increase with production. For example, you sell a home with an agent in your office. You make a $3,000 commission, but you're sharing half the commission with her. Therefore, your variable cost is $1,500. Fixed costs remain the same no matter what. If you make a $3,000 commission by yourself and your office space is $1,000 a month, your fixed costs are $1,000 a month.

This model works extremely well when you are first starting and your active listing count stays under thirty. Active listings are the amount of REOs you have listed as "active" in the multiple listing services (MLS). You can have a hundred REOs in inventory, but only thirty of those should be active on the MLS waiting for offers to be placed. Remember, after thirty, the workload gets too heavy and your quality of service will suffer.

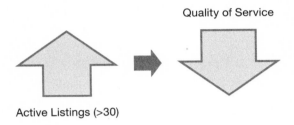

Quality of Service

Active Listings (>30)

Because you are outsourcing almost the entire REO cycle and relying on your team's skills set, you will have to hire extremely qualified, full-time, dedicated agents. Some criteria I look for in hiring listing specialists are:

- Passion for real estate/foreclosures
- Similar core values and virtues (e.g., ethical, disciplined)
- Is a team player
- Track record of prior results
- Full-time in real estate (no-part timers)
- Bachelor's degree (or certifications/designation in real estate)
- Possesses some working capital (ability to bring up to $1,000 in startup costs)

Since you will be dealing with very professional and highly educated asset managers, your team must possess skills to match your primary customer's language. One of the biggest mistakes I see in new agents is that they do not speak the same language as the banks. If the banks expect a very thorough and detailed BPO with some statistics of comparable properties, then you must provide them with exactly that, if not more.

 **INSIDER TIP**

> Always offer a unique value proposition to the banks. For example, hav-
> ing a team that all possess bachelor's degrees or certain designations
> can set you apart from the rest.

One of the companies I coached in 2009 started up with the REO
Bootstrap Model and found an excellent listing specialist (or so they
thought). His résumé was outstanding; he was a young real estate
agent just out of college and looking to get into REOs. On the first
couple of assignments, the agent did OK. He made a couple of mistakes, which is normal in the learning curve process. However, as the
work flow began to come in, he began making a lot of small mistakes:
spelling errors, incomplete sentences, missing pictures in the BPOs,
etc. Mike, as we will call him, was our REO agent who oversaw all the
work flow.

Unfortunately, one BPO slipped through the cracks with errors and
reached the asset manager. Within fifteen minutes of uploading the
BPO into their system, the asset manager emailed Mike saying that he
was "re-assigning the property because the BPO looked like a child did
it." Not only did Mike lose the property, he had to fire his listing specialist all on the same day. It wasn't a good day for Mike, but sometimes
that what happens when errors reach the top.

INSIDER TIP

> When interviewing your listing specialist, ask him or her whether they
> value efforts or results more. If they say efforts, quickly thank them
> for their time and let them go. This business is about results and
> nothing less.

If you cannot perform at 100 percent all the time, then expect to lose your listing or your bank contract. If even one deadline gets missed, the banks are holding you responsible—not the listing specialist—since you are their sole point of contact. Therefore, quality is dependent on your listing specialist. It is crucial that you bring the right people on to your team and keep a close eye on them. Your bank contract will depend on it.

 **INSIDER TIP**

> Do not give access to your log-in password on your supplier's platform to any listing specialist. Only you should be the point of contact for the banks, especially if you will be letting the specialists go after you scale your business.

One caveat when using the REO Bootstrap Model is that you will forego any communication with your secondary customers: first-time home buyers and investors. Because you are sharing 50 percent of your selling commission with a listing specialist if they find a buyer, you cannot compete directly with them by finding a buyer yourself and keeping all of the commission. You will be working as a team. Whether you or they find a buyer, you will be splitting the commission fifty-fifty. This is good and healthy, but because their name and signs will be in the field, the customers will be associating REOs with them and not with you.

 **INSIDER TIP**

> When using the REO Bootstrap Model, always put your name and number on all marketing signs along with the listing specialists' information; otherwise you will be allowing them to build a brand solely through your bank connections.

REO BOOTSTRAP MODEL PROS AND CONS

1. Entire REO cycle outsourced	1. Quality dependent on listing specialists
2. Very little cash to start	2. Sharing commissions
3. Low fixed costs	3. High variable costs
4. High motivation pool of listing specialists	4. More supervision required
5. No communications with co-operating agents or customers	5. No branding (listing specialist branded in field)
6. Limited to under 30 active	6. Capacity for volume limited

REO PLUS MODEL

One of the hardest things I had to do was transition from the REO Bootstrap Model to the REO Plus Model. It was similar to moving on to another decade in life. Remember when you turned thirty? You found your first gray hair, you felt different, maybe things started hurting a little more? That is the same feeling I experienced when I transitioned to a new REO model by letting my all-star specialist go and hiring my new dream team.

I had this one hungry lion working for me. He was a true go-getter—just out of college and ready to be the next Donald Trump. During late 2008 we started moving a lot of units. We might have closed about $25 million in gross volume. During the last week of December, I sat down with him and told him, "I'm sorry John, but you have to go." He was stunned.

No matter how many ways or times I told him he couldn't understand it. He was doing well, I was doing well, our team was doing well, so why? Because we had outgrown the business model; John just wasn't profitable to the business anymore. Sometimes great becomes the enemy of good.

His fate was written from day one of being on board; maybe not the exact date of his departure, but the actual departure itself. It was hard to break to him and hard for him to accept. In actuality, he might have gained more from the relationship than I did, because he made about

$250,000 and had an incredible résumé. What I was doing was transitioning to the REO Plus Model to begin the new year.

The model is simple. When you have thirty active listings or greater, you will terminate all your listing specialists and bring on hourly staff. You will pay them per hour (or your broker will—check your state law) and you will control your fixed costs (hourly pay) by increasing or decreasing their hours like a thermostat.

As the heat (volume of properties) is on, you turn the knob—and increase your team's hours or hire additional staff—to cool off. As the inventory begins slowing down, you turn the knob the opposite way and begin cutting hours. The key is moving your staff from part-time hours to full-time hours.

The goal is to keep all the gross commission income for yourself (no splitting of gross commissions) and hire on staff to cover your routine paperwork. Therefore, instead of outsourcing the entire REO cycle (Chapter 1), you now are in-sourcing or delegating each function of the cycle to separate staff members of your team.

This allows you to focus on what's most important—communicating to asset managers and selling homes. Your name will be branded at the retail level and your job will be to find your own in-house buyers to make both sides of the real estate commission (listing and selling) to maximize the commission. Why only make 2 or 3 percent when you can shoot for 6 percent?

As home prices continue to fall, foreclosures rise, consumer confidence drops, jobs are outsourced overseas, and unemployment rises, more people are looking for work. This is excellent news for you as an REO agent. You have an abundant supply of worker bees looking for a job and a limited number of jobs available. As a real estate entrepreneur, you will be creating jobs and getting a nice return on your investment from them. It's a true win-win.

ASSEMBLY LINE STANDARDIZATION

I want you to think of a car company or a manufacturing plant. They produce hundreds of car parts that flow down an assembly line.

Everything is standardized. They have one person doing one task the whole day, from 9 A.M. to 5 P.M.

From a distance, that person could be a robot. This is what the REO Plus Model is like. It's an assembly line. You will break each function of the REO cycle into parts and assign one staff person to be in charge of each part.

Here is how it works. You will be the main point of contact with the bank, backed up by your dream team:

- Field Inspector
- REO Analyst
- Transaction Coordinator
- Closing Coordinator
- Accounting Clerk

REO PLUS MODEL

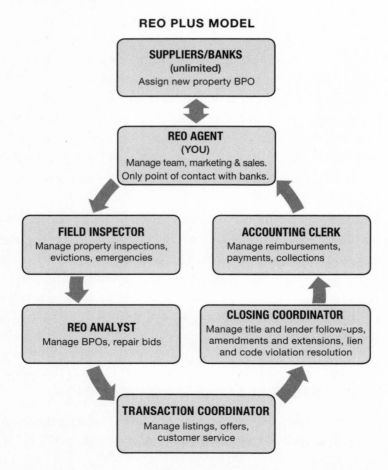

Below are the five key staff functions for your dream team:

1. **Field Inspector.** Your field inspector will visit each property weekly and perform your occupancy checks. They will determine whether the home is vacant or occupied and provide weekly reports. They will also place lockboxes and yard signs in the front lawn. As soon as a new BPO assignment comes in, they will go out to the property immediately and post any notices required by the bank. Some key activities include:

   • Initial and weekly property inspections
   • Signs, lockboxes, and replacing missing keys
   • Physical/emergency damage reports
   • Eviction and trash out assistance

2. **REO Analyst.** Your REO Analyst will perform the BPOs, prepare repair bids, and manage any contractors who are scheduled to repair your properties so they can be in marketable condition. Some key activities include:

   • Gathering comparable listing data for BPOs
   • Assessing repair damages and coordinating repair work with contractors
   • Contacting homeowner associations for estoppel information, authorization letters, access, and coordination with appraisers
   • Obtaining certificates of title when assigned new properties

3. **Transaction Coordinator.** Your transaction coordinator will enter the listings (once marketable) into the MLS and handle all offers, counter-offers, and co-operating agent communications. Finally, they will be the point of contact for the secondary customers (home owners and investors) when they call into the office. Some key activities include:

   • Entering listings and updating listings and marketing data
   • Presenting offers and counteroffers to banks

- Checking availability of properties and updating banks on status of offers
- Customer service and phones

4. **Closing Coordinator.** Your closing coordinator is the point of contact after the property is under contract. They will be the liaison between the title company, the lender (if needed), and the customer. They will handle the contracts, sales amendments, and extensions needed and will push to close the file within the deadline. Some key activities include:

- Sales amendments and closing coordination
- Managing finance and closing deadlines
- Updating bank platforms on status of closings
- Reviewing HUD-1 for accuracy

5. **Accounting Clerk.** Your accounting clerk takes over the file once the transaction closes and enters all the reimbursements into the bank's platform. Every expense you as the REO agent incur (water bills, electric, pool covers, etc.) will have to be entered with proof of service (submitting an invoice or receipt) so you can get reimbursed. This is the first staff role you will need to bring to your team. If you do not get your reimbursements in time (within their cut off period), many banks will not pay you and you will be will be stuck footing the bill. This person also collects and deposits your commission checks. Some key activities include:

- Turning on and off utilities (water/electric)
- Entering final invoices for reimbursement
- Monitoring commission checks and reimbursement checks on all closings (a/r)
- Preparing invoices to be paid to vendors

The accounting clerk is your money assistant. You must find someone with quality experience, preferably someone who has done accounting in a real estate office before. I give my accounting clerk all the tasks listed above except accounts payable. Money going out, I handle.

Once your work flow is standardized, your main function will be communicating with the banks, management of your team, and selling homes. Everything else will be in-sourced. I often get asked, "What should the pay structure be like?" Always pay hourly.

On average, each person's hourly rate will vary from $10/hour to $15/hour. I usually budget around $2,000 a month for each team member. Remember, when times are busy you will increase your staff's hours or add more people to your team. Conversely, during slow times you will cut hours. It's always better to go from full-time to part-time than removing the position entirely.

Also, I always over compensate to keep higher retention. Think about it. Two people can make $2,000 a month. The first person can make $200 an hour but only work ten hours a month. The second person can make $10 an hour and work 200 hours a month (50 hours a week). Which sounds better?

INSIDER TIP

It's always good to over pay but have the flexibility to cut hours when needed.

One caveat when using this model is that you will have to manage the high turnover of staff. Other than paying slightly above market and controlling hours, there are two additional ways to combat this. First is cross-training, and second is promoting. Each member of your staff should be cross-trained in each other's function. For example, after six months of training, your transaction coordinator can become the closing coordinator and vice versa. First, this creates challenge and excitement in the workforce, and second, it leads to putting your business on autopilot, which we will discuss in Chapter 11.

Next is promoting. Once you land your second or third account you will need to bring on an "account manager" for each account. This person will essentially replace your role. We will go into this in Chapter 11. Therefore, as you grow internally and bring on more bank accounts you can promote from within.

Another caveat when using this model is your high fixed costs. With the REO Plus Model, you are incurring high fixed costs (salaries, rent, etc.) in exchange for giving up a piece of the pie from your gross commission income (i.e., sharing listing commission), so your variable costs are next to nothing.

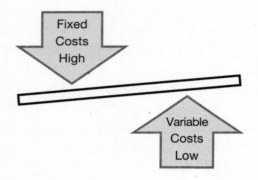

One final caveat is the size of your bankroll. You need at least $25,000 in working capital to sustain this model. You have to pay (or your broker has to pay) your staff bi-weekly. You also need money to change locks on properties and to do minor repairs, all while waiting to get reimbursed from the bank.

However, because you will only use this model after achieving thirty active MLS listings, you will have closed enough properties and made enough commissionable income to fund your business.

Regardless of the high turnover, high fixed costs, or working capital requirements, the biggest benefit of the REO Plus Model is the amount of net profit you can make per direct bank contract. Once you achieve thirty or more active listings, you will be on track to close twenty to thirty homes a month.

Remember, in the REO Bootstrap Model you are giving up 40 percent of your listing commission, which comes out to 1 percent to your listing specialists (using a conservative 2.5 percent listing commission) in addition to sharing 50 percent of your sales commission. To keep it simple, just do the math on the listing side.

Assuming the median national home sales price of $158,800, you are giving up $1,588 per deal from your top line (gross commission income). Multiply this by twenty closings a month and then by twelve months to get the yearly figure. What do you get? A whole lot of money lost:

$1,588 × 20 CLOSINGS A MONTH × 12 MONTHS = $381,120 A YEAR LOST

This is just one direct bank contract and doesn't include you receiving anything from the selling commission. Remember, to net a million in this business, you need three direct bank contracts. Therefore multiply $381,120 by three. Now what do you get?

$381,120 × 3 DIRECT BANK CONTRACTS = $1,143,360 A YEAR LOST

If you keep the REO Bootstrap Model after surpassing thirty active listed properties, you are essentially working twice as hard as you need to be. As you can see, triaging the REO Bootstrap Model is imperative to increasing your net profits.

Gross Commission Income (GCI)
(-) Variable Costs (REO Bootstrap Model)
~~(-) Fixed Costs (REO Plus Model)~~

= ↑ NET PROFIT (BEFORE TAXES)

You are trading your variable costs (splitting commissions with listing specialists) for fixed costs (paying salary to a team). You are stretching your fixed costs over volume of properties just as a production plant does; the same amount of people work on an assembly line, but the volume of car parts continues to flow in.

Also, it's almost impossible to deliver the same quality of service to banks by using the REO Bootstrap Model as you can using the REO Plus Model because you are relying on your listing specialist. Things come up. Priorities are different. Deadlines that are vital to you may be not as important to them. You cannot really control them as you do with your office staff, since you are not paying them a fixed salary.

REO PLUS MODEL PROS/CONS

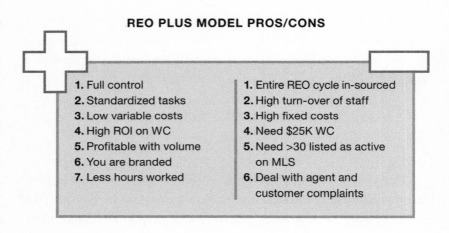

1. Full control	**1.** Entire REO cycle in-sourced
2. Standardized tasks	**2.** High turn-over of staff
3. Low variable costs	**3.** High fixed costs
4. High ROI on WC	**4.** Need $25K WC
5. Profitable with volume	**5.** Need >30 listed as active on MLS
6. You are branded	**6.** Deal with agent and customer complaints
7. Less hours worked	

HOW TO START ON A SHOE-STRING BUDGET

The biggest myth in this business is that you need a lot of money to get going. Almost all of the REO agents I coached started with less than $1,000. If you have been in the real estate business for a while, you may feel this is impossible.

Well, we want you to take your beliefs and place them in a drawer and give the key to your spouse or significant other. Below is list of tools you need to make money in the business (see appendix A for help in finding these items):

- Résumé and proposal (Chapter 2)
- Business cards (optional, 500 max)
- Digital camera (35 mm with zoom, wide angle, and date stamp feature)
- GPS
- Twenty to thirty lockboxes (Shurlok brand) and yard signs
- Smart phone (cell phone with internet capabilities)
- Desktop home computer (with Windows 7, 4gb RAM, 1 TB hard drive, Ethernet LAN, DVD +/- RW burner, and video card that supports dual monitors)
- Dual monitors (19 inches or greater)
- Website with a domain name (no AOL/Yahoo/Hotmail/Gmail accounts)
- Social media accounts (Facebook, Twitter, LinkedIn, etc.)
- MLS with tax roll search (comes with Realtor® membership)
- Microsoft Office Suite 2010 (Word/Excel/PowerPoint/Outlook/OneNote/SharePoint)
- REO forms software
- Adobe Acrobat 9 Professional
- Online fax
- VOIP toll free number
- Virtual office (brokers only—if you do not have an office yet)

This list assumes you already have a real estate license, a vehicle, and a membership with your local Realtor® board.

 **INSIDER TIP**

I require each person on my team to have dual monitors. It is extremely efficient and easier on the eyes, and it has increased my team's productivity by 50 percent.

 **INSIDER TIP**

> One of the most frustrating things is your lockboxes getting stolen. Expect about 10 percent of your lockboxes to be stolen by a customer or a competing agent. Get the Shurlok blue lockbox, which requires two codes to open up the shackles, to mitigate this risk.

Once you have your tools in place, you will need to pick the right broker to work with (if you are a broker already—great). If you are on a low commission split, anything less than 80 percent, I want you to walk into your broker's office and tell him or her you want an 80 percent or greater split because you will be doing REOs.

If they say "no," find another broker. There are hundreds of brokers who will give you an 80, 90, 95, or 100 percent commission split in exchange for volume. The REO business is strictly volume. Remember, in your first year you will be closing at least 250 transactions.

The second most important thing you need from your broker is rapid communication. If you have a broker who is not good with technology or communications, takes three or four hours to call you back, holds your commission check and pays you after a week, etc., I want you to run. The REO business is fast paced. It's conventional real estate on steroids. The last thing you need is a broker who will slow you down.

THE REO BUSINESS IS CONVENTIONAL REAL ESTATE ON STEROIDS

Next, you need to get all the insurance items mentioned in Chapter 2, along with access to a conference room. Many brokers have begun shifting their business model to virtual. This is fine as long as they have a conference room you can use free of charge.

A WORD TO BROKERS

If you are currently a principal broker, manager, or broker owner, you need to keep an eye on your fixed costs. With technology advancing at such a rapid pace, you need to forget about the first floor office space in a shopping center and the "providing your agents with desks as an incentive" mentality. That business model is close to extinct.

Your goal is to stay as financially lean as possible, which means keeping your fixed costs as low as possible. Examples of fixed costs are advertising, marketing, salaries, wages, technology, and rent. One great alternative is to use virtual offices, which are fully functional with conference rooms and live secretaries; they can run as little as $300 per month.

If you need more hours, you pay by the hour. This is all you need in an office. I used this in the beginning for the REO Bootstrap Model and it worked out wonderfully. Once I surpassed thirty active listings, I looked for a small office space with flexible lease terms.

 **INSIDER TIP**

When switching to the REO Plus Model, you will need an office space than can hold your five team members along with a conference area. Keep the office under 1,500 square feet, obtain a gross lease with your utilities included, and do not pay more than $15 per square foot. Commercial landlords are desperate for growing businesses. You are in demand.

LEVERAGING OTHER VENDORS' MONEY (OVM)

I have a very important message for you that the banks don't want you to know. You can bankroll each property with zero down. The REO business is wonderful. There are no accounts receivables, very few fixed costs, a pipeline of guaranteed income, and an unlimited stream of contractors who want to be your number one supplier. Having an REO business feels like being Walmart because of the power you have over your vendors.

If you have ever studied Walmart's business practices or simply attempted to purchase something at one of their mega stores, you can immediately feel their power. Hundreds of thousands of people shop there because of the company's everyday rock bottom prices, regardless of whether they have to park miles away or wait thirty minutes in line to check out. Walmart is a conglomerate; they have banks, credit unions, mini-stores, pharmacies, almost everything you could imagine or want at one location.

With the ability to draw so many customers Walmart can demand a lot. They tell each of their suppliers how much they will be willing to pay. They have their suppliers come in and stock their shelves and organize. If the suppliers' quality is poor or they are late on a delivery, Walmart will most likely reject the entire shipment or never do business with them again.

As an REO agent, you are a mini Walmart. Once you are known in your market as a direct REO agent, all the property preservation, rehab, and real estate vendors will be emailing you. Usually, these are the people who made a fortune during the real estate construction boom and are now on the verge of bankruptcy, looking for any type of work they can get their hands on.

Because the banks advertise you on their affiliate national website as the local broker in your market, your name and phone number will be public. This is great news. Because you will be known, you will be leveraging your mini-powerhouse REO business to squeeze a dollar out of every nickel.

When I first started with the REO business, I had a vendor who approached me for business. It was one of many. They were desperate. They were ex–home builders who thought they were on top of the world when the housing market was booming, and now they had succumbed to cleaning up foreclosures for a living with the downturn of the market. They begged me for the business. They called me weekly. They emailed me daily. They even did the unthinkable and came in to see me.

One afternoon, the owner of a company sent me a hand-written note that said, "Give me five minutes, and if you don't like what I have to say I will pay you $100 for your five minutes of time." That offer was pretty hard to turn down. I invited him into my office and I started the stopwatch.

Within five minutes, he told me his company had been a "big builder" in the past and was more than qualified to do all property preservation. He said I would not have to pay any money upfront. Further, I would only be required to pay him after I got reimbursed from the banks, up to 180 days later. Basically he was proposing open terms, with him financing my operating expenses for each property for six months. Talk about bootstrapping.

I told him, "OK, I'll give you one shot; if your quality is poor you are out." He was thrilled. Remember, as an REO agent you are responsible for maintaining each property until it sells. Don't be alarmed. Your vendor will foot the bill with open terms. Your job is to receive invoices for the work you need completed, usually minor items under $1,000 (e.g., lock changes, tarps on house, pool cages, etc.), get them approved in writing from the bank, then send an approval email to your vendor to commence work.

THREE STEPS TO OVM
1. Request invoice for job needed from vendor
2. Obtain approval in writing from bank
3. Approve vendor's invoice and order work

 **INSIDER TIP**

Accept nothing less than 120-day payment terms from your vendors and have a minimum of three vendors you can outsource your work to. Never put all your eggs in one basket.

Once a vendor has completed work, it is important for you go to the property to inspect the premises carefully. Even if it's something as small as a rekey of the front doors, you want to make sure the quality is good. Never solely rely on one vendor.

OVM RULE = 3 VENDORS
120 DAYS OR GREATER PAYMENT TERMS

Usually you will get reimbursed from your bank within ninety days. Therefore, the longer the period before you have to pay your vendor, the better. For example, if you get paid within ninety days and you pay your vendor within six months, you will have three months of free interest on your money, not to mention you will have put zero down to finance your operations.

Once you spread the word that you are an REO agent, you will be bombarded with emails. The worst thing you can do is pick the first vendor who proposes something favorable. Be cautious. A lot of times vendors can be start-up, fly-by-night companies who paid $200 for a website (or don't have one at all) and claim to be "property preservation specialists." Look at details.

Are they using an AOL or Gmail account? If you call the number, does it go to a cell phone or an office? Are they using a P.O. box for their address? Usually, reputable companies have live people answering calls, use a company email, provide a physical address you can visit, and employ a reasonably sized team or staff on site.

TOP THREE DEAL BREAKER QUESTIONS
1. Do you work weekends?
2. Which REO agents or brokerage companies are you working with now?
3. Are you approved as a preferred vendor for banks directly?

In my many attempts to find my top three vendors, I stumbled upon one vendor who told me his company did not work weekends. I told him, "You may be in the wrong business." In real estate, everyone works weekends, even if it's only one or two hours a day. His excuse was, "Since the banks are closed, we are too." Unfortunately, he didn't realize who his customers were—real estate agents, not banks.

If you come across a company that does not work weekends, run.

Emergencies happen. A flood occurs on your property. Someone steals a lockbox or key. You have an emergency eviction. You need someone reliable that can be on call 24/7. Next, make sure your top three vendors can give you real live recommendations from current REO agents. If they cannot, thank them for their time and leave. Remember, there is very little room for error with handling bank accounts. If you are meeting a vendor who just started their business, they will not be a fit for your REO business. Finally, don't forget to call the references and check them out.

A sign of a good vendor is if they are an approved in-network vendor for a bank. In Chapter 6, you will learn about managing repairs and inspections. If a bank orders a bid, you need to pick a contractor or vendor within their network. These vendors have gone through arduous qualification processes and have the financial capacity and experience to handle your day-to-day property maintenance for items under $1,000.

Top Three Shady Vendor Tactics

I cannot stress how important it is to pick the right vendors. There are many desperate and unethical vendors out there who will do anything to make a fast buck. They will throw you under the bus with a blink of an eye. These types of people will build you a house for your family with Chinese drywall and not disclose it to you.

Shady Tactic #1: Changing Terms and Holding You Hostage

The first thing to look out for is the "too good to be true" offer. If they say something like "don't worry about it, pay me whenever" or "you have a year to pay me, it's no problem," I want you to leave immediately. What shady vendors do is get you hooked on the low ball offer and then, when you have a good amount of volume coming into their office, they change payment terms on you. They will require you to pay all outstanding invoices within thirty days, or else "they no longer will service your properties." This usually happens when you need them the most, like during critical emergencies.

Even worse, they will threaten you by calling the sales manager

or director of the bank you are servicing and allege you are not paying them and are committing fraud by taking the banks money and
pocketing it (remember, the bank reimbursed you). They will hold
you hostage because they know the last thing a bank wants is to deal
with a money problem from its contracted REO agents. Many banks
are traded publicly on a stock exchange, and they abhor bad media.
Therefore, be prudent in picking the right vendors.

 **INSIDER TIP**

Always get your vendor payment terms in writing and be very specific
about what services are to be performed. If they don't have a contract
already written, they most likely are shady vendors.

Shady Tactic #2: Double Invoicing/Billing

The next shady tactic is the vendor who double bills you for the same
work. During the summer of 2009, I received a phone call from Tony,
an REO agent who needed my consulting. He had hired one vendor,
we'll call him Joe, who invoiced him for the rekeying of locks for several homes after receiving approvals from the bank.

Six months later, Tony received a statement saying he owed over
$5,000 across one hundred REOs. What Joe was doing was invoicing
Tony for the rekey of $120, which was paid within his payment terms,
but then was additionally invoicing him for "trip charges."

I quickly did the math and realized Joe was charging him an extra
$50 for each time he went out to a property. Obviously this wasn't
included within their agreement, especially since Tony had made it
very clear (in writing) that he would only pay what was approved by
the bank; so, if the bank approves only $120 to rekey a home, the ven-
dor would receive that and not a penny more or less.

I advised Tony to gather all communications in writing, email, and
fax, including the contractor agreement. During Tony's fact-finding
session, Joe had the gall to email Tony, stating, "If you do not pay the
$5,000 invoice within five days, I will report you to the director of the
XYZ bank; or we can settle this for half—$2,500 today." Basically, Joe

was attempting to extort Tony for false charges in attempt to make a fast buck.

After days of digging up old invoices and emails, Tony emailed Joe proof that he had never agreed to the trip charge services and had sent a carbon copy to his asset manager, followed by a phone call letting him know what was going on. That was the last he heard from Joe.

Six months later, Tony told me he received an email from his asset manager saying that Joe had tried becoming a direct in-network vendor for a bank when they were hiring but was rejected. It turned out, every email and conversation had been recorded in their platform. Because he had tried to make a quick buck, the shady vendor lost out on probably the biggest opportunity in his life. That goes to show you that pulling the wool over someone's eyes doesn't work. Karma caught up with Joe.

Shady Tactic #3: Offering You a Spiff

The final shady tactic is the vendor who offers you a commission spiff of each work ordered. For example, if the bank approves you to change a lock on a door and reimburses you $120 for the work, the shady vendor will offer you 10 percent off that so you only have to pay him $120 × .90 = $108.00.

If you get offered any type of spiff, commission, or referral, run as if your building were on fire. It violates your MLA bank agreement, is illegal, and is also completely unethical. Most importantly, when things go bad, as they always do with illegal activities, the vendor will claim you shorted him money and will file a complaint against you to your suppliers. It's a downward spiral that you want to avoid entirely.

USING TECHNOLOGY—FOLDERS, RULES, AND FORWARDS

The final step in setting up a lean REO machine is using technology. Most of the tasks that need to be completed for REOs are standard for each and every property; nailing down a system that works for one will usually work for others as well.

If you are like the majority of real estate agents out there, you are already incorporating a big portion of technology in your real estate business. If you work from a car, have a smart phone, and have an e-fax, then you are 50 percent done. The other 50 percent is using your current tools to their capacity. When I first started I used Microsoft Outlook, since it was included with my computer. However, I did not have the slightest clue as to the power it had. Once I learned about automating my email messages and creating filters, I freed up one or two hours a day.

If you want to save a minimum of one hour a day, you need to open up Microsoft Outlook and do the following two things. First, set up new folders. Each folder will have one REO ID as the name. Banks will assign you a REO ID (e.g., A123456), along with the street address of the REO.

The best way we have discovered for you and your team to communicate with each other is through REO IDs. Why? Because when an asset manager contacts you, that is what they will be speaking about. You need to be able to associate an REO ID with its address instantly. Besides, communicating addresses with your team only brings about confusion, as there are many similar addresses with different unit numbers in a complex, and that can waste a good fifteen to twenty minutes of your time. The easiest way is to label each folder with an REO ID as follows:

A101556-1234 Main Street Unit 22

Do this for every single property you are managing. Next, you will create a "Rule" in Microsoft outlook. Any time an email comes in your inbox with either the REO ID or the street address, it will automatically forward to your folder. Don't worry, it won't show as if you read the email. It will forward to the folder, and the folder will be highlighted as unread.

To do this, click on any email in Microsoft Outlook. Then, on the top of your screen toward the right, you will see a "Rule" folder. Click on it and hit "Create a rule." Then follow the instructions. It is pretty straightforward. At the end, your screen should look like this:

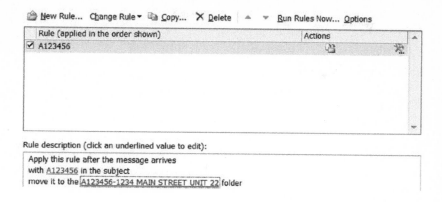

The biggest mistake I see new agents making is leaving all of their emails in their inbox. This is a recipe for disaster. At the end of the working day, you should have no new messages. Everything must be read and automatically filtered to your folders. This way, when an asset manager calls, all you do is click on that specific folder, and every single email with that REO ID or address shows up. Then you can quickly find it and be on the same page as the asset manager.

Another nice trick with rules in Microsoft Outlook is forwarding messages to your team automatically without being at a computer. For example, anytime you see an email come into your inbox with the subject "BPO," you can forward that automatically to your REO analyst or listing specialist by creating a rule.

This way, your team is not wasting time waiting for your email on the next property that is coming in. Remember, banks have a similar feature. They have scripts and programs that automatically assign properties to different REO agents and brokers the same way you will assign rules and automatic forwards to your team.

Finally, you will want to color code your inbox messages depending on importance. Click on any inbox message and then right click on your mouse. Click on "Categorize," then click on "All Categories." Follow instructions to assign different colors and short-cuts on your keyboard for different types of emails that come in.

For example, we have the following color codes and short-cut codes per type of email:

- Red—Asset Manager Inquiry (CTRL+F2)
- Green—Offer received from buyer (CTRL+F3)
- Orange—Title response needed (CTRL+F4)
- Blue—Updated needed on file (CTRL+F5)
- Purple—Executed Contract needed (CTRL+F6)

Quick Parts

Quick Parts in Microsoft Outlook is a hidden gem. How many times do you find yourself repeating the same messages to different people?

With Quick Parts from Microsoft, you can pre-type the most frequently asked or requested information about your business in advance and then, when composing or replying to an email, you can choose that message. It's like a frequently asked question turned upside down. It's your frequently typed answers or comments ready at your disposal.

QUICK PARTS IS FAQS TURNED UPSIDE DOWN

I discovered this neat feature a long time ago, and it literally shaves off about an hour and a half of time in my day—not to mention how every email I send out is consistent! I'm surprised how many agents do not use this feature.

Here is how it works. After you open up Microsoft Outlook, click "new email" as if you are composing a new message to someone. Next, in the body of the email, type the most frequent phrases you say on a day-to-day basis. Highlight (with your mouse) that phrase, click "Quick Parts" on the top of your screen, and select "Save Selection to Quick Parts Gallery." Depending on which version of Outlook you have (I use Outlook 2010), the names are slightly different but the concept is the same. You are pre-writing your responses for a future date to save you time.

Once you have all your frequent comments entered, you then can compose a new email message or reply to one. You again click on "Quick Parts" on the top, and this time instead of saving a selection, you scroll down and choose which selection you want to use.

On the next page are the most common Quick Parts I use for different phases in the REO cycle:

- GREAT NEWS! New property. Occupancy check report due in twenty-four hours; BPO due in five calendar days.
- BPO changes needed. Please re-send me the zip file within twenty-four hours.
- Complete bid (scope, contractor bid, addendums, summary sheet) due in seventy-two hours.
- Need status on repair completion by end of business day (EBD) If it wasn't done properly you need to contact the vendor and tell him to go back to property and complete work. If he objects, email me in writing the circumstances so we can update the system.
- Attached is the complete repair bid.
- X is past due. Please email me X or status on why it is late so we can update the bank platform by EBD.
- Counter offer below. Please let me know whether the buyer "accepts, rejects, or counters" by EBD.
- What is status of closing for X? We need extensions five calendar days prior to closing if it is not going to close. Please advise if we are closing or provide sales extension signed by buyer (remember to name the file correctly: AXXXXXX_Sales Amendment). Need status by 5:30 P.M. today.
- Please email me final executed HUD signed by both buyer and seller so we can turn into our asset manager within twenty-four hours as per bank policy by EBD. Also, please find our attached wiring instructions so you can wire our commissions. It was a pleasure working with you.
- Cash for keys successful. Please enter expense submissions by EBD.

 **INSIDER TIP**

Always assign a deadline in your Quick Parts, whether you're speaking internally to your team or to an outside vendor. Deadlines create call to actions.

Quick Steps

Quick Steps is an advanced function that Microsoft Outlook provides. Quick Steps allows you to perform multiple steps (forward, reply, erase, move) with multiple emails, all by making one click.

Here's how it works. Whenever you have standard steps that must be performed, pre-program them in Quick Steps. For example, as soon as you get a new assignment (new BPO order), you have to send various emails either to your listing specialist or to your staff instructing different people to inspect the property, order the rekey, turn on utilities, etc. Because of the sheer volume of properties, you can avoid forgetting certain steps such as turning on utilities by implementing a pre-programmed Quick Step.

Here's how:

1. After you open Outlook, under the HOME tab, click Quick Steps.
2. Click New > Custom. The following should show:

3. Rename the Quick Step so you can recall it and use it when needed. Example: "rekey, electric, inspection."

4. Following the example above, you want to create three actions: the first is to email your locksmith to rekey the unit, the second is to email your associate to turn on the electric, and the third is to email your associate to do the initial inspection.

5. Each action should be a forward, so when you receive your initial assignment by email, simply hit the Quick Step and the email will be forwarded to all three parties. Below is what your Quick Steps should look like, following the above example:

6. You should click "Show Options" for each action and insert the body of your message. Remember, since you will be writing practically the same message each time for each of your properties, the body should be standard text. Example for locksmith: "Please rekey the property within four hours and place a lockbox with three keys on the front door."

7. You can also add features, such as sending the message with high importance or flagging the message for review. These are available under "Show Options."
8. Click Finish.
9. Now when you receive your initial assignment, simply click on the Quick Step labeled "rekey, electric, inspection," and you will be able to send three custom pre-written email messages with the click of one button.

Now you can knock out all your emails in one shot. Your emails will be generated all at once, but you will have to use delayed delivery (see Chapter 9) to ensure that the emails are sent at the right time. For example, you want to turn on utilities after the property is rekeyed. Therefore, Quick Steps must be accompanied by delayed deliveries.

By clicking one Quick Step, you can generate pre-filled email messages to assign tasks to your team. There is no limit to the number of prefilled messages you can create. Use this tool as an advanced feature once you master Quick Parts.

Instant Messenger

The most efficient method of communicating with your listing specialists or office team is through an instant messenger chat. This way, you are not wasting valuable time on the phone. Each one of our team members is required to have Microsoft Live Instant Messenger open whenever they are in the office. This way, we can chat and communicate with our team. The greatest benefit of an instant messenger system is that it is free and it saves the entire chat history from day one of your chat. If there are any discrepancies, you can look back to the chat to determine who said what and when.

Email Accounts

Along with instant messaging you want to give each listing specialist or team member a specific company email account. Check with your broker to see if they have extra domain name accounts (for example, mary@xyzrealty.com). If not, you will need to purchase one. Create a team name for yourself and assign each member of your team an email. Example:

john@reodreamteam.com
kathy@reodreamteam.com
michael@reodreamteam.com

This is very important. Do not allow anyone in your team, including your listing specialist, to use anything other than their designated company email (no personal emails). Once you let them go, they will be constantly getting emails and customers will be contacting them, as this is the email they have associated success and REOs with. This intellectual property belongs to you and you need to protect it. Besides, your name is on the line, so you need full control.

 **INSIDER TIP**

Always make your team communicate to all parties in the REO transaction with their company email address. This includes instant messaging internally in the office as well. You will be creating a brand of your company and you want customers to associate your team's wants with that brand.

 SHARE YOUR STORY

Do you have a success story you would like to share on how you implemented the REO Bootstrap Model or REO Plus Model? How about using OVM to bankroll your business? Please logon and submit it for your chance to be featured in the next revised edition of *REO Boom*:

www.reoboom.com/story

POINTS TO REMEMBER

- The top three tech time savers that can give you an extra one to two hours a day are: folders, rules, and Quick Parts.
- OVM payables should be negotiated at a minimum of 120 days with three different vendors. Make sure you get what is promised in writing to avoid the three shady vendor tactics.
- You can start the REO business on a shoe-string budget with $1,000 or less.
- The REO Plus Model is the system of standardizing tasks and is lucrative after you achieve thirty active listings so you can spread your fixed costs over volume of properties.
- Use the REO Bootstrap Model when you first start and you have less than thirty active listings on the MLS. It saves you fixed costs (salary, rent), but you're sharing your listing commission with your team.
- The bigger your network is, the more value you will provide to banks. Build a large pool of customers to attract more banks in your REO footprint.

[PART·TWO]

MANAGING YOUR REO ATM

Receiving Your
First Assignment

I WAS UNPREPARED. I didn't know how it happened, but I know that it did. I got my first assignment. It was through an email with the subject line, "You have been selected for a new assignment." When I clicked on the email, I was sent to a link where I would have to accept or reject the assignment. The only thing I remember is hitting that accept button as fast as my eyes could blink. That was the moment. Accepting that assignment felt like making a deposit into my bank account. It felt great!

Getting an assignment takes time. It doesn't happen overnight. I remember there was a sizeable wait from the time I got in with the bank to the time I actually got the first assignment. After a couple of weeks after being approved as an REO agent with the bank and not receiving a single assignment, I thought I had done something wrong. Was it how I emailed them? Did they not like the thank-you card? I started to doubt myself.

But that was back when I first started. That was when REOs weren't a popular sport, and it was hard to get anyone else's perspective on the business—because they didn't have any! What I've learned from that time to now is that everyone gets their first assignment; some get it early and some get it later. Regardless, it is how you manage the first assignment that determines if you get more. The first assignment is your first impression. You will never get a second chance to complete your first assignment.

YOUR FIRST ASSIGNMENT IS YOUR FIRST IMPRESSION

Your first assignment must be perfect. When I coach, I always tell everyone that there is zero tolerance for delays or errors. Every component must be completed with 100 percent accuracy and timeliness. Asset managers translate excuses you make into excuses they will make when justifying why they shouldn't give you more properties. The only way you will be able to succeed is by knowing what you are doing.

When I received that very first assignment, I was uncertain about how to submit the names of the occupants, so I emailed the asset manager. He emailed me back. I responded with another question. He never emailed me back. I submitted the assignment, and it was my first and last. I did not receive another assignment from that asset manager. Now I realize why. Why would an asset manager give assignments to someone who doesn't know what they are doing when the bank has seasoned REO agents ready to handle more properties? It makes sense.

You must know what you are doing! I'll say it again, because it's so important: *There is zero tolerance for delays or errors. Every component must be completed with 100% accuracy and timeliness.* It all begins with your first occupancy check report.

OCCUPANCY CHECK REPORTS (OCRS)

After the foreclosure sale occurs, the bank will assign the property to you, the listing agent. As soon as you receive the email that with the subject that states "you have been assigned a new property," accept it. Don't think twice. The first task you will be required to do is to determine the Occupancy Check Report (OCR) for that property (see Appendix P). This task has one basic goal—to find out if the property is vacant or occupied.

OCR GOAL:
FIND OUT IF PROPERTY IS VACANT OR OCCUPIED

I used to think this task was very simple; I thought that all I had to do was mark whether the property was vacant or occupied. But I have learned since that it is necessary to be as detailed as possible. I figured out that many listing agents do not take this task seriously, and in doing so they indicate that they do not show the same appreciation for the assignment as those who are detailed. Think about it. If you are not detailed and timely, what type of impression does this make? It shows that you are not hungry. Not appreciative. Not eager to make it happen.

When I was coaching in the spring of 2009, one of my agents asked me, "Why do you think the asset manager removed my assignment?" After going through what happened, I told him, "Because it didn't seem like you wanted it." The agent was unable to get into a condo because the security guard said that that he needed a notarized letter from the bank stating he was authorized to enter. So the agent marked the property as "unknown occupied" because he couldn't get into the building to determine the occupancy. That's all he did. He didn't follow up. He didn't put forth any effort to escalate the matter. It seemed as if he didn't even want the assignment. So it was removed.

I tell my mentees to treat every assignment like their first assignment. Be detailed, communicate, and know what you are doing! Communicate with all parties before communicating with your asset manager. Try to resolve any issues that arise without the use of your asset manager's time. Leave the asset manager with the impression of "wow."

TREAT EVERY ASSIGNMENT AS IF IT IS YOUR FIRST ASSIGNMENT

Determining occupancy and completing your occupancy check report is easy. There are five simple steps you will need to follow:

1. Look at the tax record of the property.
2. Drive to the property within twenty-four hours of getting your assignment.
3. Post your occupant options letter and take a photo with a date stamp as proof.
4. Determine if the property is vacant or occupied.
5. Order the rekeying of locks from your vendor.

After you receive your assignment and accept it, you should pull up the tax records of the property. The biggest mistake you can make is to drive to the property before pulling up the tax records. On the tax records, you will look for the following items:

a. What is the name of the former owner?
b. Is the property a single family home, a condo, a duplex, a triplex, a fourplex, a co-op, a townhome, or manufactured housing?
c. How many units are there, based on the tax record?
d. If the property is a condo, what is the name of the condo?
e. What is the folio number (tax identification number) for the property?
f. Was the property previously listed on the MLS, and if so, from what dates?
g. Are there pictures of the property on the MLS, and if so, how outdated are they?

After going through the tax record, you need to physically visit the property to determine whether the property is vacant or occupied. If it is occupied, find out as many details as possible.

 INSIDER TIP

Call the local utility company to find out if there are utilities currently active at the property. By looking at the tax record, you can ask the utility company whose name the account is under. Ninety percent of the time, if the property does not have an active utility account, then the property is vacant. If the account is under the former owner, most likely the property is occupied by the former owner. If the property is not under the former owner, most likely the property is tenant occupied.

Drive to the property within twenty-four hours of getting the order from the bank. Remember, first impressions account. Always be prompt, accurate, and detailed with your work submissions. Make it very easy for the bank to understand that you work hard without having to be reminded You want it to count on you.

Most banks will have an occupant option letter flyer that they want you to post on the front door. Other banks have a door hanger that you are required to hang on the front door. The poster discusses various options the occupant(s) may have, including getting cash to leave (cash for keys), the ability to rent, and the ability to purchase the unit.

Be sure you post the flyer in both English and Spanish and take a date-stamped photo. Then, after you take a photo, knock on the door to see if anyone answers.

Also, take a photo of the exterior property showing the house and unit number. If the property is a condo, take a date-stamped photo of the building number and apartment number. In the interest of being thorough and making a great first impression, also take a date-stamped photo of the street intersection.

 **INSIDER TIP**

> Make sure you put your cell phone number on the occupant options letter. Most people who receive this on their front door will become very scared, and if you don't answer or your office is closed, they will call the bank directly. Avoid this.

THE THREE OCCUPANT OPTION POSTING RULES

When I was a rookie, I never used to put the notice on the door before knocking when doing the Occupancy Check Report. I used to knock and hand-deliver the notice. One time, the bank was in the process of doing an eviction and the judge asked the bank to give the court proof of placing the notice.

When the bank asked me for this I said, "I hand delivered it." That was a big mistake. The occupant was then able to stay in the house for another six months because there was no real proof I had given it to him! From that point on, I learned to always place the notice (in English and Spanish), take the date-stamped photo, and then knock. Follow these three steps and it will save you a lot of embarrassment!

1. PLACE OCCUPANT OPTION LETTER
2. TAKE DATE-STAMPED PHOTO
3. KNOCK ON DOOR

Sometimes you may be unable to determine occupancy. You knock and you get no response. You think someone is living in the home, but you are not certain. Here are some clues to help you determine occupancy:

- Look at the landscaping: Is it maintained?
- Are there cars in the driveway? Where are the license plates from?
- Have the neighbors seen anyone around?
- Look around the mailbox: is it empty or full? Find the mail carrier and ask if there is any activity in the house.
- Look through the windows. Is there any personal property inside?
- If it's a condo or property in a home owners association (HOA), ask the association if anyone is living there; go to the main office.

 **INSIDER TIP**

If at first you are unable to determine the property's occupancy status, return after three days to see if your letter is still posted. If it is still posted on the front door, most likely, the property is vacant.

Get as much HOA information as you can during your initial visit. Important places where HOA contact information can be found are the mailbox, common areas, the leasing office, front entrance signs, and fences. It is important that you have the HOA contact information, as you will need to update your bank platform with it. Therefore, get it on your first visit. Don't leave until you have it.

If the property is a condo, first do a quick Google search or try condocerts.com; if that does not help, look in public records for a case in which the condo association was a plaintiff. One example would be a case where the plaintiff (condo association) filed a lien or lis pendens on another party.

When you click on that case, you will see which attorney represented the condo in that lawsuit. Eight out of ten times, this will be the same attorney the condo is currently using. Call the attorney and ask them to provide you with the condo association contact information.

OCCUPANCY CHECK REPORT (OCR) PROCESS

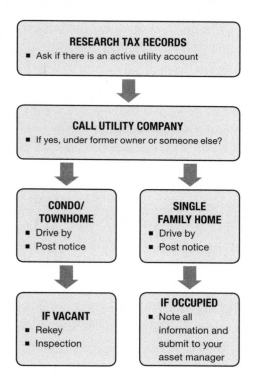

BE PREPARED AT ALL TIMES

I remember when I was on the field back in 2007 and on one of my initial OCR inspections. I was inspecting a condo located in a very nice building; the unit was on the sixth floor. I was overly excited and underprepared. I remember seeing the email on my smart phone, and instead of stopping by my office, I decided to make a U-turn and head over to the unit. I pulled up in the parking lot, hopped out of my car, and knocked on the door.

As I finished putting up the last piece of scotch tape of the bank notice on the door, a beautiful, five-foot-eleven (I'm guessing) woman with blonde hair and hazel eyes opened the door screaming, "Please don't kick me out, I was told to be here, I have no place to go." Her hair was frazzled, and she was out of breath. Also, she was topless. Yes, true story.

I said, "Uh . . . hello. I just wanted to ask you a few quick questions, are you. . . ." She quickly cut me off and began ranting about her life story, stating that she was a "model" who was in the United States illegally, and she began begging for me not to call the police. She told me how she used to "work" at the condo through an "agency," but she wasn't officially living there. As she was telling me her story, a large and muscular six-foot-six inch (guessing also) male ran to the front door with a backward-turned baseball cap and baseball bat shouting, "Get out of here before I. . ."

Before he finished his sentence I jetted down the stairs, straight to my car. I was so shocked and scared to death at the same time. The lesson I learned is this: whatever you are expecting, forget about it. You never know what can happen. Always put your safety and health first.

As time went on, I dealt with many precarious situations, such as loose dogs, barbed-wire fences, occupants with shotguns, drug addicts, squatters, etc. Working with REOs is interesting. However, never forget to be prepared; prepare for the worst and hope for the best.

Not every case will be as crazy as the "model" story. Most of the time you will have people occupying the home. If the property is occupied, be sure to have a pencil and paper to write as much information as you can from the occupants. Here is what you will need to jot down:

- Occupant names
- Phone numbers
- Email addresses
- Are occupants tenants or former owners?
- If tenants, do they have a bona-fide lease? (Is the lease in good faith? For example, is there written documentation, proof of

past payments, other items showing that the lease was executed in good faith?)

- Are there any children living in the home? What ages?
- Are there any occupants under the age of six?
- How long have the occupants been residing at the property?
- Are any of the occupants receiving government assistance?
- Any other pertinent information the occupants are willing to provide.

Once you have your data from the occupants, you will have twenty-four hours or less to complete your Occupancy Check Report (OCR) report. This is done by transferring your data from your visit to your bank's platform. Remember to be extra detailed. The more comments you have, the better.

If you are unsure of the occupancy and are planning to revisit the property after a couple of days, you should still complete the OCR within twenty-four hours and note in the comments that you are planning to go back. The more detailed and thorough you are with the comments, the more likely you will be to get the property vacant, marketed, and ultimately sold.

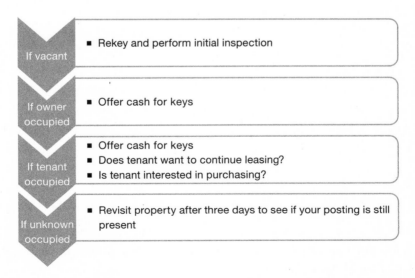

The best news is if the property is vacant. You will be one step closer to closing and cashing in on your ATM. If the property is vacant, order the property to be rekeyed by contacting your vendor (i.e., your locksmith). Be sure the locksmith puts a lockbox on the door with three keys inside the lockbox.

Which locksmith should you use? You can find a locksmith from your local yellow pages, angieslist.com, or craigslist.com. Make sure you interview the locksmith to check that they are capable of performing rekeys on the same business day of you placing the order, and that they will not make any excuses such as "I couldn't get in through the building." Tell your locksmith to "make it happen" and negotiate with them so they put the lockbox on the front door of the home, along with three keys inside. Remember, keys get stolen.

Often there will be properties that are vacant, but upon further exploration, you will find that there is personal property inside. You can often tell by looking through the windows if any personal property is inside the home. If you notice that there is personal property even though the home is vacant, only rekey the back door. This is because if you rekey the front door as well, you can be liable for illegal forcible entry. If you do rekey a back door, be sure to post a notice on the front door stating that you have rekeyed the property, and provide contact information so that occupants can call you. Most times, they will call you to retrieve their personal property.

Once the property is rekeyed, perform the initial interior inspection. Note that if there are any personal property items left inside the home, special laws that vary from state to state require certain actions. Check with your local municipality or state ordinance to determine what threshold of personal property requires a court order to remove.

PERFORMING THE INITIAL INTERIOR INSPECTION

Once the property is rekeyed, you will most likely be instructed to place bank signs all across the home—at the front, back, and sides. These are signs with your contact information that warn people not to trespass. When you have access to the inside of the property, don't expect to see a spotless home that is ready to be moved into. Most of the time, the homes will be damaged and in need of repair.

From the initial interior inspection, you should be able to determine the extent of necessary repairs, any potential liability issues, whether personal property exists, if any immediate emergency repairs are required, and what is needed to ensure that the property itself is secured.

INITIAL INSPECTION

☐ **Note if any emergency repairs are needed**
 - Any leaks or emergency repairs that you discover should be reported immediately to the asset manager. Most of the time you will be authorized to complete these emergency repairs immediately.

☐ **Is subject safe and secure?**
 - If there is a gate, is it locked?
 - Are all doors secured?
 - Are all entry points sealed?

☐ **What is the garage sale value of the personal property?**
 - If personal property exceeds $500, a legal personal property eviction is most often required. Inform your asset manager immediately.

☐ **Are there any potential liability issues?**
 - Examples: unsecure pool, broken glass, broken windows, exposed wires

---

Finally, update your bank's platform with the results of your initial inspection to ensure that the bank is aware of any special circumstances.

MANAGING CASH FOR KEYS

If the property isn't vacant, most banks have several options that they offer occupants. Most of the time, the occupant will be offered cash for keys. Cash for keys is a program that gives relocation assistance to the occupant if the occupant is willing to move out of the home and give their keys to the bank. Usually, the sooner the occupant is able to move out, the larger the cash for keys amount they can get. If the occupants do choose cash for keys, they are responsible for leaving the property in "broom swept condition," which means move-in ready.

The cash for keys process is very simple. You will get the negotiated amount approved by your bank, and you will meet with the occupants to provide the bank forms they need to sign and a check from your office. Before the occupants sign and hand over the keys, you will have to perform an inspection to make sure the property is left in broom-swept condition.

Many occupants feel the need to take all the appliances, hardware, fixtures, and faucets when they leave the property. It is best to let them know from the very beginning that they are receiving cash for keys with the agreement that they are only to take their personal belongings from the house; nothing else.

As a listing agent, you may feel the need to avoid paying cash for keys and letting the bank formally evict the occupants, even though you will be reimbursed for it. However, that will hurt your pocket book, performance, and statistics in the long run. Cash for keys, even though amounts can vary from $1,000 to $5,000, is a win-win-win situation.

First, the occupants win. They don't want to deal with a sheriff or a police officer with a badge and a gun. Most likely they have been living in the property for quite some time without having paid their mortgage or rent (maybe even years). Many consumers take advantage of the daunting foreclosure process and choose to stay in their homes. This is a strategic default. By the time you come to the door, they are already content with living for free and are thrilled that you now are actually paying them to leave.

Second, the bank wins. Banks avoid having to litigate in court. Offering cash for keys is a faster and more economical solution. It saves them attorney's fees and minimizes the time in which the property can further depreciate. Also, it preserves the property (e.g., appliances stay intact, fixtures aren't stolen, etc.)

Finally, you win. As the bank's REO listing agent, you will get reim-bursed 100 percent for the negotiated cash for keys amount. You get a vacant property, get a head start on the valuation, marketing, and placing a buyer in the home, and have better turnaround-time statistics to show your asset manager. Remember the ultimate bank rule: maximize value and minimize disposition time. The cash for keys exchange actually speeds up the cash flow for you despite the initial cash outlay.

 **INSIDER TIP**

Always try to convince a hesitant occupant to do cash for keys. Tell them, "Would you rather work with a sheriff that has a badge or gun, or with me?"

On the other hand, if after determining that the property is occupied and the occupants are uncooperative (i.e., they do not want cash for keys), then you must proceed with an eviction. Remember the occupant options letter that you took a date stamp of? Well, the foreclosing attorney will need it to "file a motion" in court. In court, the number one defense story from an occupant is "I never got the notice"; therefore some banks will also require you to take a date-stamp picture of the envelope that you mailed.

INSIDER TIP

If required to mail the occupant options letter to the physical address, take a date-stamped photo of the envelope with a stamp prior to mailing it.

If there are any illegal units (e.g., illegal rooms, efficiencies, etc.) in the property, it is important to include those illegal units as if they were part of the original home. For example, if there is a duplex with two illegal units, note for your bank platform that the property is a four-plex. In the comments, state that units three and four are illegal. Most courts will require an eviction to serve all units in the home, even if the units are illegal.

ATTENDING EVICTIONS

Unfortunately, sometimes the bank has no choice but to start an eviction, and at that point, the bank's attorney will go to court. The bank's goal will be to get the occupant out of the property so you can market and sell it. This is why you must be on their team and help them with the eviction.

When do you attend the eviction? You will most likely receive an email or a phone call from the foreclosing attorney telling you what date and time the evictions is being held. Since you are the listing agent for the bank, you must be present at the eviction, or else the local sheriff will cancel the order. You will be given a time frame of two to six hours when the sheriff can arrive and do the eviction. This will take a large chunk out of your day, so plan ahead of time.

Before the sheriff actually executes the eviction, he or she will issue several warnings to the occupants. The last and final warning, sometimes referred to as a "writ of possession," informs the occupant that they have a short timeframe (e.g., twenty-four hours) before the sheriff returns and moves their personal belongings out of the house.

A locksmith must also be present for the eviction. At the eviction, the locksmith will change the locks, and you will be responsible for moving the personal property to the front curb; however, this rule varies from state to state, so check the law beforehand. We also recommend scheduling a moving crew to move furniture on to the front lawn. I have been at evictions where I had to move an entire bedroom and living room set. It was not fun. Remember, before incurring any expense, get it approved by your asset manager for reimbursement.

The occupants will then have another twenty-four to thirty-six hours to collect their personal belongings. The property should then be secured (locks changed).

If you had it marked off in your bank platform as "tenant occupied," change it to "vacant" and write a detailed description with time tables describing what happened during the eviction process ("I arrived to the house at 8:30 A.M., waited for the sheriff for two hours, locksmith arrived at 9:15 A.M., tenants were peeking through the window," etc.).

HOW TO GET INTO CONDOS AND GAIN COOPERATION FROM HOAS

Condo associations or HOAs are sometimes very difficult to work with. However, to gain cooperation, you must get the association on your side. Sometimes condo managers will refuse to let anyone access the unit until they have a notarized authorization letter faxed to them along with the "certificate of title" showing that the bank that is authorizing you to access the unit. When sending information to the condo, be sure to include the following three items:

1. Certificate of title, or instrument showing the bank as the owner of record.
2. Letter from the bank/asset manager giving you permission to rekey, access, market, and maintain the property.
3. Letter from you to the condo granting all other real estate agents, utility workers, contractors, etc., permission to access the unit.

 **INSIDER TIP**

When sending authorization letters to the condo associations, be sure to leave out the asset manager's email and phone number. If the condo ever gets upset, the last thing you want is for them to contact the asset manager/bank directly to file a complaint.

To gain the cooperation of the property manager at the condo, you have to show them a couple of things besides the items we just discussed. First, show them you really appreciate their cooperation. Do not act like it is their duty to give you access. If you do, they will be very difficult to deal with. Appreciate their cooperativeness. Act like they are doing you a favor.

Second, show them that you are willing to entertain any offers the property manager may have. Sometimes, property managers are targeted heavily by investors who tell them to notify the investor as soon as an REO is up for sale so they can buy it. Telling the manager that you will entertain any of their offers is critical in gaining their trust. They will like you.

Finally, you are, in fact, authorized to access, rekey, and list the unit for sale. Make sure you fax and email the property manager the authorization letter and certificate of title. Please see a sample authorization letter below:

SAMPLE AUTHORIZATION LETTER FROM LA TO CONDO

3/1/2011

██████████████

Attn: Broker Services
████ Addison Circle, Suite 400
Addison, TX 75001

Dear ████████████████,

This letter is serves as effective constructive notice that I hereby authorize any <u>and all</u> visitors to the property located at: ████████████████████

The visitors include, but are not limited to, other realtors, repairmen, maintenance workers, FPL, Comcast, etc... For me to call you to advise when each person would arrive would be inefficient. Therefore, I am authorizing <u>ALL</u> parties to this address. I will hold ██████████████. harmless for any liability that may be caused to subject property.

Please understand that my intent is to get the previous past-due payments for ████████████ ████████. paid off and help you bring the association to a better financial standpoint. Should you have any questions, please feel free to call me on my cell at: ██████████

Sincerely,

████████

Licensed Real Estate Agent

PH: ████████
CELL: ████████
FAX: ████████

🏠 INSIDER TIP

Be sure to set up a gate code when you are getting authorization from the condo for you to access the unit. You want to make sure that you obtain everything in one shot so you minimize the time you require from the property manager at that association.

CHECKING CERTIFICATES OF TITLE

Certificate of title is a crucial document that shows the owner of record at the time you are notified by the bank to market the property. There are a couple of ways to retrieve a certificate of title. First, you can call the foreclosing attorney who represented the bank in the civil pleading. Alternatively, you can go online to your local court clerk's website to look up the public records database.

Search by the former owner, as there will most likely be a court docket online showing the progress of the foreclosure case. In many counties, the certificate of title will be readily available on the court's website, so you can download it immediately without having to call the foreclosing attorney.

 **INSIDER TIP**

When reviewing the certificate of title, please make sure the legal description is correct. If not, this will pose a big problem at closing. Getting any issues resolved prior to listing the REO for sale is a very important skill that will transition an executed contract into a closing seamlessly.

OBTAINING ESTOPPELS

Some associations are growing increasingly strict about past-due HOA payments, and as such are preventing banks from accessing the unit until all past-due HOA fees have been paid off. Therefore, an estoppel is needed. An estoppel is a document that informs all parties of the amount of past-due payments that are missing and the need to be brought current.

Estoppels are required for the bank to provide a free and clear title (no encumbrances or liens) to the new buyer. The new buyer should not be responsible for any past-due HOA or condo fees that were not paid. Therefore, estoppels are used in order for the new buyer to own the property free and clear without having obligatory back-payments due in the future.

One thing to note is that HOAs have becoming increasingly aware of the potential to make a lot of money from the past due fees by adding "special assessments and attorney's fees" to the estoppel pay-off amount. It is critical to set the upfront agreement when initially requesting the estoppel to let the HOA know that the bank will not pay for an estoppel that does not comply with "statutory regulations" or whatever the state law says.

States have statutes that limit the amount of estoppel a condo or HOA can collect. Regardless, always negotiate to waive the late fees and penalties on the estoppel letter by explaining that the property was in a foreclosure. Most of the time, the HOA or condo will be able to waive part of the fee.

Estoppels will usually be handled on behalf of the HOA or condo by their attorney or a third party. When you contact the appropriate party to request an estoppel letter, they will charge you a fee. The best thing to do is ask them to add the fee to the actual estoppel pay-off (the final bill). This will help save you the up-front cost of ordering the estoppel. Also, be sure to confirm if there is more than one association that requires estoppels. Some condos are governed by multiple associations.

 **INSIDER TIP**

Let the association know you want to expedite payment of the past-due HOA fees, but you need their compliance to do so. Let them understand that by getting the past-due fees paid for on time, their own job security will be assured. Also, let them know that in order for you to pay the fees promptly, you need their full cooperation. Establishing rapport with the actual person who completes the estoppel for you will save you time and frustration.

Below is a sample estoppel request form (also found in Appendix Q) that you will need the HOA's attorney or property management to complete:

Please complete the following information.

1. Maintenance amount
2. Water included in maintenance (y/n)?
3. Intervals that payments are due (annually/quarterly/monthly)
4. What date is maintenance paid through?
5. What date is your estoppel letter good through?
6. Are there any accrued late fees due (y/n)?
   a. If yes, amount due?
7. Total amount now due (attach a breakdown and a W9 form)
8. Are there any special assessments due (y/n)?
   a. If yes, date assessments were passed?
   b. If yes, are assessments payable in installments (y/n)?
   c. Total amount to pay now in full
   d. Date due
9. Written condo approval required (y/n)?
   a. If so, has buyer been approved (y/n)?
10. Any other associations or clubs to the referenced unit (y/n)? If yes:
    a. Name of association/club
    b. Contact person name
    c. Phone
    d. Fax
    e. Email
11. Name of master hazard insurance policy company
    a. Name of agent
    b. Address
    c. Phone
    d. Fax
    e. Email
12. Name of master flood insurance policy company
    a. Name of agent
    b. Address
    c. Phone
    d. Fax
    e. Email

13. Is there a recreation lease (y/n)?
    a. If yes, payment amount?
14. If there a leasehold interest (y/n)? If yes:
    a. Is there an existing lease (y/n)?
    b. Amount of lease payment
    c. Is this payment included with maintenance?

Also, when ordering the estoppel, make sure you order the W-9 and ledger too. A W-9 is a form used for tax purposes so the bank can write off its payments to the association as an expense. A ledger will detail each charge the association is claiming as past due. Make sure there is no balance being carried forward from a time period in which the condo should not have been collecting dues.

For example, if your state statutes indicate that past-due payments can only be collected a maximum of one year back, make sure that the ledger does not carry forward a balance in the first month. The first month should start with a zero past-due balance and then accumulate the allowed amount of past-due payments throughout the following months. The ledger will detail this precisely, so pay close attention to it.

MANAGING UTILITIES

After you finally get access to the house and mark off on your bank's platform that the property is vacant, you will need to turn on the utilities (water/electric) to the unit. Utilities are a very important aspect of making your REO presentable, as they discourage pests, rodents, and mold from lurking on the property. Also, the bank's in-network cleaning crew (discussed later) will not be able to clean the unit until utilities are set up, as they need access to water and electricity.

However, note that many electric companies will not be able to turn on the electricity if the breaker switches are in the "on" position. Therefore, it is imperative that the listing specialist or field rep making the initial inspection always turns the breaker switches to "off."

In addition, it is critical that the field rep turns all water valves off. Do not leave any water faucets or valves on. Avoiding this mistake is simple, but you'll be surprised at how many agents actually don't get it right.

 **INSIDER TIP**

> Before turning on the utilities, make sure you turn breaker switches and water valves off.

One question I get asked all the time is, "Should I open up a temporary electric account or a permanent one?" Always open a permanent account.

Many agents choose not to open up a permanent utilities account because these accounts require a deposit, and sometimes a very large deposit. But temporary accounts only remain good for thirty to sixty days, and the electric company will turn the service off as soon as these accounts expire. Also, remember from Chapter 1 that you are looking at a ninety-day turnaround time to close on your first property. Therefore, you must have the utilities on until the buyer's ink is dried at the closing table.

Also, there are unforeseen circumstances that arise out of all transactions, even the cash ones (e.g., title hold ups). The last thing you want is for your home not to have utilities, which causes a delay in closing. Do not let this happen.

More importantly, for certain types of financing, such as the Federal Housing Administration (FHA) mortgage insurance, appraisals must have access to both water and electricity. Also, if your property needs repairs or a home buyer is doing an inspection, utilities will be needed; therefore, no utilities, no closing. Turn on the utilities immediately. Don't fret over it. You will be reimbursed for it by the bank.

 **INSIDER TIP**

> Use e-bills to keep track of expenditures. Many banks have a deadline
> that they require for you to submit final utility bills. Having electronic
> billing will help you efficiently meet those timelines.

One recommendation we can give you is to not sign up for auto-
pay. Sometimes there are unforeseen instances where water is being
stolen and you end up with an unusually large bill. The last thing you
want is to have to explain to the bank why you are demanding a larger-
than-usual reimbursement.

 **INSIDER TIP**

> Many utility companies allow you to create a master account whereby
> they will waive the deposit requirement if you are able to obtain a surety
> bond or letter of credit from a financial institution. This may be a way of
> preserving your cash instead of using it to pay deposits.

We also recommend setting up a master utilities account if it's available in your area. Having a master account will sometimes enable
you to apply a deposit for a property that you have already sold to a
new property that you are about to list. This can help save time and
resources by automating the deposits to roll over from one property
to the next. In addition, this will efficiently help you control your cash
flow by keeping your cash in your pocket instead of having it somewhere in the mail.

A few final words about utilities: most of the time, the property will
have a main water shut-off valve on the outside of the house. Don't get
baffled if you have turned on the water and there is no water coming
from the faucets. Check the outside for the main water shut-off valve
and make sure the valve is not off. Also, keep the home at 74 degrees
Fahrenheit. Based on my experience and research, this temperature
meets the perfect balance between marketability and cost effectiveness.

AGENT SIGN-OFF SHEETS

Once you leave the property and head back to your office to upload your OCR into the bank platform, you will be emailed one final task to complete. This happens if the property you visited was marked "vacant." Once the bank platform shows the property is unoccupied, it automatically triggers an email to their in-network cleaning crew to visit the property and clean it. Your job is to re-visit the property within twenty-four hours and rate the cleaning.

If the cleaning was done sloppily, or if the cleaning was incomplete, you need to note the deficiencies in an agent sign off. This sheet has everything that you will look for when checking the cleaning work. If everything is good, you will sign off on the cleaning job. If the cleaners need to go back to finish, then you will not sign off on the cleaning job and will mark what needs to be redone.

It is important that you do not base the rating on the condition of the property. The rating should be based only on the initial cleaning, trash out, and landscaping (if any) performed by the cleaning company. If you have a property that has a concaved roof, it should not influence your rating on the quality of work the cleaning company did. Banks have a lot of checks and balances in place. You will check the cleaning company's work while an appraiser will check your BPO to make sure you are not low-balling the value.

Don't let cleaning companies take advantage of your eagerness to list the property for sale and do a low-quality job. Cleaning companies know that after a property is cleaned, it will be listed for sale (assuming there are no repairs needed), and if you're in a hurry to list the property you might overlook a less-than-professional effort. However, as the listing agent, it is your responsibility to make sure that you check the quality of their work and ensure that all items have been cleaned to satisfactory conditions.

Even if one item is deficient, you must flag it. Let them make a second trip out there to fix it. Remember, it can only help you market the property to a customer and will help the bank achieve a maximum value for it. No one wants to open a door and have a spider fall on them or have a dead rat in the middle of the living room. I have experienced both. It is not pretty.

Below is a sample agent sign-off sheet checklist (see Appendix N) that you can use when inspecting cleaning. You will be required to confirm that each area has been cleaned to satisfactory conditions. If it hasn't, you are to mark the respective area as "deficient," so the cleaning company can redo the cleaning in that area.

Agent Sign-Off Sheet

Cleaning—Initial (Completed __/___/____):

Entry Way (Circle deficiencies if any)
    Floor swept and mopped
    Cobwebs removed from corners and ceilings
    Baseboards and walls wiped down
    Light fixtures, switch and outlet covers are wiped down
    Storm door glass is cleaned

Living Room (Circle deficiencies if any)
    Floor swept and mopped
    Carpet vacuumed (if any)
    Cobwebs removed from corners and ceilings
    Baseboards and walls wiped down
    Light fixtures, switch and outlet covers are wiped down
    Windows are clean (no streaks)
    Window sills are wiped off
    Door frames are free of dust
    Fireplace is cleaned out (if any)
    Ceiling fan blades are clean

Family Room (Circle deficiencies if any)
    Floor swept and mopped
    Carpet vacuumed (if any)
    Cobwebs removed from corners and ceilings

Baseboards and walls wiped down

Light fixtures, switch and outlet covers are wiped down

Windows are clean (no streaks)

Window sills are wiped off

Door frames are free of dust

Fireplace is cleaned out (if any)

Ceiling fan blades are clean

Master Bedroom (Circle deficiencies if any)

Floor swept and mopped

Carpet vacuumed (if any)

Cobwebs removed from corners and ceilings

Baseboards and walls wiped down

Light fixtures, switch and outlet covers are wiped down

Windows are clean (no streaks)

Window sills are wiped off

Door frames are free of dust

Fireplace is cleaned out (if any)

Ceiling fan blades are clean

Other Bedrooms (Circle deficiencies if any)

Floor swept and mopped

Carpet vacuumed (if any)

Cobwebs removed from corners and ceilings

Baseboards and walls wiped down

Light fixtures, switch and outlet covers are wiped down

Windows are clean (no streaks)

Window sills are wiped off

Door frames are free of dust

Fireplace is cleaned out (if any)

Ceiling fan blades are clean

Kitchen (Circle deficiencies if any)

Sink is cleaned

Stove and oven are cleaned both inside and out

Microwave is cleaned both inside and out (if any)

Dishwasher is cleaned both inside and out

Refrigerator is cleaned both inside and out

Floor is swept and mopped

Windows are cleaned (no streaks)

Window sills are wiped off

Counters are clean (no grease)

Cobwebs are removed from corners and ceiling

Baseboards and walls are wiped down

Light fixtures, switch and outlet covers are wiped down

Ceiling fan blades are clean

Porch-Enclosed (Circle deficiencies if any)

Floor swept and mopped

Cobwebs removed from corners and ceilings

Baseboards and walls wiped down

Light fixtures, switch and outlet covers are wiped down

Windows are clean (no streaks)

Window sills are wiped off

Door frames are free of dust

Ceiling fan blades are clean

Master Bathroom (Circle deficiencies if any)

Floor swept and mopped

Cobwebs removed from corners and ceilings

Baseboards and walls wiped down

Light fixtures, switch and outlet covers are wiped down

Windows are clean (no streaks)

Window sills are wiped off

Door frames are free of dust

Sinks and faucets are clean

Toilet is clean

Tub and shower are clean

Surrounding area is clean and free of dust

Mirrors, cabinets, drawers, and shelves are clean

Other Bathroom (Circle deficiencies if any)

    Floor swept and mopped

    Cobwebs removed from corners and ceilings

    Baseboards and walls wiped down

    Light fixtures, switch and outlet covers are wiped down

    Windows are clean (no streaks)

    Window sills are wiped off

    Door frames are free of dust

    Sinks and faucets are clean

    Toilet is clean

    Tub and shower are clean

    Surrounding area is clean and free of dust

    Mirrors, cabinets, drawers, and shelves are clean

Landscaping (Circle deficiencies if any)

    Flower beds are free of debris

    Grass is cut

    Debris removed from driveway and yard

    Weeds are trimmed around foundation and fence line

    Weeds are removed from driveway and yard

    Walkways, driveways, sidewalks, and yard are edged

    Shrubs are trimmed below window sill

Misc. (Circle deficiencies if any)

    Handrails are present (if any)

    Exposed wires are capped

    Windows are boarded if cracked

    Broken glass is swept and noted

    Battery operated smoke detectors are installed

    Air fresheners are present

Some agent sign-off sheets will ask you to give an overall rating as a big picture consensus. When providing an overall rating for the initial cleaning, be sure you keep these categories in mind:

- Excellent: all cleaning criteria were completed to satisfactory conditions. No areas were deficient; the subject is clean, safe, and presentable.
- Good: most of the cleaning criteria were completed to satisfactory conditions. If only one area was deficient, then you should mark the overall rating as "good."
- Fair: some deficiencies require the cleaning company to go back to resolve the cleaning issues. If two or more areas are deficient, you should mark the overall rating as "fair."
- Poor: serious deficiencies are present and the cleaning company must go back to immediately resolve the deficiencies. Mark the overall rating as "poor" when there more than three line items are marked as deficient.

Also, inform the cleaning company of any special requests that you have. Remember, since you will be completing the initial inspection before the cleaning services are approved, you will be able to assess the condition of the property. Here are some items you may ask the cleaning company to take care of:

- Replace any light bulbs
- Replace any air conditioning filters
- Remove any appliances that are a safety hazard or that depreciate the value and appeal of the subject
- Remove any curtains or blinds that may be outdated
- Remove mail and trash from the property
- Secure any outside gates
- Board up any broken windows
- Fix any toilet valves that do not allow toilets to be flushed
- Add air fresheners to a particular part of the home
- Fix any exposed wires
- Add receptacle plates
- Add smoke detectors, or add batteries to remove any "chirping"
- Provide landscape package

Be sure that the cleaning company bills your bank directly. Most banks have an allowance that they provide cleaning companies with.

Remember, the first assignment that you receive is the most important assignment you will ever get. Treat it with as much detail, precision, and care as you can. Using the previous guidelines will be to your benefit. You will soon see assignments start piling up. Remember to treat each new assignment with the same diligence and precision as your first one. But before getting excited about future assignments, it's time to learn about Step 2 of the REO Cycle: Conducting the Perfect BPO.

 SHARE YOUR STORY

Do you have a success story you would like to share about receiving your first assignment? Any crazy occupancy checks situations or evictions? Please log on and submit it for your chance to be featured in the next revised edition of *REO Boom*:

www.reoboom.com/story

POINTS TO REMEMBER

- Add special requests to your agent sign offs. Start thinking of marketing when doing your agent sign-off sheet so you can find a buyer fast.
- Be very detailed when signing off on the cleaning. You don't want to put your name on the line when something is deficient and requires attention.
- Turn breaker switches and water valves off before turning on utilities.
- Set up a master account for your utilities but do not use auto pay.
- Have the estoppel bill added to the final pay-off amount so you do not incur the costs upfront.
- Gain cooperation from managers at condos and HOAs. Explain that you want to help them get all their past-due amounts paid

and current. Establish rapport, smile, and don't argue unless you have to.

- Schedule your locksmith or cleaning crew in advance for a property eviction, as the sheriff or police can take two to six hours to show up.
- Resist the temptation to not complete cash for keys. Even though your cost is the time in which it will take to be reimbursed, the benefits far outweigh the negatives.
- Know the three occupant options posting rules: tape the letter, take a date-stamped photo, and then knock on the door; the number one defense in court is, "I never received the notice."
- Know what you're getting into before making your first trip. Check out the tax record, call the association, call the utility company, and find out as much information as possible so your trip will be efficient and worthwhile.

Conducting the Perfect BPO

THE PERFECT BROKER PRICE OPINION (BPO)

I remember when I first learned about BPOs. I had no idea what it was. One person told me it stood for "best price obtainable." Someone else told me a BPO is only used for short sales. After several months, I realized that BPO stands for "Broker Price Opinion" and it was one of the biggest assignments I ever had. It was tough. On my first BPO, I spent two nights back to back changing and revising, thinking out loud, "What does the bank want to see?" I had no idea. I was scared, but at the same time, I was excited.

The broker's price opinion is used by the bank as a resource to determine the list price of the property. Banks want to maximize the sales price for a property, but at the same time, they don't want to be priced out of the market. In a market where prices are going down, not having the optimal price the first time around can lead to a series of price cuts in order for the property to get sold.

This is what the banks don't want. They don't want the property to be priced too high, or they will have to slash and burn the list price in order to get an offer. They also don't want to price their home too low. The broker's price opinion is not just your opinion on the value of the home. It's more than that.

The BPO is one of the most important assignments that you will complete. You must be accurate and detailed. Remember, you are not an appraiser, but you need to give your opinion on the value of the property. You are the expert in your area. The banks trust your expertise.

The BPO that you complete is a direct representation of your ability to successfully sell a home for the bank. How else would you be able to sell a home without knowing its true valuation? Always check your BPO twice before uploading it to your bank's platform; there is zero room for error.

In your BPO, you will determine the as-is and repaired value of the property, recommend a marketing strategy for pricing to the bank based on the target buyer, outline and comment on repairs and suggested repair inspections, and present extensive photos that show completed repairs, potential liabilities, and a detailed representation of the interior home.

After completing about a thousand BPOs, I finally understood how to perfect them. In the beginning, when I first started doing BPOs, my only concern was choosing the best comparable property (comps) and pinpointing the correct values. Then, after a while, I started to focus more on the repairs and marketing strategy part of the BPO. Finally, I was able to put it all together to complete the perfect BPO. It's actually an easy process; I'll walk you through it step-by-step.

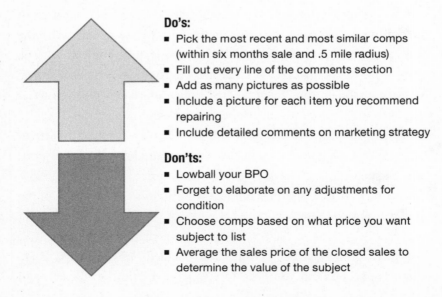

Do's:
- Pick the most recent and most similar comps (within six months sale and .5 mile radius)
- Fill out every line of the comments section
- Add as many pictures as possible
- Include a picture for each item you recommend repairing
- Include detailed comments on marketing strategy

Don'ts:
- Lowball your BPO
- Forget to elaborate on any adjustments for condition
- Choose comps based on what price you want subject to list
- Average the sales price of the closed sales to determine the value of the subject

 **INSIDER TIP**

Never try to lowball a BPO. Banks want to maximize the sales price from each asset without being priced out of the market. However, keep in mind that banks will order a state certified appraisal for the property to compare your valuation with. If your valuation differs substantially from the appraised valuation, that raises a big red flag.

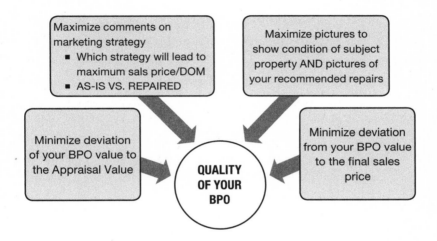

YOUR BPO PICTURES

When I first started doing BPOs, I was not efficient. I was not taught how to do a perfect BPO, so I made mistakes, learned, made more mistakes, and finally got it right. I remember when I first started I would have to make five trips to the subject property (my REO) because I would always forget to do something. For example, I forgot to take a picture of the breaker panel open, so I went back. Or I forgot to take a picture of the street view, so I went back again. Finally, I learned it because I became more efficient. I found a way to do the perfect BPO without having to worry about making mistakes or forgetting something.

The first tool you need when conducting your BPO is a good camera. You need a digital camera, wide angle or lens, 35 mm, with a zoom and date-stamp feature. When you stand in the corner of a room, for example, only a wide lens camera will allow you to capture the depth of the room. The flash on the camera must be bright. However, don't simply rely on your flash. You must have good lighting throughout the home—this is part of the reason it's so important to have the utilities turned on. Expect to take about fifty pictures per property, if not more. If you think you've taken enough, take some more. Look at every detail.

Pretend the bank is in a foreign country and it wants to know every single detail about the property, from the color of the roses in the front lawn to the dust in the corners of the garage. It wants photos of everything. If your REO has three bedrooms and two and a half baths, you must take pictures of each room, including the extra half-bath. If you see a dead rat, rodents, a green pool with mold (pools must be blue), or a beehive, take a picture of it. Remember the "model" story from Chapter 4? Well, once that condo was vacant, guess what I found lying around everywhere? Used condoms. Yes, I took a picture of them.

When you first go to the property, take as many photos as you can. Then when you go home you can choose which ones you want to include in the BPO. It's better to be safe than sorry. The three photos I most frequently see missing from new REO agents' BPOs are:

1. Breaker box (with electrical box open to view breaker switches)
2. AC/internal air handlers for condos (sometimes they are located in the attic or ceiling compartment)
3. Water heater (sometimes one water heater can be for the entire floor in a condo)

 INSIDER TIP

Tankless water heaters are now becoming popular in homes, so look out for them and make sure to get a photograph.

Your pictures should also have a clear transition. For example, don't take a picture of the balcony view after taking a picture of the living room, especially when you still have to include the family room. The goal with your BPO pictures is to story-tell. Start with the front lawn, then take a picture of the front door, then the living room, and work your way to the backyard.

If an asset manager is sitting in a different state or even a different country for that matter, they must be able to envision walking through the house and feeling the wood on the floor through your pictures. You must be a storyteller.

THE GOAL WITH YOUR BPO PICTURES IS TO STORYTELL

Pictures should be bright and clear. Do not include pictures that are blurry. If you need to go back to the property, go back—it's OK. In the beginning, you may feel nervous and forget a couple of things. It's normal; it happens all the time.

When taking pictures of rooms, you want to show the depth of the room, so open up all the closets, cabinetry, doors, etc. Stand in at least two corners of the room and take a picture of the entire room. Make sure the blinds are open; otherwise it will look like you are taking the pictures in a rush.

When you take pictures in the kitchen, include a separate picture of each appliance. This is important, because if the appliances get stolen in the future, you know exactly what replacements are necessary. Also, open the refrigerator, microwave, and oven doors, as well as the cabinets, to show the depth of the kitchen, cabinetry, and appliances.

Always include a picture of the breaker panel, thermostat, interior and exterior air conditioner units, water heater, and any other detailed aspects of the home. Personal property (e.g., left behind furniture) pictures should be taken and included at the end of the BPO pictures section with captions that illustrate the estimated value of the personal property. When determining the value of personal property, always take into consideration the garage sale value, not fair market price that you could sell the items for on eBay. Usually, the price is twenty-five cents on the dollar of what you can buy at a furniture store.

Don't forget to take multiple pictures of the street views, so the asset manager can get an idea of the curb appeal and level of traffic that may or may not affect the value of the property. Stand in front of the driveway and face all directions (north, south, east, west). Think of yourself as a professional photographer, and your REO is the model. It's better to take a hundred photos than to drive back to the property because you forgot one or two.

In your BPO, you will be recommending repairs. Therefore, it is crucial to include pictures for every repair that you recommend. Also, banks are huge on liability issues. Anything you see that screams "law suit" must be shot and labeled clearly. For example, a pool without a cage or cover poses a huge liability issue if a family views the home and brings their children—the children could fall in and drown. Think of it as if you were doing a final walk-through for a home buyer. What would you see that you would want to get replaced for your customer?

Finally, you must take pictures of your competing (comps) properties and active (actives) properties. You will have three comps and three actives in your BPO. Do not just download a picture from the MLS. Physically drive to all six properties and shoot the front door. Your comps and actives should all be within a half-mile radius. We have included a BPO Photo Checklist for you to print out and take with you in the field (see Appendix S).

BPO PHOTO CHECKLIST

☐ Exterior front

☐ Rear view

☐ Steeet view (multiple views)

☐ Picture of the street intersection

☐ Picture of any highways or commercial buildings that are in direct view from subject

☐ Entrance view

☐ At least two pictures of every room (bathroom and bedrooms)

☐ Picture of balcony and/or door leading to balcony

☐ Picture of balcony view (left, middle, right)

☐ Backyard

☐ Interior AC handler

☐ External AC unit

☐ Water heater

☐ Breaker panel

- [ ] At least two pictures of every area (dining area, living area, etc.)

- [ ] At least two pictures of the kitchen

- [ ] Picture of each appliance

- [ ] Washer and dryer

- [ ] Breakfast nook

- [ ] Den

- [ ] Stairs

- [ ] Electrical meter

- [ ] Any damage to the property

- [ ] Include a picture for each repair you recommend

- [ ] Pictures of the warning signs you have placed around the property

- [ ] Pictures of all three comparable closed sales

- [ ] Picture of all three competitive listings

- [ ] Picture of personal property— added to the end with estimated garage sale value of each item

After you have taken all the pictures, you will have to go home and choose the ones to present with your BPO. But first, reduce the file size of the pictures. The last thing you want is to upload all these pictures and then realize that the size of the BPO is too large to upload. You can find a free resizer software program online by searching Google.

When you finally do upload, make sure all your pictures are right side up. Your goal should be to turn around a BPO within forty-eight hours, regardless of whether the bank gives you more time. Some banks can give you up to seven days, and some will only give you forty-eight hours.

Also, always remember to include three pictures per page. Do not submit a BPO with a blank picture or blank white space. This looks like you put in only minimal effort. If you are stuck, re-use an exterior front picture to fill up the page.

The BPO is composed of different sections, all of which tie in together to give the bank as much information as possible on the property, its value, your recommended marketing price strategy, and ultimately what you plan to do to take the asset from its initial state to a successful sale.

When filling out the BPO, you will need forms that are consistent with your bank. Usually your bank will provide you with the forms or will direct you to use "forms software." We have included some different software providers in Appendix A so you can shop around.

Also, we have included a sample BPO form (Appendix K) that you can follow along with in each section. For a free download, please visit reoboom.com. Note, each bank and BPO form is different. Therefore, we go over the most important sections in *all* BPO forms, not any particular ones. Now with that being said, let's start with the first section: Client and General Information.

BPO SECTION 1: CLIENT AND GENERAL INFO

The first section contains pertinent information related to the property or asset you are valuing. Please remember the following when filling out section one:

- Make sure the REO ID number is 100 percent accurate. For example, do not confuse 0 with O. Always copy this ID from your original assignment letter, then paste it onto your BPO form.
- The asset manager's name must be 100 percent spelled correctly. Do not insult your asset manager by not knowing how to spell his or her name.
- Completion Date: Aim to have this date no later than forty-eight hours from your initial assignment. DO NOT put a completion date prior to your assignment date; this is a big red flag.
- Remember to indicate which BPO you are completing; this is especially important when conducting an "updated BPO." If you are doing an updated BPO or second BPO (remember the REO Lunch Method strategy from Chapter 2?), then switch the box from "initial" to "updated."

REO Number	[_____]
Completed By	[_____]
Loan Number	[_____]
Property Address	[_____]
Phone Number	[_____]
Property, State, and Zip	[_____]

Completion Date [_____] mm/dd/yyyy

BPO ☐ Initial ☐ 2nd Opinion ☐ Update ☐ Exterior Only

Sales Representative [_____]

Client Name [_____]

Broker Office [_____]

Completed By [_____]

Fax No [_____]

Email [_____]

BPO SECTION 2: GENERAL MARKET CONDITIONS

The second section deals with the details on the general market conditions in which the subject property is located. These are the general conditions that may affect how you would currently market the property. The bank wants to know the general market trends in the neighborhood for which the subject is located.

- In today's economy, most of the time the market condition will be "depressed." This is good for you.
- Employment conditions will usually be "declining." I believe we are at a national unemployment level of 9 percent as of the middle of 2011.
- Market price usually shows "decreased." To determine what percentage the price has decreased, compare the difference of

the tax assessed value for the subject in the past year (i.e., tax assessed value one year ago to the tax assessed value this year) divided by the tax assessed value one year ago.

> **Example:**
> 2011 tax assessed value = $100,000
> 2012 tax assessed value = $85,000
> **Difference = $15,000**
> **Divided by previous Year's value ($15,000/$100,000) = 15% loss**

- Calculate what percentage of tenants and owners reside in the neighborhood. Most MLS have functions that provide this information automatically. If your local MLS does not, consider looking at the sales versus rentals in the past twelve months for the neighborhood. Most likely, there will be a greater percentage of owners to tenants in the neighborhood.

- Calculate the supply of competitive listings (active and pending sales).
  - Normal Supply = 6 to 50 (Needs marketing updates every 25 days, if still on market. We discuss this in Chapter 7.)
  - Over Supply = 51 + (Need to prevent overexposure to market, differentiate asset through repairs, marketing strategy, etc.)
  - Shortage Supply = 0 to 5 (Can be priced with a longer time frame such as a 120-day marketing time period and can be sold "as-is.")
  - How many total competitive listings?
  - Of which, how many are REOs?
  - The more competitive the REO listings, the more attention you should pay to your marketing strategy/recommendation.
  - How many are boarded up? Look at MLS pictures for listings to determine this.

 **INSIDER TIP**

Be sure that the supply of properties (normal, over, or shortage) does not conflict with the number of comparable listings.

Market conditions:

     ☑ Depressed   ☐ Slow   ☐ Stable   ☐ Improving   ☐ Excellent

Employment conditions:

     ☑ Declining   ☐ Stable   ☐ Improving

Market price has: ☑ Decreased   ☐ Increased   ☐ Remained stable

[_____]% in past [_____] months

Owners vs Tenants:

    [_____] % owner occupant [_____] % tenant

Supply ☐   ☐ Over   ☐ Shortage of comparable listing in neighborhood

Normal

\# Sale comp. units:

[_____]

\# REO/Corp. listings:

[_____]

\# Boarded/Block-up:

[_____]

BPO SECTION 3: YOUR SUBJECT PROPERTY

This section deals with your REO property (also called the "subject property") and the general marketability of it. Components include how the subject property compares to other comparable properties, financing types available for the property, when the property was last listed for sale, and what, if any, reasons there are for its failure to sell, the type of property (e.g., condo, single family home, duplex, etc.), and the Homeowner's Association information. Below are some important tips to consider while you are filling out this section:

- Range of values should be the range of closed comparable sales.
- Subject's improvement: usually marked as "appropriate" unless subject is much superior or much inferior in quality relative to the comps.

- Average marketing time: Take the average of the days on market (DOM) for the closed comparable sales in the last six months. Use the three comps you will use for the BPO.
- Indicate if subject has been on market for the last twelve months and under what category (as a short sale, conventional sale, etc.). Also, was it listed by another broker? If subject was on property, indicate why didn't it sell (i.e., it was over-priced, not repaired, not marketed appropriately).
- What types of financing are available? Please note here if subject does not qualify for FHA (Federal Housing Administration mortgage insurance backed mortgage loan) due to the community not being approved or if repairs are needed to make it conform to lending requirements. Typically, FHA loans apply to those properties that are in habitable condition. Also, if subject is a condo, is the current master insurance policy up to date?
- Unit type: Look at the tax records to determine if subject is single family detached versus attached (i.e., zero lot and block), multi-family, condo, co-op, mobile home (include mobile home serial number in comments and take a photo), condotel (condo that is operated as a hotel), townhome, modular, or other.
- Specify the accurate HOA/condo fee. Call the HOA and/or condo and ask:
  - What is the current monthly/quarterly fee for your unit?
  - What does this fee cover?
  - Are there any other associations that govern the subject? What are their fees?
  - Include the phone number for the condo you just called. This will be used by many parties to communicate with the HOA/Condo. Verify that the phone number works before entering it into your BPO.

 **INSIDER TIP**

Do not go on the MLS to find out the fee based on what other agents have put in the MLS. Always call and verify the current fee(s) for your subject property. Include the name of the contact person in addition to the name of the HOA/condo.

Value range: $ [＿＿＿＿＿] to $ [＿＿＿＿＿]

Subject improvement: ☐ Over   ☐ Under   ☐ Appropriate for the neighborhood

Area marketing time: [＿＿＿＿＿] Days

Financing available: ☐ Yes   ☐ No   If no, explain: [＿＿＿＿＿]

Last 12 mo. on market ☐ Yes   ☐ No   If yes, price $ [＿＿＿＿＿]

Reason for no sale: [＿＿＿＿＿]

Unit type: ☐ Single family detached   ☐ Condo   ☐ Co-op   ☐ Mobile Home
            ☐ Single family detached   ☐ Townhouse   ☐ Modular   ☐ Condotel

Fee: ☐ Monthly   ☐ Annually   **Fee $:** [＿＿＿＿＿]

Current: ☐ Yes   ☐ No   **Delinquent $:** [＿＿＿＿＿]

Fee includes: ☐ Insurance   ☐ Landscape   ☐ Pool   ☐ Tennis   ☐ Other

Association name/ contact: [＿＿＿＿＿]

Phone no: [＿＿＿＿＿]

BPO SECTION 4: YOUR COMPETITION

Competitive Sold Properties (Comps)

This section deals with inputting data from three comparable closed sales. You will find your comps on the MLS. The key is to compare apples to apples. The best comparables are those that are most similar, most recent, and have a reasonable amount of days on market. Usually, when the DOM is very low, it is likely that the property was priced too low. However, to determine if this is true, you would have to look at the spread in list price versus sales price of these low DOM properties.

 **INSIDER TIP**

Choose the most recent and most comparable sales (must have been sold in last six months and within a half-mile radius of subject). If the comps you select are not within these guidelines, you must make a comment stating so.

Here are some guidelines to follow when choosing comps:

1. Your local MLS will have various ways for you to find the best comps. In many cities, your local MLS will have a feature for you to draw a radius around your subject property. It's best to use a half-mile circle radius.
2. Choose comps with similar conditions.
   - REO comps are the best choice (remember, compare apples to apples)
   - Similar age +/- 10 years
   - Adjusted square feet within 15 percent of your subject property's square footage
   - Similar bed and bath count to your subject
   - Similar design (number of stories), construction, garage, lot size, and amenities
3. Address: Enter each address with correct state abbreviation. The

three comparable sales should be located in the same building as subject (if a condo) or at least located in same subdivision if a house.

4. Proximity: Choose to write in distance per miles or blocks. If the comps are in the same building, write "same bldg;" if they are in the same subdivision, write "same sdev."

5. Place a check mark in each of the comps that were REOs.

6. Write the sales price for each of the three comps.

7. Price/Gross Living Area (GLA): This is automatically calculated after you enter the GLA and sales price for each of the comps. If not, simply divide each sales price by the respective gross living area.

8. Data Source: Include the MLS number.

9. Sale Date and DOM: Sales date should be the closing date (some MLS refer to this as "CD"). Days on market should be calculated as the total days on market from the initial listing date to the sales date. Some agents may have expired listings that they have to relist, and thus DOM can be misinterpreted if you don't manually verify the days on market. Always double check DOM to ensure accurate figures.

 **INSIDER TIP**

When verifying the sales price, look in the tax records, not the MLS, as the MLS may not always be accurate. Garbage in is garbage out. Always double check to validate your figures.

Making Adjustments

Before moving on to your marketing pricing strategy (Section 5), I want to discuss making "adjustments" to your comps to match your subject. Adjustments are needed to compensate for differences of features between your comps and your REO home. Remember, your subject property is the base or standard. Therefore, you will be adjusting the value of the comparable sales to reflect the standard. Never, under any circumstances, make adjustments to your subject property. Think of it as a finished statue. Here are the two basic adjustment rules:

> *Rule #1*: If your comparable sale includes a superior quality, then a negative adjustment is required.
>
> *Rule #2*: If your comparable sale includes an inferior quality, then a positive adjustment is required.

I included some typical adjustments items you will see when conducting your BPO:

- Sales or Financing Concessions: If the comparable sale included any seller contributions, make a negative adjustment for that amount.
- Location: All comparable sales should be in the same location; thus this field should be the same for all properties. Select: Suburban, Rural, Resort, Rural Sub, Downtown, Urban, etc.
- Site: Indicate size of the lot in terms of acres. You can also use square feet. Remember to be consistent across all comparable sales and competitive listings when choosing how to specify site. For condos, include the percentage of ownership to common elements.
- View: Very important for high rise, lake homes, and units where view is a major component of the homebuyer's decision to purchase one unit versus another unit in the same subdivision/condo. Always check the comparable sales listing and photos. Do not just rely on the listing remarks. Verify with the photos that the comparable sale has the view it claimed in the listing. When in doubt, err on the side of conservativeness. Carefully determine how much of an adjustment you are providing to "view." Guideline: Keep the view adjustment within 10 percent of the competitive sale's price.
- Design/Appeal: Indicate whether it is one story, two story, split level, etc. Try to use comparable sales of the same design/appeal. If you know your home is two stories, look for two-story

comparable sales from the beginning. Don't get to this point only to realize, "Oh, this is a one-story home."

- Quality of Construction: Indicate type and quality of construction. For example, concrete block structures (CBS)/typical, stucco/wood-frame, etc. Try to compare CBS construction homes to CBS construction homes.
- Age versus Year Built: Be sure you input what the required field is asking. Note that age is the number of years since the subject was originally constructed, while year built is the exact year the property was built. Do not confuse the two.
- Condition:
  - Poor: Boarded up, uninhabitable, hazardous conditions, severe structural damage.
  - Fair: Habitable but not well maintained.
  - Average: Generally well maintained, no updates visible in interior or exterior.
  - Good: Improvements to property including roof, interior, exterior. Very well maintained.
  - Excellent: Excellent workmanship and all major facets of home updated. Visually above par from exterior and interior.
- Room Count:
  - Total: include living room, dining room, kitchen, bedrooms, bathrooms, etc.
  - Bedrooms: Include total number of bedrooms.
  - Bathrooms: Include total number of bathrooms (use .5 to add half bathrooms).
- Gross Living Area:
  - Include the total gross living area. Be consistent. Always compare GLA to GLA.
- Functional Utility:
  - Described as "good," "typical," "average," "excellent." Most comparables should have the same functional utility as subject.

- Heating/Cooling:
  - Describe the heating and cooling. For example, central heating and cooling (CHAC) that runs on electricity versus CHAC running on gas, window air conditioner, base board electric, etc.
- Energy Efficient Items: Is there a tankless water heater? Include it.
- Garage/Carport: Include if property has a carport or a single/double/triple car garage; if the property is a condo, how many parking spaces, detached or attached garage?
- Pool/Fence: Indicate which comparable sales have a pool or fence and adjust accordingly.

It is very important to never double adjust. For example, if you are adjusting for square footage and adjusting for bed and bath, make sure that the additional adjustment is valid and necessary. Most often, an adjustment for interior square footage encompasses adjustments for bed and bath.

Below are some common maximum adjustments you can make to your comps. I have included a full chart in Appendix M, or feel free to download a free chart from reoboom.com.

COMMON ADJUSTMENTS

IF SUBJECT HAS:	AND COMPARABLE HAS:	ADJUST THE COMP:
N/A	Over 300 DOM	MAX: 10% of sales price (-)
Residential view	Lake view	MAX: -$20,000
DESIGN: One story	DESIGN: Two stories	MAX: -$10,000
AGE: N/A	AGE: Ten years older than subject	MAX: +$10,000

CONDITION: Fair	Poor	+$4,000
	Fair	N/A
	Average	-$4,000
	Good	-$8,000
	Excellent	-$12,000
HTNG/CLNG: Window	CHAC/Elec	MAX: -$6,000
No pool	Pool	MAX: -$12,000
No fence	Fence	MAX: -$10,000
1 car garage	2 car garage	MAX: -$4,000
Porch	No porch	MAX: +$2,500
Carport	No carport/no garage	MAX: +$3,000

Competitive Listings (Actives)

The competing active listings are similar to your sold comps but require you to input data on the properties that are listed for sale. This gives you a better understanding of the competition you will face when you do, in fact, list the property for sale. Knowing what other properties are listed for is extremely important. Words of caution: Some properties are listed at very high prices and have been on the market for a while. It is important to find properties that have a reasonable amount of days on the market.

Follow the same guidelines for closed sales (comps) as you would for actives. Note: If you are having a difficult time finding comparable active listings, you may also use "pending sales," but this must be disclosed in the comments section of your BPO.

BPO SECTION 5: YOUR REPAIR STRATEGY

In the repair section, you will list the necessary repairs for the property. Even if you do not recommend doing certain repairs, you should still list them so your asset manager knows what could be done.

In addition to listing the repairs, you will estimate the cost of repairs. Finally, if you are recommending repairing the items, be sure to place a checkmark on each repair you are recommending for the bank to complete. Typically, you should not include regular maintenance as part of the repairs, since these items will automatically be addressed by the cleaning company.

It is critical to include a picture for every repair that you are recommending. The asset manager needs to see to what extent the repairs you mention are necessary. You also want to include any type of inspection that you recommend, including termite, roof, structural HVAC, etc.

I have included some general benchmarks for you to use. See Appendix M for a full list of repairs.

- Carpet replacement can be estimated at .75 × Adj. Sq. Ft.
- Interior paint can be estimated at 1.5 × Adj. Sq. Ft.
- Water heater can be estimated at $450
- Appliances can be estimated at $600
- Interior and Exterior AC units can be estimated at $3,500

Many agents prefer to recommend interior paint and new carpets (if applicable) at the very minimum. The rationale is that the cost of interior paint and carpet replacement is so nominal that it is worth the extra marketability it brings. Remember to target your recommended repairs to your target buyer (home owner or investor).

If targeting homeowners, think neutrality. You don't want to reduce the marketability of your subject by having bold colors in the home. If the colors aren't neutral, recommend re-painting the interior. Also, consider the time involved. If you are recommending any repairs such as interior paint, you may as well recommend carpet replacement.

If your target buyer is an investor, you may recommend an as-is strategy, because investors usually have their own contractors and their own way of doing repairs.

BPO SECTION 6: YOUR MARKET PRICING STRATEGY

In the market pricing strategy section, you are recommending the best way to sell your REO. Should you complete repairs? Or should you sell it as-is? Who is the target buyer (home owner or investor)? Who is the most likely buyer? Will the cost of repairs be outweighed by the return from the additional spread in sales price? If so, to what extent?

Think about all these factors when you choose which marketing strategy to recommend. If you are recommending doing repairs, verify that the cost of repairing your subject property is outweighed by the increased value, less the cost of keeping the property off the market for the time it takes to complete the repairs.

For example, let's assume you have:

As-Is Value: $100,000
Cost of Repairs: $5,000
Time to Do Repair (est. at $1,000/day): 5 days
As-Repaired Value: $115,000

In this case, it is a good idea to recommend repairs, because by doing $5,000 of repairs, you are increasing the value of the home by $15,000, a difference of $10,000 that required only five days of time.

On the contrary, let's assume you have:

As-Is Value: $100,000
Cost of Repairs: $5,000
Time to Do Repair (est. at $1,000/day): 5 days
As-Repaired Value: $102,500

In this case, it will not be a good idea to recommend repairs, because by doing $5,000 of repairs, you are increasing the value of the home by $2,500, plus losing an additional five days that could have been used to market the property.

There are eight factors indicating that the most likely customer of your REO will be an investor:

1. Excessive repairs are needed.
2. Subject property has several liens.
3. There is no financing available.
4. Condo or townhome does not have a master insurance policy.
5. Subject property is in an area that is predominantly tenant occupied.
6. Subject has two or more illegal units.
7. Subject is currently occupied and the purchaser is responsible for removing occupants.
8. Cost of repairs does not outweigh the difference in what a homeowner versus an investor would pay.

Most BPOs will require that you insert the "as-is" and "repaired" market value, and, in addition, the "suggested listing price." Remember that competitive active listings do not have a strong indication of value because those properties have not sold. Closed comps, on the other hand, give you a better indication of what the market is willing to pay for similar properties. In the market value comments section, you must include why you recommend to market the property "as-is" or "repaired." You have to state your case.

INSIDER TIP

Make sure your BPO value is in line with the adjusted market value of comparable closed sales.

Some common reasons for marketing "as-is" are: very little repairs are required, the increase from value of repairs is not outweighed by costs, and the subject property is in a high demand area. Similarly, some common reasons for marketing the REO as "repaired" are that financing will require repairs, and the marginal difference between the additional sales price and cost of repairs is worth the time investment to complete the repairs.

BPO SECTION 7: FINAL COMMENTS

When I first started, I used to take four hours to complete a BPO. After doing hundreds of BPOs, it now takes me less than an hour for a condo or a townhome and less than an hour and a half for a single family home. This does not include the time spent inspecting and taking pictures of the REO. What takes me under an hour and a half to complete takes an asset manager less than a minute and a half to review. The first thing they glance at is the opinion of value, followed by the comments section.

In the comments section, you should include which of the properties were "short sales" versus "conventional sales" versus "REOs." It is important to realize that comparing an REO to an REO is better than comparing an REO to a short sale. To put it another way, if you are doing a BPO on a condo, and there is a similar unit in the same building that is an REO, when selling agents show your unit, they will compare it to the other REO.

So, your property must have a differential advantage, either in price or marketability. Use the comments section to include comments that aren't otherwise explicit in the BPO. Try not to be redundant, and use the section to make comments on items that can't be found by reading the data of your BPO. Some key components of your comments section are:

- Speak about which comparable you gave the most weight to in order to come up with your final valuation.
- Mention why your marketing strategy (as-is or repaired) is best to reach your target buyer (homeowner or investor).
- Speak about the competition. Is there a surplus of competitive listings? What does the asset manager need to know that can't be seen from the data?

- Speak about the return on repairs, if you recommend repairs. What type of return (in the form of increased sales price) will repairs bring?
- Note the days on market of your competitive sales, and how those days and marketing strategies affect your bank's marketing strategy. For example, some banks want to market an REO for sixty to ninety days. Refer back to the closed sales and their marketing strategies to infer which marketing strategy will work best for the subject.
- Mention any other market specific comments, such as location, economic justification on marketing strategy, and demand factors.

PUTTING IT ALL TOGETHER

As you can see, the BPO is just more than an opinion of value. It includes many points: details on the subject property (your REO), nature of the competition as a whole and specific comparable listings and sales, the best marketing strategy to target the most likely buyer, repairs that are needed versus repairs that are recommended, and factors that support your price and marketing strategy given the specific guidelines of the bank.

Some say that the BPO is the most important part of the REO cycle. An asset manager can tell a good BPO from a poor BPO right away. A good BPO will not look like it was done in a rush; rather, it will be detailed and have valid points and fundamental elements as described earlier. As the bank's REO listing agent, you should strive to impress your asset manager by mastering the BPO elements in this chapter. You should be visualizing the best way to market the property to maximize the sales price for the bank. It's important to understand that REOs do not compete only on price.

In my history of selling REOs, I'd say about 75 percent of them went through repairs. Because of the way I marketed the repairs, and how I used our marketing strengths to advertise how my REOs were superior to the competitive REOs, it was very easy and worthwhile to justify doing repairs.

In fact, I realized that many of the deals that went through were because of my ability to speak to a cooperating agent or homebuyer and tell them about how we repaired the property and how it was in "move-in condition." To attract the most buyers and the best offers, you need to know how to leverage the repairs that you've done to magnify your marketing. But before I delve into the marketing madness, let's learn how to manager repairs and inspections, which is Step 3 of the REO cycle.

 SHARE YOUR STORY

Do you have a success story you'd like to share about conducting your first BPO? Any wild pictures you took or adjustments you made? Please log on and submit it for your chance to be featured in the next revised edition of *REO Boom*:

www.reoboom.com/story

POINTS TO REMEMBER

- Make sure your final BPO value is in line with your closed comps.
- When making adjustments if your comps are superior, adjust downwards, and if your comps are inferior adjust upwards. Never make adjustments to your subject property.
- Use comparables in the same building/subdivision as frequently as possible.
- Look at the condition of the comparable by going through the MLS pictures, calling up the listing agent, searching tax records, and noting these remarks in the comments section of your BPO.
- Every recommended repair must have a photo showing the repair needed.
- Your turnaround time on BPOs should be no more than forty-eight hours.
- Make sure the electricity is on when you do your BPO so you can include pictures of the interior with lighted background.

- The meat of the BPO is the comps, and the potatoes are the photos. Choose the best comps and make sure your photos are detailed, clean, and organized.

Managing Repairs and Inspections

"The time to repair the roof is when the sun is shining."

—JOHN F. KENNEDY

AGENTS TRADITIONALLY HATE doing repairs. It takes more time, more work, and is sometimes truly a headache. Before REOs became so popular, I remember advertising "as-is, cash sale, quick closing." But then everyone began doing that, so the appeal of the "as-is cash only" sale began to fall through the cracks.

Now, REOs are everywhere, and buyers have a choice. Sometimes there may be more than a dozen listings on a block in the same month. If that's the case, the listing agents who don't repair will most likely get the short end of the stick.

Repairs are sometimes necessary. But I typically coach my agents to think of repairs as going above and beyond. Even if they aren't necessary, it's great to maximize every chance of getting an offer for your listing. As a listing agent, you are going to make a recommendation to the bank, detailing exactly what you think the bank should do in order to maximize the net sales price from the sale of the home.

Keep in mind that repairs cost time, money, liability, ongoing maintenance, and other miscellaneous costs that banks must put up with if they choose to make repairs to a property. However, repairs lead to better marketability, stronger likelihood that buyers will stay in a deal, and higher sales prices, and are sometimes necessary to make in order to comply with certain municipality requirements.

As agents, you have to balance the competing responsibility of getting the property closed as quickly as possible versus maximizing the sales price. It goes back to the time versus money conundrum. Yes, it takes extra time to make repairs and to check that repairs were done according to standards. But is the time spent doing the repairs worth the extra money that you would receive from the sale of the home? Will the repairs make a difference as to what people will offer for the home?

Below are some of the pros and cons of doing repairs.

PROS	CONS
■ More appeal and a better first impression ■ Makes it more likely to convert a showing into an offer ■ Differentiates your property from other active properties and any future properties that will be listed ■ Improves financing availability ■ More likely to lead into multiple offers ■ Weekly inspections are more likely to be favorable after repairs since many deficiencies will have been repaired	■ Creates more work for you ■ Requires that you inspect the property at least twice before repairs are complete and once more after repaires are complete ■ Requires you to list the property for a higher price than you would have listed it as-is ■ Delays the cash flow turnover of selling your REO and earning your commission ■ May require upfront expenditures on your part

AS-IS VERSUS REPAIRED

Banks don't want to throw good money after bad. They don't have an unlimited budget. As much as they want to get the highest sales price, they also want to make sure that they are disposing of their REOs as quickly as they can. Sometimes banks will sell "as-is," but it's becoming more popular for banks to repair properties before they list them for sale.

Therefore, it is very important to have a good foundation on the repair process, which will differ for the various banks you work with. As part of your commitment to helping the banks minimize their credit loss for the property, you want to make a recommendation to them on whether repairs should be completed on the property.

 **INSIDER TIP**

A good rule of thumb is that if repair costs exceed 15 percent of the subject property's BPO "as-is" value, then an "as-is" marketing strategy should be recommended.

There are many benefits of completing repairs to the subject property; they include:

1. Making the property more presentable and more attractive to end buyers.
2. Buyers will be inclined to offer a price above what the property is listed for, especially when selling agents can highlight the repairs that were done.
3. Retaining buyers who would have otherwise terminated their contract due to external circumstances that sometimes delay closing. Buyers will have a good first impression and that impression will carry forward to the day of closing. Without repairs, the buyers may become indifferent to your property versus the property down the street. I've had many deals that stayed together simply because the property was repaired.
4. Broadening the market for the types of purchasers, especially when repairs are made to meet minimum lender requirements.
5. Avoiding per diem fines (fines that accrue daily) imposed by municipalities for code violations that require repairs or permits until your REO is in compliance.

There are buyers who make decisions only on price. Sometimes, buyers choose one home over another based on the lower price. These price-sensitive consumers tend to change their minds a lot, but they love to purchase REOs. However, banks are aware that they can't compete on price. Think about it—if every bank started lowering its price because of another bank, the whole market would collapse. So that's why having repairs and enhancements done to your property will give your property a competitive advantage compared to the other property down the street. You won't be able to get that competitive advantage by lowering your price.

 **INSIDER TIP**

> For condos located in an FHA approved development, we recommend minimum repairs to meet lender requirements. We strongly advise not to market these properties as-is, because doing so will limit your target market and most likely not lead to the optimal sales price for the seller.

For all your properties, we recommend at a minimum:

1. Fresh paint
    - For walls: Moderate White SW 6140 (flat finish)
    - For baseboards, casings, and doors: Pure White SW 7005 (semi-gloss finish)
2. New carpets and/or carpet cleaning
3. Pool cleaning/preservation
4. Acid wash bathtub
5. Smoke detectors

Believe it or not, as the number of foreclosures start to rise steadily in the upcoming years, it will be more difficult to differentiate one house from another, especially in locales where the houses conform to a standard. Curb appeal, therefore, is very important to the ability of getting the maximum price possible for the bank.

We also recommend completing a "landscape package" on all single-family homes where the landscaping is not managed by the HOA. A typical landscape package would include approximately two cubic yards of mulch, application of weed killer in the beds, and an installation of weed barrier in the beds. Leaves and weeds should also be removed. Also, pressure washing driveways and front areas of the home will lead to better curb appeal for a reasonable cost.

 **INSIDER TIP**

Make sure all electric and water accounts are opened by the time you send a contractor to provide you with a bid.

AS-IS VERSUS REPAIRED

AS-IS	REPAIRED
■ Cost of repairs exceed 15% of subject's value ■ Comparables in BPO were all sold as-is ■ Permits required that will prolong marketability ■ HOA approval required for repairs	■ Located in FHA approved building ■ Comparables in BPO were repaired compared to subject ■ Need to comply with HOA/municipality violations ■ Repairs will increase the target market for subject, thereby increasing demand

Refer back to your BPO for another very important factor to consider when choosing whether or not to repair your subject property. If the comps that you used on your BPO were in "average" condition and had less than ninety days on market, then it would be in your best interest to bring your subject property to "average" condition.

If your property is already in average condition (i.e., the same condition as the comps you used on your BPO), then you may want to stick with an "as-is" strategy. On the other hand, if your comps had less than ninety days on market, on average, and they were in "good" condition, it may be in your best interest to bring the subject property to the same "good" condition.

Back in the summer of 2009, one of my mentees, who I will refer to as Chris, told me that he had just lost $1,500 for a silly mistake that he made. Chris was a top producer and very good at sales. He wasn't, however, good at operations. Chris was so excited about a new assignment that he had received from a new account, plus he had his own customer for the REO.

So he was naturally in a rush to get the property on the market and under contract with his customer. The customer told him that he wanted carpentry repairs in the home, and if Chris did that the customer told him he would make an offer right away. Chris was such a sales-oriented guy that all he could think of was getting the repairs done and getting his customer under contract. So he called up a local contractor and asked him for an estimate. The contractor gave him a bid over the phone, and Chris said, "Sounds good, let me know when the job is done."

Unfortunately, the contractor that Chris used wasn't approved to work with the bank. In addition, Chris never got the repairs approved prior to authorizing the repairs. So after Chris informed the asset manager that he had begun repairs, the asset manager said, "I didn't authorize any repairs yet. You haven't even given me a bid package." Chris was shocked. Not only did he look like an amateur, but he ended up incurring those expenses out of his own pocket after the bank chose to sell the property as-is. What's worse: Chris's customer backed out of the deal. Chris was devastated.

He felt like a failure. When he called me, I told him, "You're not the only one." I've heard story after story about how REO agents incorrectly or inadvertently complete repairs and then pay (sometimes literally) for their mistakes. I will show you how to avoid these mistakes, save your dignity, and successfully complete repairs without risking your hardearned money.

Keep in mind, though, that in most instances the listing agent is not the party who makes the final decision on whether to complete repairs or not. The asset manager is the actual party who will authorize the repairs. Most of the time, they will make a decision based on what you recommend. The more detailed you are on the BPO comments (see Chapter 5), the more likely it is that your recommendation comes to fruition.

THE BID SCOPE AND REPAIR PROCESS

If you make a recommendation to make repairs, the asset manager will review and approve the recommendation. The first thing they will do is email you and request "bids" for them. Basically, this means that the asset manager is asking you to send them an estimate on how much it would cost to make the suggested repairs. Many banks use in-network contractors who they already have a relationship with. Think of this in terms of healthcare providers. Some insurance companies require you to use in-network providers to qualify for their insurance. These contractors are limited in what they can charge the bank for many of the repairs, but since they are in-network, agents are required to use them.

If the bank you are working with does not have such an agreement, they will most likely require you to obtain bids from two different contractors. We have itemized three guidelines for choosing contractors:

- The contractors you choose should have no relationship with you or anyone from your company.
- Contractors must be licensed and insured.
- Obtain contractors' W-9s (an important tax document that allows banks to write-off their repair expenses).

The process to obtain a bid is summarized below.

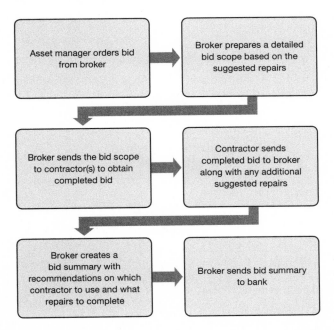

So here's how it works: As the listing agent, you provide the general contractor(s) with a "bid scope," which details exactly what the contractor is bidding for. Typically, you will send this by email, on a standard form (see Appendix R). You should be very detailed in your scope and include repairs that were recommended on your BPO (assuming you are not using an as-is marketing strategy).

The bid scope should not have any costs whatsoever, only detailed repairs for the contractor to bid on. Remember, the purpose of the bid scope is for you to tell the contractor what repairs you want them to bid on, not the other way around.

 **INSIDER TIP**

Do not let the contractor tell you what repairs should go on the bid scope. You are in charge. You must advise them. You are the marketing expert.

When obtaining bids from contractors who have an agreement with the bank and are in-network, it is important not to order bids from two different general contractors. Since these contractors have a service agreement with the banks, most of the bids they complete are converted into orders. Therefore, you only need to choose one in-network provider, as their bid amounts are capped off at a certain amount. In addition, if the total repairs are less than a certain amount (e.g., $500), banks typically only request one bid.

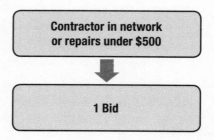

If, however, you are obtaining bids from contractors who have no relationship to the bank, or if the repairs are greater than $1,000, then it is customary to order two bids from two different contractors. Essentially, you will be looking for the best price if you are not using in-network providers. If you estimate repairs to be more than $10,000 and you are not using an in-network provider, it is best to obtain three bids.

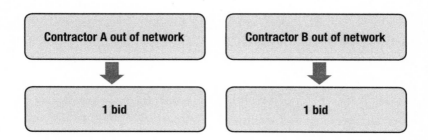

If HVAC (heating, ventilation, and air conditioning) or flooring repairs are necessary, the bank may require that you use a different contractor who specializes in HVAC or flooring. In this case, you would send each contractor a bid scope with what you want them to bid on. For example, if you want to repair the air conditioner (AC), carpets, and kitchen, you may be required to send three separate bids: (1) AC—bid requested from HVAC contractor, (2) Carpets—bid requested from flooring contractor, and (3) Kitchen—bid requested from general contractor.

INSIDER TIP

Each repair on the bid scope must be as detailed as possible, indicating the quantity, type, and extent of each repair. Examples of inferior labeling: repair door, repair wall, repair fence. These are so broad that contractors tend to "exaggerate" the cost of such repairs when they are not detailed initially, because they're not sure what to expect. However, when the listing agent details these repairs, contractors tend not to exaggerate the cost of repairs, because they know that the asset manager will see exactly what needs to be repaired and that asset managers are aware of appropriate pricing.

Once the contractor receives your bid request, the contractor will then visit the property and bid on the items you requested. When the contractor determines how much they will charge for the repairs, they will complete the bid (i.e., fill in the costs for the repairs you included on the bid scope) and email it to you. The general contractor will also typically include an appliance sheet attached to the bid they send you, which will include the cost of any appliances they are recommending. Many banks require contractors to sign and date their completed bid.

The contractor may also provide you with an addendum in which they will recommend additional repairs that are not included in your bid scope. Once you compile this bid scope, the addendum, and any other bids you received from other contractors (HVAC and/or flooring), it is your responsibility to relay to the bank which repairs you recommend. You do this on a "summary of bids form," typically supplied by the bank that is going to authorize the repairs.

REPAIR BID PROCESS

△ Listing Agent	◻ Contractor	◁ Listing Agent	◯ Asset Manager
■ Performs initial inspection	■ Performs initial inspection	■ Reviews contractor's bid(s)	■ Reviews bid
■ Recommends Marketing strategy and repairs	■ Completes bid	■ Prepares summary	■ Makes final decision on what repairs will be approved
■ Receives bid order from asset manager/ bank	■ Adds any additional repairs recommended by contractor	■ Compiles all documents and makes recommendation on which repairs to complete	■ Authorizes and approves repairs

SUBMITTING COMPLETED BID PACKAGES

Once you have received all the bid documents back from the contractors, it is your responsibility to assemble a summary of bids so that you can pass the following along to the asset manager:

1. Cost of repairs from the bid scope.
2. Cost and details of any repairs recommended by contractor but which were not included in original bid scope.

3. Your recommendation as to what should be repaired and why. Sample summary of bids form:

PROPERTY INFORMATION	PREPARED BY
REO #:	Company Name:
Address:	Address:
Bedrooms:	Phone:
Bathrooms:	Fax:

REPAIR BIDS	BID 1	BID 2
CONTRACTOR NAME		
	AMOUNT	AMOUNT
1. Floors	$	$
2. Interior Walls/Ceilings	$	$
3. Interior Paint	$	$
4. Exterior Paint	$	$
5. Appliances	$	$
6. Cleaning	$	$
7. Electrical	$	$
8. Heating/Air	$	$
9. Plumbing	$	$
10. Roof	$	$
11. Structural	$	$
12. Carpentry Interior/Exterior	$	$
13. Other	$	$
14. Supplemental Recommendations	$	$
TOTAL BID:	$	$

BID RECOMMENDATION	
Bid # Recommended:	Contractor Name:
Listing Agent:	In-Network Vendor#:
Comments:	
Submitted By:	Date:

If you disagree with certain repairs, you should note why. State your case.

In the repairs bid package, include the following items (in order):

1. Summary of bid (discussed above)
2. Bid scope that contractor filled out
3. Addendum provided by contractor with additional recommended repairs
4. Flooring bid (if using a separate contractor)
5. HVAC bid (if using a separate contractor)
6. Appliance costs (general contractor will include an appliance form)

Be sure to attach the previous items into one PDF. Once you compile the repairs bid package, email it to your asset manager. The asset manager will then review the costs along with your comments to determine which repairs to approve. It is a good idea to make a note in the bank platform you use that the summary bid was sent on the specified date you emailed your asset manager.

Within two days, you should receive authorization from the bank to begin repairs. It is a good practice to follow up on the third day, should you not receive any authorization by that point. For many banks and asset managers, bids exceeding $8,500 require management approval.

So that's the first half of the repair bid process. The next half is managing the contractors after the repairs get approved. Once the repairs are approved, you should tell the contractors to start work immediately.

A general rule of thumb on the timeframe contractors take to complete repairs is one day per one thousand dollars. So, if your repairs amount to $5,000, then repairs should be completed within five days.

FOR EVERY ONE THOUSAND DOLLARS IN REPAIRS, GIVE YOUR CONTRACTOR ONE DAY TO COMPLETE THE JOB. IF THE REPAIRS COSTS $5,000, IT SHOULD TAKE FIVE DAYS TO COMPLETE THE REHAB.

MANAGING CONTRACTOR AND REPAIR TIMELINES

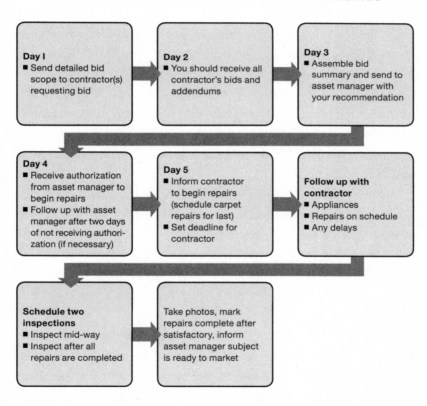

Day 1
- Send detailed bid scope to contractor(s) requesting bid

Day 2
- You should receive all contractor's bids and addendums

Day 3
- Assemble bid summary and send to asset manager with your recommendation

Day 4
- Receive authorization from asset manager to begin repairs
- Follow up with asset manager after two days of not receiving authorization (if necessary)

Day 5
- Inform contractor to begin repairs (schedule carpet repairs for last)
- Set deadline for contractor

Follow up with contractor
- Appliances
- Repairs on schedule
- Any delays

Schedule two inspections
- Inspect mid-way
- Inspect after all repairs are completed

Take photos, mark repairs complete after satisfactory, inform asset manager subject is ready to market

CONTRACTOR MANAGEMENT

I remember getting into an argument with a contractor who I started to do business with. The argument was silly, and I regret getting into it. I was pushing the contractor to finish faster. But the more I pushed him, the less it worked. In fact, he ignored my emails and calls. We argued. He finished the job late. Needless to say, I never used him again, and the relationship was lost. It happens. It's business.

In the REO business you will face many battles. You cannot win them all. You must realize which ones to fight and which ones to let go. With bad comes good. When you find great contractors, build strong relationships with them, because they are the ones who will decide whether to do your job first over another job. Cultivating these relationships is something that will take time, but overall it will be worth it.

Contractors have a certain timeframe in which they are expected to complete their work. Each day a property is off the market it costs the bank more and more to maintain. Therefore, make sure that repairs are completed to satisfactory condition and on time. These are critical skills you must master.

Once you have established yourself in the REO market as a superb listing agent, contractors will become accustomed to what you expect of them. Always set your expectations high. They will deliver. At the end of the day, contractors need business; if you are the last one standing because of your high-quality work ethic and performance, they will be appreciative to receive work orders from you regardless of how demanding you may be.

Always perform inspections on repairs. Never mark repairs complete until you have performed inspections and taken date-stamped pictures of the completed repairs. It is very tempting to not send a field rep out to inspect repairs, especially when the repairs are so basic and inexpensive that you may feel it's not worth the time. However, many times contractors make mistakes.

You are responsible for inspecting the property within forty-eight hours of being told that the repairs are complete. Before going to inspect repairs, print out the repair bid package so you can check the repairs line item by line item. Once you inspect, take a picture of all items that were repaired. This is very important. If repairs were done to satisfactory conditions, you will need the pictures to prove it.

BEFORE INSPECTING THE PROPERTY, WITHIN FORTY-EIGHT HOURS, PRINT OUT YOUR REPAIR BID PACKAGE AND TAKE PICTURES OF ALL ITEMS THAT WERE REPAIRED

Then, after you verify that repairs were done correctly and you have taken pictures, mark the repairs "complete" in your bank's online platform. Keep in mind that once you mark repairs complete, the contractor's job is done. Don't expect them to go back out to fix items if you mark them complete.

Case in point: A contractor is to complete roughly $10,000 worth of repairs on a certain property. Some of the repairs include paint, structural repairs, installation of cabinets, installation of one range, etc. After inspecting the property, you are amazed at the quality of workmanship and you know in your heart that this property is ready to market.

However, what you fail to realize is the fact that the contractor forgot to order the range for the kitchen. The range is part of the approved repairs. You end up marking all repairs "complete," but then your asset manager contacts you to let you know that the property was re-assigned to another broker because you marked off showing that all repairs were completed when, in fact, the range was never installed.

Because of this careless mistake of not checking each and every repair to ensure that all repairs have been completed to satisfactory conditions, you end up losing the property and tarnishing your reputation. It takes years to build your reputation, and one careless mistake to ruin it.

Remember, build a relationship with the contractor. Contractors think along the lines of: "Oh, this is a new listing agent, so I can get away with anything." Counter that fallacy by building a relationship with the contractor; tell them that you look forward to doing a lot of business with them in the future. Make sure you emphasize these points.

MANAGING CONTRACTORS

Set up-front agreement with contractor

- You are expecting high quality work in a timely maner.
- You will be inspecting the property multiple times.
- If the repairs are done to your satisfaction, you look forward to sending more bids to the contractor in the future.

Make sure the contractor meets deadlines

- Inform contractor that they are expected to complete the job within a set time-frame.
- Follow up with contractor to make sure there are no delays in meeting that deadline.
- Request that the contractor contact you should they expect any delays.

Communicate after inspections

- Inform contractor of the results of your inspections.
- Advise contractor if any items need to be corrected before you mark repairs complete.
- After you mark repairs complete, thank the contractor and inform them that you have marked the repairs complete in the system.

APPLIANCE ORDERING

Many times, ordering appliances is necessary to meet minimum lender required repairs, especially when appliances are missing from the subject property. I recommend ordering appliances in these two situations:

1. You are choosing a strategy to meet minimum lender required repairs and there are no appliances in the subject property.

2. You are completing other repairs to the subject property; even if subject has appliances, we recommend replacing them with new appliances.

The costs of appliances are inexpensive to banks, as they have contracts with large appliance manufacturers such as Whirlpool and have access to wholesale pricing. As such, most of the time ordering appliances is well worth the discounted cost for the bank. Contractors really do not make money from the appliances. They typically make money on the other repairs that are sometimes added on, such as interior paint. However, contractors have the responsibility of ensuring that appliances are delivered and installed at the subject property. You, as the listing agent, have the responsibility of verifying and checking to see if the contractor has completed the approved repairs.

Sometimes it is a good practice to ask the contractor via email if the appliances have been delivered to the subject property. This way, they will automatically check to verify that the appliances were ordered and installed.

 **INSIDER TIP**

Make sure the contractors leave the warranty information inside the appliances so that the new homeowners can register the devices and have access to their warranties.

Types and costs of appliances typically ordered:

1. Electric Range	$268
2. Dishwasher	$186
3. Microwave	$173

Note that refrigerators are typically not ordered, as they are not required by FHA. Installation costs for these appliances are estimated to be around $100 to $150 total (regardless of the amount of appliances to be installed. As stated earlier, contractors do not make much money on appliances, and oftentimes they "forget" about them; therefore, make sure you diligently verify that they completed their appliance installation. It is important for you to let them know not to "forget," or else they can "forget" about getting more work from you!

APPLIANCE GUIDELINES

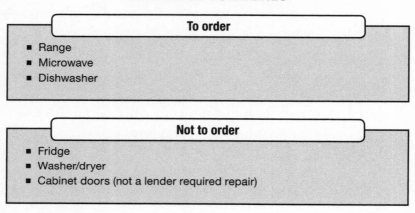

To order

- Range
- Microwave
- Dishwasher

Not to order

- Fridge
- Washer/dryer
- Cabinet doors (not a lender required repair)

SAMPLE REPAIR COSTS

You need a good foundation on what the average repairs costs are in the market that you currently serve. Typically, the costs vary from state to state, but most contractors are restricted as to how they can charge per their service agreement with the bank.

 **INSIDER TIP**

When summarizing the repairs and your recommendation to the bank in the comments section, make sure you emphasize how well you know your market. Show it off. It always impresses asset managers when they read comments showing that you know what you are doing!

REPAIR BID MAIN COMPONENTS

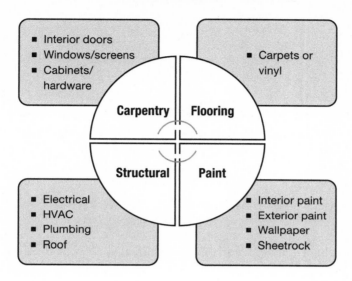

- Interior doors
- Windows/screens
- Cabinets/ hardware

Carpentry

- Carpets or vinyl

Flooring

Structural

- Electrical
- HVAC
- Plumbing
- Roof

Paint

- Interior paint
- Exterior paint
- Wallpaper
- Sheetrock

In addition to the components above, we recommend adding appliances and a final sales clean to all repair bids you request from contractors. A final sales clean is completed after all repairs are made, and it is to remove any debris left after the repairs are completed to ensure that the subject is in marketable condition.

COMMON COSTS ASSOCIATED WITH TYPICAL REPAIRS

Appliance labor	$125	**Labor only**
Interior painting	$1.50 per square foot	**Includes labor**
Carpet replacement	$.75 per square foot	**Includes labor**
Final sales clean	$200	**Includes labor**
Water heater	$450	**Includes labor**
AC handler and condenser	$3,000	**Includes labor**
Screens	$100/screen	**Includes labor**

Note that painting will include minor sheetrock repairs, prime coat if necessary, and sanding and caulking as needed. Paint will be applied in sufficient coats to thoroughly cover existing conditions and produce a quality appearance.

The contractor should also clean (or replace) light cover plates and doorstops. Also, HVAC vent covers should be cleaned and painted to look new in appearance or replaced if necessary. Always make sure all electrical outlets and plates are cleaned or replaced, as they are usually included with the interior painting price.

MANAGING AND INSPECTING CONTRACTOR TIMELINES

Getting high-quality repairs done accurately and with timeliness is a challenge, especially when contractors have multiple jobs and inadequate staff. However, this should not affect your ability as a listing agent to enforce the timelines that banks require contractors to complete jobs in. Let the contractors know from the beginning what your expectations are, so they make your property a priority over other listing agents who haven't read this book or who are careless as to what reality calls for.

You should plan at least two inspections during the repairs and at least one inspection after you are notified that repairs are complete. Communication and follow-up is an integral part of minimizing the time for repairs to be completed. As quickly as you want repairs to be done, keep in mind that if the repairs aren't satisfactory, the contractor will have to go back out and re-do the repairs. Inspecting the repairs process will allow you to point out any repairs that you feel may not be done correctly.

If, however, you only inspect after you are notified that repairs are complete, it may delay the repairs even further, as the contractor will have to make a special trip out to the property to fix unsatisfactory work. The earlier you notify the contractor of any deficiencies, the less time it will take overall to finish all repairs.

Communication is huge. If multiple contractors are scheduled to do repairs, make sure you are coordinating the repairs for them. For example, if flooring work is to be completed, make sure that the painting and other repairs are completed prior to the flooring being installed. This will make repairs more efficient and the general contractor will really appreciate it. It saves them from having to wrap plastic all around the carpets when they paint. So the best bet is to have the carpets replaced last.

ALWAYS ORDER THE INSTALLATION OF CARPETS OR FLOORING LAST, AFTER PAINTING AND GENERAL REPAIRS ARE COMPLETED

In order to ensure that repairs are done to the highest quality and with the least turnaround time, be sure to follow these guidelines:

- Notify the contractor immediately upon repairs being approved.
- Call the contractor and ask what day the repairs are scheduled for
- Remind the contractor that you expect them to complete the repairs by said date.
- Complete inspections before contractor completes repairs so you can make them aware of any deficiencies.
- Follow up to make sure contractors are meeting their timeline.
- Complete the final inspection the same day of being notified that repairs are complete.

Make sure you inspect all repairs to make sure they were completed to satisfactory conditions. You don't want to give contractors the impression that you are lax about their work. Set the upfront agreement with them and tell them you expect high quality workmanship, that you will conduct multiple inspections, and that they will not be paid until you are satisfied with their work. Be firm and be fair.

DEALING WITH REPAIR CHANGE ORDERS

A "change order" is necessary when the contractor forgets to include a cost in the bid. Typically, the contractor is asking for more money to do the repairs than he originally estimated. Change orders are common in situations where contractors are bidding to fix violations. Because the extent of repairs is not known until an inspector goes out and either approves or disapproves the repairs, the initial bid can be imprecise. In such situations, the contractor will send you an email stating that they need to send a change order to the bank.

The change order is completed in the same way the original bid was completed. However, the difference is that you will not send a bid scope to the contractor. Instead, the contractor will send you a completed bid with the additional repairs that he is requiring in order to finish the repair job. Upon receipt of this change order, you should create a summary of repair bids. On the summary, include the total cost of the change order and your recommendation as to whether the bank should approve or reject the change order.

Once you complete the summary of repair bids, attach the change order, and then combine the two documents into one PDF. Send this to the asset manager for approval. Once it is approved, notify the contractor so he can proceed with completing repairs.

PERFORMING WEEKLY PROPERTY INSPECTIONS

Weekly inspections are a very important component of maintaining your listings. As an REO listing agent, it is important to keep a log of all weekly inspections and input this data into your system of communication so that the asset manager is aware that you are keeping track of the property's progress.

As stated before, perception is reality in this business; if you are being compared to another REO agent who appears to be equal in all other performance measures, having the weekly updates will magnify your performance and work ethic. Constantly putting updates into the bank platform will enable you to build trust. Your asset managers will know that they won't have to doubt your performance.

Each week your field inspector(s) should visit all your properties that are listed, under contract, and temporarily off the market. Off the market properties are those that are not listed yet, either because of repairs being completed and/or other items pending for the property to be listed (for example, the certificate of title). It is important to also inspect your properties after it has rained. If you notice water seeping through the roof, place a tarp over it ASAP!

Why are weekly inspections so important? Put yourself in this scenario: You get a call from an occupant in a condo building directly underneath where you have your REO property. The occupant is screaming belligerently at you, claiming that he has been trying to get in touch with you for a week. The occupant is stating that you owe them $5,000 due to a leak coming from the unit you are listing.

The occupant claims that someone left the water faucet on sometime on Friday and the water ran the entire weekend and seeped through the floor. Now there is extensive damage to his unit and the possibility of mold growth. The occupant's uncle is an attorney, and the attorney has already filed a litigious complaint to the bank.

Meanwhile, when the bank receives the complaint, it checks the comments for the property (in the bank platform) and does not see anything that indicates you have completed weekly inspections. The asset manager is now in trouble because they were relying on you to preserve and sell the asset, and the bank itself is in trouble.

Further, the HOA refuses to approve the new buyer until the issue is fixed. The occupant, who is president of the HOA, will not accept anything except cash to fix the unit. Don't think this can happen to you? Think again!

When your field rep completes weekly inspections, it is critical to take date-stamped photos showing the property was inspected on that day. Doing the best you can to minimize any break-ins, vandalism, theft, and repairs to the property is critical. Weekly inspections will help achieve this and also will help ensure that the marketing of the property is satisfactory.

WEEKLY INSPECTIONS MUST HAVE DATE-STAMPED PHOTOS.

So now let's assume your weekly inspections are completed and you notice that some of your properties require further cleaning because of the length of time the properties have been sitting on the market. Most asset management companies and banks have a large property preservation company that they contract for properties.

It is important to contact these companies immediately and let them know that the home requires a cleaning follow-up. Also, be sure to note the email in the bank platform where your asset manager sees the general notes for the property. It is very easy to update the system with a note. All you have to do is click on the email you sent, then click "reply" and copy and paste everything from the entire communication. Here is an example:

From: REO AGENT [mailto:XXXX@AGENT.COM]
Sent: Monday, March 21, 2012 5:38 p.m.
To: Property Preservation Company
Subject: RE: REO ID: A123456 | 1234 Mainstreet #007, any town USA | Post cleaning required

Please note: During our weekly inspection on the week of X, we noticed debris and dirt in the living and dining areas. Photos are attached. Please send someone to perform maintenance cleaning ASAP and let us know once complete.

Below is a sample checklist that you can use when completing weekly inspections. You should be on the lookout for certain items:

1. Confirm utilities are on (water and electric).
2. Confirm property is secure and marketable (if listed).
3. Confirm that the property is clean and presentable.
   a. Yard work

   b. No trash, debris, misc. items

   c. Pool is clean

4. Keys are in lockbox (We always recommend putting three keys in the lockbox). Keys are very cheap to replace versus driving somewhere on demand at $4/gallon.

5. Light bulbs work.

6. Yard sign and marketing material is present.

7. Any pests/termite intrusions should be noted and communicated to the asset manager.

8. Any repairs that appear during the inspection but that were not already noted during a previous inspection and/or during your initial inspection.

9. Toilets are flushed and toilet lids are down.

10. Bank signs are readable and present.

11. All screen doors and windows are secured.

12. Property is in marketable condition (even after property is under contract).

13. No newspapers present around entrance way.

14. Mailbox is clear and clean.

15. Grass is cut and all clippings are removed from sidewalks, driveways, and lawns.

16. Grass is edged on driveways, walkways, and sidewalks.

Congratulations! You just finished a very important chapter on repairs. You have mastered Step 3 of the REO Cycle—managing repairs and contractors. Now it's time to put your marketing cap on. With the repairs and weekly inspections, I am sure your property is in tip-top shape. Now, you need to get buyers to go see the property so they can be convinced that this property is for them. To do that, it's all about the marketing. Want to learn how to attract buyers like magnets? Keep reading—the magnet marketing plan is next!

SHARE YOUR STORY

Do you have a success story you would like to share about conducting repairs on your REO? Any nightmare contractor issues you had and resolved? Please log on and submit it for your chance to be featured in the next revised edition of *REO Boom*:

www.reoboom.com/story

POINTS TO REMEMBER

- Weekly inspections and updates are necessary; they are not optional.
- Complete a "change order" the same way you complete an original repair bid. Remember, a change order is a way for a contractor to get more money to do the repairs.
- Always install flooring or carpets last, after general repairs are completed.
- Build relationships with contractors, so they can deliver to your expectations every time.
- A rule of thumb for contractor completion is that for every $1,000 of repairs you give one day for completion. So, a $5,000 repair job should be completed in five days.
- If repairing, at minimum include interior paint, carpet replacement, and appliance replacement.
- If a contractor is "in-network," order one bid. If they do not have a service agreement with the bank, order two bids from different contractors.
- Always schedule a minimum of two inspections, one mid-way and one final inspection. Take photographs each trip.
- Managing repairs is a three-step process: bid scope, bid, and bid summary.
- Use a "minimum repair strategy" versus "as-is" repair strategy for condos located in an FHA approved development.
- Consider the condition of the comparable you used in your BPO to determine whether repairs are needed for your property to reach marketable condition.

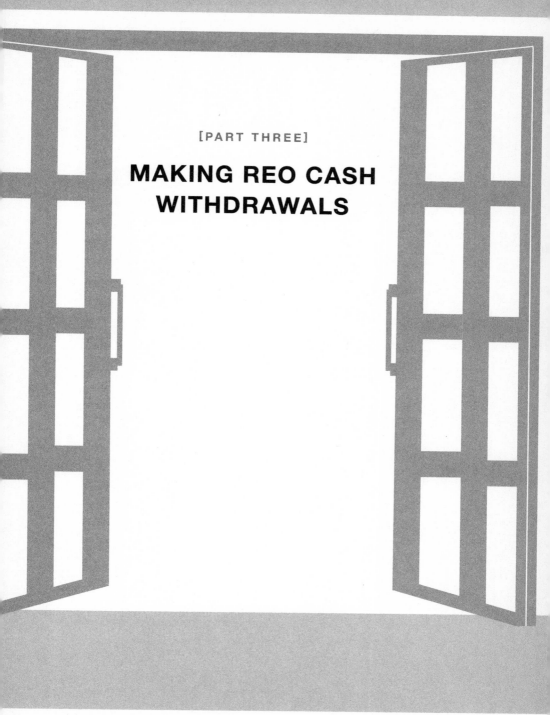

[PART THREE]

MAKING REO CASH
WITHDRAWALS

Mastering Listings and Marketing

LISTINGS AND MARKETING go hand in hand. You cannot have one without the other. A stellar marketing plan will do you no good if you do not have a listing to market. Further, a listing will result in no contracts if there is no marketing. In Chapter 6 you learned about recommending the property's marketing strategy for pricing: either listing the property as-is or with repairs.

Regardless of which marketing strategy for pricing you choose, the majority of your success will come from a knockout listing and marketing presentation. In the REO business, the REOs are the steak and the marketing is the sizzle. Your goal as an REO agent is to create a magnet marketing appeal—a marketing plan so luxurious you attract buyers like magnets.

MAGNET MARKETING APPEAL = LUXURIOUS MARKETING PLAN

Listing REOs is all about presenting the marketability of your property. As an REO agent, you want to bring in as many offers as possible. Meanwhile, the bank's goal is to maximize the sales price of the home. They want and expect you to bring in offers at list price or above.

You are their eyes and ears to the streets. There's an old adage that says, "Be careful what you wish for, because it may come true." Whether you recommended an as-is or with repaired pricing marketing strategy, you must be ready back up the recommendation by bringing in customers. Once the property is on the market, you need to get it off the market as soon as possible.

With the magnet marketing plan you should expect to see properties under contract on average within twenty-one days. This is the time from when you receive the list price from the bank and place it on the MLS to the time the bank accepts the offer and designates the property as "pending sale" in the MLS.

MAGNET MARKETING PLAN = 21 DAYS ON MARKET

THE MAGNET MARKETING PLAN

The days of listing your REO on the MLS and allowing the property to sell itself are over. With the abundance of REOs in today's market, your competition will be fierce. Therefore, you need to take an aggressive marketing stance to procure a buyer within twenty-one days. This is done by creating a magnet marketing plan that encompasses the four Ps of marketing for each REO to attract buyers:

The Four Ps of REOs
1. Product
2. Price
3. Promotion
4. Placement

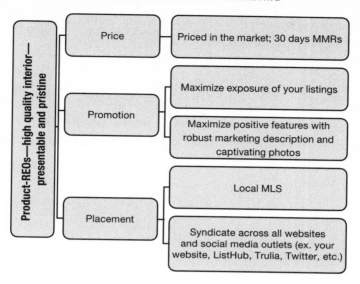

Product

The great news is that you are selling a product that is hot in demand. The tricky part is how fast it will take you to cash in on the REO. If you have done a good job recommending a pricing strategy from your BPO (see Chapter 5), then you should be priced at the market and aligned with your competition. Therefore, if pricing is good, your need to make sure the quality of the home is as well. Every REO you have must be presentable and in pristine condition. Depending on which model you are using, either your listing specialist or field inspector will be responsible for the following.

THE TWENTY-POINT INTERIOR CHECKLIST

1. Blinds are pulled up in all the rooms, including the living room, for enhanced picture lighting.
2. Air fresheners are placed in each room.
3. Smoke alarms have batteries and are not chirping.
4. Light bulbs are functioning in each room.
5. Each room is left in broom swept condition, including balconies and railings.

6. Mirrors in each room are clean and without streak marks.

7. Carpets are vacuumed.

8. Pungent odors are removed from the home.

9. Hard surface floors are polished or washed.

10. All cabinets, drawers, and toilet seats are closed.

11. Window sills are free of dust, cobwebs, bugs, dirt, etc.

12. No broken windows, glass, or unsecured areas throughout the home.

13. All doors are hung properly, including closet bi-folds.

14. Utilities (electric/water) are on to make the home bright and inviting.

15. AC is on and set to a neutral 74 degrees Fahrenheit, with the heat set to 64 degrees during winter months.

16. Bank "warning signs" are placed on the outside of the front door and on windows on all sides of the home. This includes both English and Spanish versions of the sign. Caution: some condos may prohibit you from putting any signage in front of your condo. Always follow all by-laws and association rules.

17. Lockbox is working properly and an extra set of keys is placed inside the lockbox (many keys will be misplaced, lost, etc.).

18. Bank's marketing/finance flyers are on placed on the kitchen countertops (to encourage prospective home buyers to obtain financing; approximately ten flyers).

19. Your customized property flyer is placed in a folder on the kitchen countertop (approximately ten folders with flyers).

20. Old signage is removed (old eviction notices, previous broker's marketing signs, etc.).

 INSIDER TIP

Treat every REO as a luxury home when it comes to marketing to achieve the Magnet Marketing Appeal. If you would do it for a luxury home, you must do it for your REO listing.

THE TEN-POINT EXTERIOR CHECKLIST

1. Sprinkler systems are functioning properly.
2. Lawn is trimmed/mowed/hedged.
3. Gutters are cleaned.
4. Flower beds are mulched.
5. No termites or mold are present.
6. Abandoned items such as broken sheds, cars, and appliances are removed (check bank policy first).
7. Walkway, porches, and decks are clean.
8. Roof is secured. No roof damage, such as missing shingles or tiles.
9. No illegal additions or modifications.
10. No structural defects to vinyl, siding, brick, etc.

In addition, make sure you place a yard sign outside in the front of the home with your contact information, picture, toll-free automated recording highlighting property features, bank riders (if any), and a quick response QR code (see Appendix A). This is a fairly new concept that allows consumers to scan with their camera phone or smart phone (iPhone, Blackberry, etc.) the QR barcode you created to instantly download property information, websites, contact information, etc. Whatever you want them to download, they can do so instantly by just scanning.

Where do consumers find this program? They can log into an application store (app store) from their smart phone and search for a free QR reader. Once they have downloaded the app, they can open the program, hold the smart phone up to the barcode, and scan it. Do this with your smart phone and scan this bar code now. What do you get?

For each home, I create a unique QR code to highlight the features of the home: spacious layouts, wrap-around balconies, luscious back yards, never-ending hallways, etc. This will enable selling agents and customers to quickly find out details on my REO listing when they are pulling in the driveway. Do this the same way no matter what type of property—townhome, condo, duplex, loft, etc. You may have to adjust the information provided to meet the rules and regulations for each governing body regulating the property.

Remember, certain items on the checklist may be farmed out to specific bank partners. If this is the case, and the work isn't completed or is not completed to your satisfaction as a marketing expert (you are the marketing expert for your listing), then notify the vendor or your asset manager immediately. For example, perhaps the home is missing interior appliances or has holes in the wall, dead animals, water stains on ceiling, cracks in walls, exposed wiring (must be capped), panel damage, missing outlet covers, carpet tears, etc.

In addition to the home's interior and exterior checklists, a staging checklist is important, especially if the bank has elected to rehab the home (versus selling it as-is). Putting an attractive plant in a spacious corner of a home with fresh new paint, carpets, and new appliances (i.e., rehabbed) can be a deal maker. Emotions sell. You want to tap into the buyer's heart first, then their mind. Each home buyer must be motivated to buy *before* they think about the price.

EMOTIONS SELL; MOTIVATION BEFORE MONEY

THE TOP TEN STAGING CHECKLIST ITEMS

1. Attractive plant in a spacious corner of the home (e.g., near fireplace, visible corner, etc.). Less is more. Limit the quantity to one.
2. Decorative logs or candles in fireplace and firebox.
3. Bathroom décor is a must (e.g., attractive hand towels with custom-made tied ribbons, tied bow on the toilet seat, fresh soap in the tub, etc.).
4. Baked fresh cookies to add a warm, welcoming aroma in the air (also great for open houses).
5. Wreath or a welcome mat placed outside the front door.
6. Bright planters filled with flowers placed on the doorstep.
7. Dull light bulbs changed with high quality wattage bulbs.
8. Stylish retail bags in different sizes placed throughout the home and on the shelves.
9. Attractive paper or napkins in the kitchen with your company's logo etched on them.
10. Classical music playing on low in the background.

PRICE

Performing Monthly Marketing Reports (MMRs)

Every now and then, some REOs will slip through the cracks and take longer than twenty-one days to get under contract. There could be an oversupply, an underpriced new comparable that just hit the market, a property hazard such as mold throughout the unit that turns off buyers, or your bank simply priced the property above market price. Sometimes they do this to test the market. They will intentionally price it 10 to 15 percent above market to see what happens. They can always drop the price later, so they take the gamble.

Sometimes it works and sometimes it backfires, resulting in an unsold property that lingers on the market for months. Regardless, the way you combat this is by keeping the bank abreast of the marketplace at all times. This is done by performing a monthly marketing report (MMR) every thirty days with the goal of receiving a list price reduction when the market demands it.

MMRs are a critical function that will define a great REO listing agent from a good REO agent. Giving your asset manager complete information at all times is a necessity. Because the supply of REOs is so unpredictable (you can go from five new properties a week to twenty), there is no certainty of what will be in the market at any given time. The unknown factor of time plays a crucial role in determining what a good list price for a property is. Many times new REO agents who are starting off put this on the bottom of their to-do list. This is primarily because they feel overwhelmed or they don't have the resources (money, time, or staff) to invest in an MMR.

Unfortunately, if you do not do an MMR, you risk the chance of your property not selling, being re-assigned to another competing REO listing agent, or going to auction. A lot of determinants on the price relate to what comparables are on the market or what comparables have recently sold—statistics which are constantly changing.

Imagine doing all the work on a property (everything in this book) and at the last minute a property gets yanked from you. Yes, it can happen, and that is the cost of doing business. The only way to prevent it is by staying on top of your MMRs (see template in Appendix I).

We like to think of MMRs as your best friend, because they will be there when you need them the most—when it's time to get a list price reduction (LPR).

MMR GOAL = LIST PRICE REDUCTION (LPR)

 **INSIDER TIP**

If you begin to feel overwhelmed and dread doing an MMR, form a positive association with the outcome: getting your list price reduced, selling the home, and making your commission faster. The extra thirty minutes is well worth the tradeoff.

The Eight MMR Requirements

1. Number of times the property was shown.
2. Three current active listings (address, list price, square footage differences compared to subject, current days on market, condition of unit, and any special remarks).
3. Three recent closed sales (address, closing date, square footage differences compared to subject, any special remarks if applicable).
4. Selling agent feedback.
5. Buyer feedback.
6. Your recommendation on marketing strategy.
7. Your recommendation on a new listing price.
8. Repair status (if applicable).

 **INSIDER TIP**

Create a one-page flyer that condenses the eight MMR requirements with your logo and one to three pictures of the property. Email it in PDF format to your asset manager. It is professional, clean, and easier on the eyes to read.

In order to find the number of times the property was shown, you can consult your local MLS board for help. They usually have a showing tracker program that tracks automatically how many times selling agents request lockbox codes. This information is usually found in the statistics section in your MLS reports page.

When obtaining current actives and recent sold properties, follow the same criteria you would use to select properties when conducting your BPO (see Chapter 5). Most importantly you want to include information on any new sales that occurred after your initial BPO or subsequent MMRs. Also include the condition of the new comparable.

When conducting an MMR for condos, note that condos with few comparable units tend to stay on the market a bit longer than those condos with an abundance of comparable units. Selling agents usually have a difficult time convincing their customer they are getting a good deal because there is little to compare to. They can't say, for example,

"Someone bought a unit last month for $150,000, and this is condo is priced to sell at $130,000. What a great deal! We need to put an offer in today before it's under contract."

Therefore, because of the lack of comparable sales, both selling agents and consumers may be a bit hesitant to break the ice and purchase a condo in that particular building. On the plus side, a building that has few comparable sales may have an association that is more healthy than one that has many more REO sales and defaults. The tradeoff will be valued by the market. Each day an asset carries forward without being sold, many costs are associated with the upkeep of it; there are preservation expenses and other expenses such as code violations, assessments, etc., that continue to occur until the asset is sold.

Ultimately, your job as the REO listing agent is to make sure you maximize the proceeds from the sale of the home and minimize the days on market. Regardless of the tradeoff, make sure you state all the facts in your MMR.

Detailed feedback from other real estate agents and buyers who demonstrated interest in the property is also critical to report. Maybe a property is difficult to gain access to. Keys are missing. There is an emergency due to damage. Perhaps the rooms are too small or big, or the layout is not functional, etc. The more ammo and details you can get from both the selling agent and buyers, the better prepared you are to argue for a LPR.

After you gather your facts, you want to provide your recommendation on the marketing strategy of the property and a recommendation on a new listing price. You must recommend items that will improve the marketability of the home within the next thirty days. This is the time to change your marketing strategy if you feel it does not work. For example, if you feel the "as-is" strategy is not working and instead you want to pursue an "as-repaired" strategy, please elaborate on why. Always support your MMR with facts.

Many times, banks request MMRs within a thirty-day window, but sometimes you may need to conduct an MMR sooner. I usually do them around day twenty-five, or sometimes as early as day twenty if there is a lot of activity in the neighborhood or building (if the property is a condo).

If the property still has not received a contract within thirty days after your first MMR (i.e., after you received your first list price reduction), you need to repeat the process until it is under contract. If it's priced right, the quality of the home is good, and you implement the magnet marketing plan, the property will be picked up.

LPR + HIGH QUALITY INTERIOR + MAGNET MARKETING PLAN = REO UNDER CONTRACT!

List Price Reductions (LPR)

The final phase of an MMR is requesting a new list price. Though it is true that banks generally do not want to conduct a slash and burn sale, it is important to note that banks are not in the business of selling homes—rather, they are in the business of minimizing credit loss and disposing of these assets in a timely fashion.

Many banks have a preferred "days on market" that they expect assets to have. Having an asset on the market for more than ninety days may indicate that the marketing is poor, communication to the listing agent is poor, access to the home is difficult, and/or the property is priced out of the market; most of the time it is the latter.

With monthly marketing reports, you have the responsibility of recommending a list price reduction to the asset manager. This is an MMR's best feature! For example, suppose at the time of your initial BPO order, you found only one additional comparable sale within the same building of the subject.

You then receive the list price five days after completing your BPO. Fifteen days later, you notice there was a new sale in the building—more specifically an REO sale in the same condition as your subject home, but sold for much less than what your property is currently listed for.

Now you are priced out of the market, because the new REO sale will set precedence as the new comparable. This is why it is critical to produce a high quality MMR, especially for condos whereby you can inform your asset manager of new sales within the subject's building.

Why would an asset manager reduce their list price based on a new sale? Well, because the supply of REOs is unpredictable. Hypothetically, a property can sell for completely different values based on when it was listed and what the demand is at that time. However, if an asset is priced well above what the market is willing to pay, most likely the asset manager will miss out on the opportunity to capture a sale even while prices are depreciating.

Let's look at an example: You list a condo for $100,000 on March 1, 2012, at which time there was only one other sale in the building of the condo, which occurred on January 15, 2012, at a sales price of $85,000. Let's assume that the comparable sale was equal in all characteristics to the property you just listed.

You also notice that there were many pending sales within the subjects building, but those pending sales are not concrete data because you don't know if the deal will close and don't know what sales price it will close for.

On April 1, 2012, you notice another sale that was recorded that occurred on March 20, 2010 for $75,000, with equal characteristics to both your unit and the other unit that sold on January 15, 2012. So now your condo is priced above the most recent comparable sale, and selling agents are turned off by the fact that your unit is priced too high.

- Your List Price: $100,000 (3/1/12)
- Comp 1 = $85,000 (1/15/12)
- Comp 2 = $75,000 (3/20/12)

Meanwhile, there are more active REO listings that are being valued by other listing agents for much less than what your unit is currently listed for during the same time frame.

- Active REO 1 = $85,500
- Active REO 2 = $78,000
- Active REO 3 = $89,000

Thus, your unit is not only priced high relative to the most recent sales (comps), but is also priced high relative to the most recently listed REO listings.

Ultimately, the longer you wait to reduce the list price, the less of a chance you will have to sell your unit at the current list price and the more likely it is that the unit will end up selling for less than what it would have sold for if you had done a timely and high-quality MMR.

For asset managers to grant you a list price reduction, they look at certain elements such as:

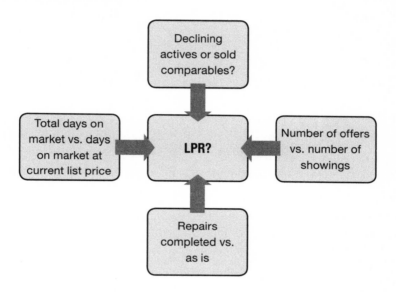

 **INSIDER TIP**

Expect to receive an LPR of no more than 5 to 10 percent every thirty days.

Your actives, closed sales, days on market at current listing price, days on market overall, number of showings, number of offers, and whether the property is repaired or left in as-is condition are all elements in determining a list price reduction. Each item above must be explained in detail in your MMR.

If you find a comparable that sold in the same building or subdivision in the same condition for 30 percent less than your REO listing, you can expect a bigger LPR. However, generally from my experience, you will only receive anywhere between a 5 to 10 percent reduction in price every thirty days. This assumes you produce a high-quality MMR fulfilling all eight requirements.

Sometimes, the asset managers may feel the pressure when they have to hit their sales quotas or need to meet their monthly bonuses because they have personal expenses just like you or I. Expect for them to vent and let out some steam. You may hear, "Well, market the property better," or something to that effect out of pure emotion. Do not take it personally.

Asset managers are people too with more pressure than REO listing agents. Always remain diplomatic, and make a recommendation based on several factors supported by facts. No one can argue with facts, right?

Eventually MMRs and valuing a property become more of an art than a science. Once you finish this book, you will have the methods behind the madness to conduct any BPO or MMR and to manage any REO from A to Z. However, the style or swagger comes with time.

Good listing agents are able to sell properties without lowering prices, and even better listing agents are able to sell properties without needing to perform MMRs; they manage to get the property under contract within twenty-one days, as they have mastered the four Ps of REOs. Receiving an optimal price the first time around is a skill that you will develop as your REO experience progresses and you become seasoned.

PROMOTION

Next, if pricing is par and quality is good, what separates your REO from competing REOs, short-sales, or conventional listings is your sizzle or promotions. How will you promote your REO? Just listing them on the MLS will not work. You will need to maximize the exposure to your listings both online and offline.

Increasing exposure online will include maximizing your MLS exposure by exploiting your REOs' positive features; this is done through selecting and implementing captivating photos and creating a robust marketing description so rich with content that it creates urgency for selling agents to show your listing. Increasing exposure offline will include marketing and staging on-site at the property incorporating both the interior and exterior of the property.

To effectively promote both online and offline, you must start by developing marketing plan for each REO listing. Whether the pricing strategy is repaired or as-is, your goal is to procure a buyer at list price or above in the shortest amount of time. For each REO, I implement the magnet marketing checklist:

Top Twenty Magnet Marketing Checklists

1. Identify five key value proposition points for each property. What are the unique points of difference? What's special? What are the positive features of the home?
2. Place a detailed and flawless MLS listing with a rich marketing description and a minimum of twelve pictures.
3. Implement the interior, exterior, and staging checklists (above).
4. Create a customized flyer in English and in Spanish for each property.
5. Conduct two open houses a month.
6. Conduct one broker's open house a month.
7. Implement a direct email campaign to selling agents automatically utilizing services such as happygrasshopper.com (purchase email lists through your local board).
8. Implement a direct email campaign to your buyer leads using attractive letterheads utilizing services such as fabusend.com (e.g., newsletters, property flyers in both English and Spanish, property of the week, etc.).
9. Place one hundred yard signs on the weekends within a one-mile radius (see Chapter 2).
10. Post yard signs with QR code, sign rider, and toll-free 800 number that illustrates the attractive features of the home.
11. Become an affiliate for various real estate–related websites such as trulia.com, listhub.com, etc.
12. Create a modern customized website on Wordpress with IDX syndication (no templates) by hiring someone overseas from odesk.com or Elance.com. Include lots of video, podcasts,

webinars, e-zine articles, etc. Highlight why you are the marketing expert. Attract buyers; the more the better.

13. Implement a search engine optimization campaign (Google
    AdWords, landing pages, strong key words, deep back links,
    etc.). Your goal is to get high organic ranking for your website
    to be placed on page one or two of major search engines.

14. Post virtual tours on your website.

15. Create a YouTube video showcasing the home from the front
    door to the backyard.

16. Create screencasts that you can send to both selling agents and
    buyers (e.g., screenr.com).

17. Respond to all selling agent inquiries and buyers within twenty-
    four hours or sooner (highlight value proposition, discuss spe-
    cial incentives, financing, or repairs made, if any).

18. Implement an electronic lockbox on the front door.

19. Network with investor groups at local real estate meetings
    announcing you are the REO listing agent expert.

20. Implement social media marketing (utilize Wordpress blogging,
    Facebook, Twitter, Digg.com, etc., and update daily).

A Picture Is Worth a Thousand Words

Marketing pictures are extremely important when it comes to making your listing attractive to selling agents and maximizing the sales
price of your property. Pictures are worth a thousand words. How
many times have you ignored a listing because there were no pictures?
How about searching through MLS listings and checking off the criteria "one picture minimum"? The picture game is about quantity; the
more the better. Buyers like it, banks like it, and, most importantly,
selling agents like it.

Remember, when you sell a property for a higher price than it is
listed, your agent score card (see Chapter 11) becomes more favorable, and, in turn, you get more properties. In addition, closing ahead

of time allows you to make a solid and reputable case to obtain more inventory, which will essentially grow your business into a larger REO money-making machine.

In Chapter 1, we discussed how each REO is an ATM. Your goal now is to combine each ATM and turn it into a bank. You will be playing Monopoly, except this time with REOs. You want to trade in several ATMs for a regional bank. Once you have three direct bank contracts, you can trade in your regional bank for a national bank.

It all begins with the pictures. For example, the most critical picture is your first. It must lure the buyer in and make them fall in love with the home. The picture can be of a spectacular front lawn, an ocean view, or an upgraded kitchen. Pictures are what separate you from your competition.

I have seen many times when REO listing agents post pictures that do them a lot more harm than good. Imagine looking at an REO listing where there are only four pictures: one is of the exterior, the other two are of the interior with trash and debris scattered around the picture, and the last is of the common area. What does that tell you about the property? That you shouldn't show it!

If the bank were to find out that their REO listing agent used rudimentary pictures to market their property, that agent would most likely be disciplined and/or terminated. By implementing the twelve marketing magnet photo tips, you will maximize the dollar value of each property, achieve your twenty-one DOM turnaround, and give your supplier a higher gross execution percentage (see Chapter 11).

 **INSIDER TIP**

REOs do not sell on price. They are not a commodity. Market them with the same level as you would if it were your own home.

The Twelve Magnet Marketing Photo Tips

The difference between you and someone else who hasn't read *REO Boom* will be demonstrated in the pictures. Make sure you utilize this top twelve magnet marketing checklist before finalizing your MLS listing. Each picture must have a date-stamp on it, as you need to keep the banks updated. Therefore, make sure your digital camera has this feature turned on.

1. Take a minimum of twelve photos with a focused lens (no blurry or distorted pictures).
2. Take photos on a clear, bright, and sunny day or with flash (no dark/night photos).
3. Take photos with a wide lens—step on the sidewalk and take a picture of the exterior front of the home encompassing the landscaping and surrounding. With a wide lens camera, you can step in closer and capture the same effect.
4. Take photos without any obstructions—no cars parked in front of the house, no trash in the pictures, no dead animals, etc.
5. Take photos only after the interior is flawless and staging is complete. Avoid any seasonal displays of holiday spirit (Christmas lights, etc.). Be as neutral as possible. Remember, you need the consumer to feel like it is their home, not someone else's home.
6. Story tell with your photos. The photos from the time you open the front door to the time you are in the backyard should unfold like those in a storybook. Capture every room and any unique features. This includes street views. Stand on the front lawn of home, face the street, and snap away in all directions.
7. Order your photos—the first one should be the front of the home and the last one should be the back of the home. Also have a smooth transition from room to room. For example, don't go from the backyard to the washer/dryer room, or from bathroom one to the exterior front of the home.
8. Take photos with toilet seats and cabinets closed.

9. Take photos from a floor view—bend or sit down so you can capture the entire room mid-level. This is better than tilting the camera to take pictures. Make sure focal point is mid-point, not the floor.

10. Take more than one photo of the property, especially for nice views (e.g., ocean or city views from the balcony). This also saves time in case one of the pictures comes out blurry or incorrect.

11. Label the photos with appealing words that highlight the positives features of the home. Also label the direction (ocean view facing east, south, etc.) so there is no confusion from selling agents. This will also help selling agents sell your listing as they can describe the spectacular view by reading the description. Don't forget to double check grammar and spelling.

12. Resize your photos. Download a free image resizer program online and shrink your photos so each photo is under 300 kilobytes.

There are a minimum of three times when you need to take pictures. The first is when you first visit the home and conduct your broker price opinion (BPO). The second is after the bank orders the clean-out of the home from their contracted vendors. The final time is after any repairs are done to the home. Always use the post-repair pictures. If the property is marketed "as-is," use post clean-out pictures. While much of my advice for taking BPO pictures and taking marketing photos is similar, never use original BPO pictures for your MLS listings.

 **INSIDER TIP**

If repairs are made to the property, use the post-repair pictures for your marketing. Never use the original pictures from your BPO.

Writing the Perfect Marketing Description

Marketing descriptions are your chance to showcase your property in the MLS to homebuyers as well as to co-operating agents. Most marketing descriptions are limited to 510 characters. This means that you must maximize the effectiveness of each character you enter in your marketing description for the MLS. Your goal is to use your marketing description as a device to capture a buyer's attention like a magnet. It must scream SHOW ME. From there, your marketing photos will pique more of their interest, ultimately leading them to see the property, make a high offer, and close quickly. Listings must have a robust marketing description that promotes the positive features of the property.

Marketing Description Do's & Don'ts
DO's

1. Be as detailed as possible. Maximize each character in the MLS description field.
2. Use adjectives as well as descriptive and appealing words to help buyers envision themselves living in the home (e.g., luscious landscapes, never-ending hallways, breathtaking views, cozy fireplace, state-of-the-art fitness center, etc.).
3. Highlight property's value proposition and attractive features in the home (e.g., fully upgraded with stainless steel appliances).
4. Mention and keep updated any special incentives, financing specials, or offer statuses your bank offers (e.g., close by April 2012 and receive up to $6,000 toward closing costs).
5. Do mention if property is vacant or tenant occupied (sometimes banks sell "as-is" with tenants living in home).
6. Double check your spelling and grammar.

DON'Ts

1. Abbreviate words or put trade acronyms (e.g., great for FHB or needs TLC).
2. Highlight any negatives of home (e.g., not attractive but decent, buyer beware, must have thick skin, cheap fixer upper, investor's dream, etc.).

3. State opinions (e.g., don't say the property has mold unless you are also a state licensed mold specialist).

4. Put lockbox codes or earnest money requirements in description.

5. Limit any buyers by disqualifying them on financing (e.g., only cash buyers accepted or must submit pre-qualification letter for offers to be submitted).

6. Force buyers to use a specific lender or title company (e.g., must close with seller-chosen title or lender).

Your goal with the marketing description is to have buyers envision themselves living in the home. Your pictures are what catch their eyes, and your descriptions are what grab their hearts. Always ask yourself, would you use this description if it was your own home for sale? Always highlight positive features and value propositions of the listing and never discuss any negative features. Saying something such as "needs TLC, health hazard be careful" is not inviting to consumers.

Some banks even prefer listings to omit words such as "foreclosure," "corporate owned," or "bank-owned" because this has a connotation of bringing in low-ball offers. Since the bank's goals are to maximize its proceeds, it is looking for offers at list price or above. Therefore, your marketing description will play a crucial role. Be sure to review your master listing agreement to verify the policy of the bank you are working with to meet its minimum requirements for marketing the properties appropriately.

An example of a perfect marketing description:

Your buyer will fall in love with this spacious floor plan. With over 3,200 square feet spread over two stories, this luxurious home features marble and wood floors, floor-to-ceiling windows overlooking a gorgeous bay, and has over six bedrooms and three baths. Enjoy a nice breakfast out on the balcony from your master suite overlooking the sunrise or take a dip in the pool and cool off on the deck. Close by June 30, 2012, and request 3 percent of the final sales price to be used as closing costs assistance. Eligibility restrictions apply. Call today.

Many banks will automatically link your MLS listing with affiliated sites and your marketing description will be placed on national
sites such as Zillow.com, Realtytrac.com, Listhub.com, etc. The more
detailed and creative your marketing description is, the greater the
chance of you attracting your own buyer from the online leads.

PLACEMENT

Where will your home be featured? This includes your website and all
of the syndicated websites you are affiliated with. The great news about
the internet is that it's an even playing field. With a little bit of marketing money, you can get a whole lot of bang for your buck compared to
purchasing a print ad. Once again, quantity is the name of the game
here. The more exposure you have, the more likely you are to find a
buyer—fast. It's a numbers game. Placement starts with properly listing a property in the MLS.

The Listing Building Blocks

After you receive a list price from the bank, you will be required to
place the REO into the MLS. You will receive a formal listing letter (see
Appendix H) that indicates the following:

1. Property information (address, REO ID, legal, folio #, type,
   internal loan numbers, etc.)
2. Price
3. Terms (start date/expiration date)
4. Conditions (exclusivity, repair conditions, occupancy conditions)
5. Commissions and bonuses (if any)
6. MLS basic instructions
7. Financing eligibility (e.g., FHA approved, etc.)
8. Servicing information (if property was serviced by a different
   company)
9. REO agent signature box
10. Asset manager contact information

Usually you have twenty-four hours to enter the listing (with pictures, marketing descriptions, offer attachments, etc.) and submit a listing package to your asset manager. Note: The offer packet for selling agents or buyers to submit offers is different than the listing packet. The listing package must be combined into one PDF and have your PDF signature.

The listing package includes:

1. Listing letter with your PDF signature
2. Copy of MLS listing (broker view or full view)
3. Copy of MLS listing picture

 **INSIDER TIP**

In your listing package, highlight via Adobe PDF Professional the following: 1) REO ID, 2) listing price, 3) listing and selling side commission, 4) list date, 5) MLS number. This makes it easier for your asset manager to quickly verify your listing packet and saves them time.

If you are working with an outsourcer or with a direct bank, they will have different rules. Some direct accounts do not want to add another email to their hundreds a day and will trust that you will submit the listing into the MLS within your timeframe.

Many outsourcers require you to submit a copy of the listing packet to them so they can cover their assets (CTA) when they deal directly with the banks in case something goes wrong. You're an easier scapegoat to blame, as well as an easy wild card for them to apologize for while shifting the blame: "My apologies, bank, we will reprimand or fire the REO agent." Outsourcers also require the listing packet to minimize error from the REO agent, as it makes the agent submit all the required documents in a timely fashion rather than making the careless mistakes that accompany procrastination.

A couple of years ago, I was required to submit all MLS listings directly to the bank. This included the initial listing, photos, signed documents, updated listing price changes, showing request stats, etc. Every time there was a change in a list price, a new showing request, or if an offer fell through and I was required to re-list the property, they wanted new listing packets as well. It took about six months before they realized it was not worth their time and canceled the policy. About eight months after, they re-instated the policy again.

When dealing with banks you have to realize they are like a living and breathing organism. Rules are constantly changing. I have seen rules change from year to year or even week to week. A new director steps in, policy changes, and everything trickles down to the field where you and I operate.

The Tenant Occupied Listing

Sometimes you may be required to market a property occupied by a tenant. Each bank and policy will be different. For example, some banks require you to handle the tenants and eviction process during your occupancy checks (see Chapter 4) and others will assign the property to a property management company that will negotiate lease terms, etc.

With tenant occupied properties, because people are living there you cannot install any lockboxes. If the bank works with a property management company, they will usually forward a copy of the lease to you so you know if it's a month-to-month or a term lease (e.g., six months or one year).

Below are some general tenant occupied rules:

1. No lockboxes or yard signs on the home.
2. Appointments needed for showing at least forty-eight hours in advance.
3. Tenant information kept private (do not place in MLS).
4. Showings must be confirmed by tenants residing over the age of eighteen (no children).
5. A special addendum must be placed in the MLS attachment.

Once a prospective buyer decides to purchase an REO listing with a tenant and their offer is accepted (see Chapter 8), you will have to provide them with a copy of the lease. This is between either the bank and the tenant or the property manager representing the bank and the tenant. Most likely, the lease will be a sample blank lease so that the privacy of the tenant can remain intact.

INSIDER TIP

Expect no more than 10 percent of your REO listings to be tenant occupied. Unless the tenants themselves want to purchase, more likely than not you will be working with a selling agent in the transaction.

Once your listing is live, make sure you have your magnet marketing plan ready and phone lines open, because you will be in for a surprise. Have your Red Bulls and espressos handy, as you will be crossing the chasm into the multiple offer arenas.

INSIDER TIP

Listing letters are generally computer generated and can come during odd times. Because many asset managers work from home on their laptops, they tend to review listing prices during odd hours, such as Friday after 5 P.M. or Saturday mornings. Be prepared at all times, 24/7.

The Top Ten HOA and Condo Pre-Listing Checklist

For single-family homes governed by an HOA and condominiums governed by an association, rules and regulations affect the marketability of your property. Prior to listing, you should have the following information and verify that it is accurate and current:

1. Monthly/quarterly HOA dues
2. Any rental/restrictions

3. Pet restrictions
4. Number of parking spaces
5. Unit view
6. Amenities
7. Special assessments (current and expected future assessments)
8. Number of garage spaces (if any)
9. Approval timeframe
10. HOA/condo application

The earlier you receive these items the better, so you can add them to MLS. Buyers can then be aware of the application and fees prior to submitting an offer; this will also help ensure timely closings, as buyers will be ahead of the game with their application to the condo requesting a certificate of approval to reside in the property.

Almost every market utilizes the MLS or a similar service to enter listings. If the MLS is not available, make sure you update your asset manager. Keep in mind the following when listing properties for sale:

1. Selling agents have set automated searches that will send them your listing the first time you submit it to the MLS. Changes made after that may or may not be seen by selling agents and/ or their buyers.
2. Listings inside condos will most likely face competition from other condos (even if the competition comes from short sales). Regardless of whether one condo is a short sale and one is an REO, they are both in direct competition. Banks are open to both when considering list prices, as they have begun to realize the costs associated with carrying properties too long after they repossess them.

As a selling agent, if you take a customer to a condo building, you may as well see all the listings in that building. It's just good time management. Therefore, as an REO agent, you must make sure your property has the magnet marketing appeal so that the first impression selling agents and buyers get when they walk into one of your listings is an impression that will carry them through the closing stage.

The two critical stages (deal breakers) of properly listing the REO on the market are pictures and the marketing description. If these two elements are not flawless, you will not procure a buyer and you may get your listing re-assigned to another competing REO agent.

 **INSIDER TIP**

Be sure your listings provide complete information to buyers; you don't want to mislead or misrepresent your property by including information that has not been verified for accuracy.

Once your listing is placed on the MLS, it will trigger your bank's affiliated network. Some banks have partnerships with companies like listhub.com that take live feeds from the MLS and blast out the listing online through websites like Google, Yahoo Real Estate, etc. Many websites (see Appendix A) will let you post your listing for free or for a nominal cost.

The biggest lead source to help you achieve your twenty-one DOM goal will be through your website. It must be affiliated with as many real estate sites as possible. Having a website is necessary. Usually, your broker has capabilities to provide you with a template that branches off their own company website. However, we do not recommend this.

Instead, invest in a high-quality website (made on Wordpress) with an IDX feed so you can pull all listings from the MLS into your site. Make sure you follow all state real estate laws and always put your brokerage name, address, and phone number on the site. In addition, make sure your email address is your name @ website (mary@xyzbrokerage.com).

When setting up your email, do not use your personal free email such as AOL.com, Yahoo.com, Hotmail.com, or Gmail.com. This does not look professional. You need to brand yourself as a seasoned REO agent. Get a domain name for $12 a year from companies like Go

Daddy.com and pick a nice domain name for yourself. In our business, perception is reality, and you have only one chance to impress your customers (both banks and buyers).

I usually coach my REO agents to look for names they would like to brand in their market. If they are having a hard time thinking of possible website names, I advise them to use wordoid.com to make up catchy words for them.

For example, instead of thinking about words and manually jotting them down on a notepad, let the computer do it for you. Once you have a list of catchy words (e.g. reomover, reolist, reoking, etc.), check out domainsbot.com to see availability. Finally, we recommend buying your domain on GoDaddy.com, as it is a trusted site.

🏠 INSIDER TIP

Be creative online. Buy five to ten catchy domain names and auto-forward them to your website; the more sites that can have high organic page rankings, the better.

Your goal with your website is to achieve a high page rank in search engines such as Google (i.e., land on page one or two). When someone types in "REO" in your city and state, your company/name should pop up. This is not the paid advertising on the top or right hand side. This is in the middle of the page organically; the higher the page rank the better.

Hire someone from odesk.com or elance.com for less than $5 an hour and tell them you want a website built along with search engine optimization (SEO). They will teach you about Google AdWords, landing pages, using strong key words, back linking, etc. You'll be surprised at how inexpensively you can hire a specialist who can make you and your company a star online.

Securing quantity placements for your REOs is critical in gaining buyer leads. Once you have the hot product, you need it on as many websites as possible. The MLS is the first major step. Your bank will link the REO to its affiliates. Finally, your job is to partner with other agents, websites, etc., to gain maximum exposure. This includes using and exploiting all social media, from Facebook to blogging.

Think of it as an REO bridge. On one side are your high-quality bank REOs waiting to be sold. On the other side are hungry home buyers and investors (your customers). Your high-quality, pristine REOs that are perfectly priced, properly promoted, and persistently placed on the MLS and all online media outlets are the bridge that connects.

THE FOUR P'S OF REOS

- Product (High-Quality REO)
- Price (MMR/LPR)
- Promo (Magnet Marketing Checklist)
- Placement (MLS/Website/Affiliates)

THE SIX BIGGEST MARKETING AND LISTING EXPECTATIONS FROM BANKS

Marketing and listing are one of the most critical parts of REO management. Without a proper magnet marketing plan or perfect listing there will be a very slim chance you will be able to get a property under contract within twenty-one days. While there are many expectations in marketing and listings, below are the top six that banks look for:

1. **Make sure the property is clean and presentable before listing.** Banks want to ensure that when buyers and selling agents view the property, they have a good first impression. The home must be staged and pass the 20-point interior and 10-point exterior checklists. They don't want buyers to enter a property that has debris or clutter, or any other issues that will hinder the marketability of the property.

2. **Maximize the number of photos that enhance the property's marketability.** Banks want to minimize their disposition time on the market from the property. By having as many clean and

presentable pictures as possible (minimum of twelve) that enhance the property's marketability, you are positioning the bank's property to be a better choice than the next bank-owned property down the street.

3. **Provide a rich and detailed marketing description.** Banks want a magnet marketing appeal and marketing description that catches buyers' attention. To do this, they want you to maximize the home's key positive features or value propositions. Any special repairs done? Any special financing offers or buyer incentives? Any unique amenities the home has to offer, such as an elevator or built-in gym? Imagine being a buyer and looking at twenty-plus REO listings. The one that will catch your eye will use stunning descriptive words that invite buyers to inquire further.

4. **Ensure access is available to every selling agent/buyer who is interested in viewing the property in order to maximize the likelihood of getting offers.** This one is critical. Some of the biggest complaints from banks are listing agents who hide listings or do not offer selling agents a fair chance at showing the listing. Some listing agents provide as little information as possible or ignore phone calls when they see another brokerage company in the caller ID. Others intentionally remove lock-boxes or keys if they have their own in-house buyer.

   Withholding pertinent information, not placing pictures on the MLS, not returning phone calls, and not submitting offers is a sure way of losing your bank contract. REOs are in abundance. The more you give out, the more you get back. Play fair and by the rules and watch how your business expands exponentially.

5. **Create a marketing plan for each property.** Banks want to use every avenue available to maximize exposure of their property. Quantity is the game; the more exposure the better. Each REO you list must have a marketing plan (product, price, promotion, and placement). Implement the Top 20 Magnet Marketing Checklist on each REO you manage, from placing yard signs outside to doing search engine optimization.

6. **Ensure that listings are entered into MLS within twenty-four hours and are constantly updated.** Asset managers face a lot of pressure. They have goals and quotas to meet. If a listing is delayed by even one day, it's as good as it being delayed by a week or a month, as buyers have many REOs to choose from. Keep your listings up-to-date with any special incentives or offers, and continuously track and monitor your marketing efforts. If your REO is not picked up within thirty days, submit an MMR immediately with your new strategy and new pricing recommendation (i.e., list price reduction request). Remember to back it up with facts.

SHARE YOUR STORY

Do you have a success story you would like to share about the Four Ps of REOs? How about achieving a record breaking DOM time? Do you have any list price reduction stories? Please log on and submit it for your chance to be featured in the next revised edition of *REO Boom*:

www.reoboom.com/story

POINTS TO REMEMBER

- Submit your listing packet within twenty-four hours to your asset manager.
- The Four Ps of REOs is the bridge that connects bank REOs to hungry home buyers and investors.
- Gather the top ten HOA and condo pre-listing checklist early for MLS input.
- Have a minimum of twelve photos in the MLS, following the Magnet Marketing Photo Tips.
- Make sure that you have a robust marketing description that is detailed, descriptive, and appealing.
- Maximize exposure of your listing by implementing the Top 20 Magnet Marketing Checklist.

- Conduct a monthly marketing report (MMR) every thirty days to achieve a list price reduction (LPR).
- Expect a LPR of 5 to 10 percent every thirty days.
- Each REO listing must have a magnet marketing plan to achieve a twenty-one-day turnaround time.
- Market each REO with magnet marketing appeal (a luxurious marketing plan) as if you were marketing your own home for sale, incorporating the interior, exterior, and staging checklists.

The Art of Offers

OFFER EXPECTATIONS

The secret to making a million dollars in this business is mastering offers. The buck stops here. You can have the perfect BPO, have the best listing price, have a pristine condition home, but if you cannot quickly screen buyers or give good recommendations to asset managers, then all the work you have done will be in vain. There is one thing that the public doesn't know about the offer process—the listing agent has power.

You have come a long way in the REO cycle. You have learned to master the BPO, as well as how to get a property repaired and ready for the market, and now you are at the most critical part standing in the way of closing the deal. The offer process is nothing like the offer process in conventional real estate. It is quick and dirty. Banks will not cross out and initial on your standard contract and send it back. They will email you one line or enter one comment in their online platform, and you will have to dictate that to the buyer or other cooperating agent.

Most banks have their own addendum that supersedes any state-regulated real estate contract. They also have a waiver in which the buyer waives all rights to sue the bank after the sale of the property for whatever reason.

Below is the order of the offer process:

REO Offer Process
- Initial Offer
- Counter Offer
- Multiple Offer

REO Offer Actions
- Accepted
- Rejected
- Countered

As an REO listing agent, you will be responsible for managing the entire offer process. If you are using the REO Bootstrap Model, you will be the one entering in the offers in your bank's platform. If you surpassed thirty active listings and are using the REO Plus Model, you will have your transaction coordinator handle the offer process.

The offer process begins only after you have a listing price and the property is placed on the MLS. Until then, banks will not entertain any offers. Remember, banks promote home ownership and neighborhood stabilization, so they want an even playing field for all parties.

From the bank's perspective, it does them no good to take a low-ball offer; therefore, they usually have a requirement to let a property stay on the market for a certain time period before entertaining any offers. Some banks require that the property stay on the market for three full days before any offers will be considered.

BANK THREE-DAY RULE: PROPERTY MUST STAY ACTIVE ON MLS FOR THREE FULL CALENDAR DAYS. NO OFFERS WILL BE CONSIDERED DURING THIS TIME.

Each bank is different, but they all generally have a first-time home buyer (FHB) privilege period, where they give bona-fide first-time home buyers (i.e., owner occupants who intend to purchase a home as their primary residence) a chance to bid on the REO before they open up the doors to investors. Typically this period is the first fifteen days from the time the property is listed.

FHBs are usually required to sign an occupancy certificate or affidavit stating their intent to use the home as their primary residence. Sometimes, consumers who have purchased a home before but are looking to upgrade their home may be eligible to qualify as an FHB. However, because you do not make decisions for the bank (remember, you are not the seller) your job is to present the facts to the banks and let them decide. Never act as a seller by speaking for them or making decisions for them; it is a sure way of losing your bank contract.

In addition, public entities (PE) such as cities, counties, etc., that are using special types of government-sponsored or subsidized public funds (e.g., HUD neighborhood stabilization program, grants, housing trust funds, etc.) also have preferential treatment in purchasing homes within the first fifteen days. This also includes homeowners who intend to occupy the home using public funds.

After day fifteen, all offers are considered. Investor offers come from private individuals, syndicate corporations, and even second-time home buyers looking to park their money in real estate are fair game. Investors are defined as buyers not looking to occupy the property themselves.

BANK FIFTEEN-DAY RULE: ONLY OFFERS FROM BONA-FIDE HOMEOWNERS AND PUBLIC ENTITIES WILL BE CONSIDERED WITHIN THE FIRST FIFTEEN DAYS OF THE PROPERTY BEING ACTIVE ON MLS

OFFER ACCEPTED TIMELINE

If there is one take-away message you must learn in this chapter, it is to present every single offer. First-time home buyer, second-time home buyer, corporations, public entities or individuals using public funds, the mayor, a senator, or even the president—it doesn't matter. Even though you know an offer will be rejected within the first three days, you must present it.

Remember, you are not the seller. You do not own the property, therefore, you cannot decide its fate. Email your asset manager the facts, update your online platform, and let the bank decide. Always cover your assets (CYA).

Hiding offers or going back to cooperating agents and prolonging their offer because of a technical error (missing a document, spelling error, missing initial, etc.) is the fastest way of losing your bank contract.

Banks usually have one perspective when dealing with offers: give everyone a fair chance with impartial consideration to maximize the sales price of a given home. Therefore, every offer must always be presented, no matter when it was received (even if it's before the listing price is given to you), for what amount it is, or from whom it was sent by.

PRESENT EVERY OFFER TO MAXIMIZE SALES PRICE

A very important element in handling offers is keeping clean records of all emails, faxes, and conversations. Updating your asset manager and your online platform is critical. At the end of the day, it's whatever is in writing that counts.

Make sure when dealing with offers that you have written proof. Verbal offers are generally not accepted along with offers without consideration (earnest money deposits, or EMDs). Expect a minimum of forty-eight hours for the banks to respond to your offers.

There are seven general expectations (E's) the banks look for in offers submitted to them. The best thing you can do is set the upfront expectations for your buyers and other selling agents in the marketplace; otherwise, you will be setting yourself up for failure.

- **E1:** Banks want to maximize their sales price.
- **E2:** Banks have no preference whether offer is cash or financing.
- **E3:** Banks want all offers submitted to them within twenty-four hours.
- **E4:** Banks want to minimize their liability and therefore require every offer submitted, regardless of the circumstance or time.
- **E5:** Banks generally prefer first-time home buyers to support local housing initiatives and therefore may require a ninety-day or greater deed restriction prohibiting the resale of a home for investor offers.
- **E6:** Banks will only execute their attorney-drafted documents in a "take it or leave it" stance.
- **E7:** Banks will sell their properties as-is and will make a buyer sign a waiver at closing.

THE OFFER PACKAGE

Every bank is different, but generally the majority of them want to promote homeownership and want to give a fair shot to the public, especially first-time home buyers and public entities that use public funds subsidized by the government to purchase homes. Your offer package should consist of the following elements:

- State or local promulgated contract
- Bank addendum and disclosures
- Any owner occupied certifications or affidavits
- Earnest money deposit (EMD) copy
- Pre-qualification letter (optional)
- Proof of funds (POF) for cash offers (optional)

 **INSIDER TIP**

Create a very transparent offer package for selling agents to use. Less is more. The easier the package is for a selling agent and buyer to fill out, the faster you will get the REO under contract.

The pre-qualification letter for financing offers and proof of funds for cash offers are required for some banks but not for all. They may allow an offer to be submitted, but they won't accept the offer until it is produced. Usually if a selling agent or buyer presents an offer without a pre-qualification letter or proof of funds and it is the highest offer, the bank will counter, asking for the missing document. Even though the banks want the highest and best price for the home, they do not want to waste time with an unqualified buyer. A thorough pre-qualification letter or proof of funds should include:

- Maximum loan qualification based on monthly income-to-debt ratios (e.g., can qualify up to $150,000)
- Credit bureau report or credit score
- Verification of paycheck stubs
- Recent bank statement showing sufficient monies for down payment and closing costs
- Recent bank statement showing sufficient funds for purchase of entire home plus closing costs (cash offers)

With earnest money deposits, most banks simply require a copy of the check. It would be nice if the majority of banks required an earnest money escrow statement or certified funds, but because the demand is so high for REOs, they usually require only a copy of a check even if there is no money in the bank account. That is an inherent risk that has to be dealt with. Expect one out of ten winning bidders to fall out. Many buyers place offers on multiple properties without physically seeing them to ensure they get something.

 **INSIDER TIP**

FHBs usually give 1 to 3 percent of the offer amount or greater as consideration for their EMD. Investors usually give 10 percent as consideration. EMDs are usually payable to the bank's designated settlement agent or the listing brokerage company (you).

If you have a public entity or individual using public funds, their EMD requirement may be waived or reduced to as low as $500. This is the case if they have an approval letter indicating the source of funds (from whom, amount, etc.).

REVIEWING OFFERS

Your offer packet can be streamlined and perfect. You can have perfect instructions on the MLS and still have selling agents who will butcher the offer packet (putting numbers in wrong lines, missing initials on pages, missing spouses' names on contract and addendums, leaving sections blank, overlooking expired pre-approval letters or post-dated earnest money checks, etc.).

Below is an internal offer checklist you can use to ensure the offer you receive is as complete as possible before sending it to the bank. Remember, even if the offer is not perfect, you still must present it to the bank. Simply notify your asset manager of the specific items that may be missing.

Internal Offer Checklist

1. Price
2. Seller concessions amount
3. Offer type: FHB, PE, INVESTOR
4. Owner occupied certificate or affidavit (y/n)
5. Copy of EMD (y/n)
6. Copy of POF if cash (y/n)
7. Closing date
8. Loan type (FHA/VA/conventional, cash)
9. Public funds used (y/n)
10. Selling agent involved (y/n)
11. Pre-qualification letter (y/n)
12. All pages initialed and signed in contract and bank addendum

 **INSIDER TIP**

> Submit all offers to the bank within one day of receipt; the sooner the
> better. Even if it's missing a document from your offer packet, submit
> it and email your asset manager what is missing (e.g., proof of funds,
> owner occupied certificate, etc.). When in doubt, submit it.

Who pays closing costs and who chooses the settlement agent? There is only one answer: whatever is negotiated between the buyer and seller. Sometimes counties require the seller to pay title fees or vice versa. If you receive an offer that doesn't mention the bank is to pay the buyer's closing costs and it gets accepted, the bank will not pay the closing costs.

If a selling agent asks you about closing costs, you need them to put them in writing with the offer. Generally, banks pay up to 6 percent toward the buyer's closing costs and other concessions such as repairs. Please be as detailed as possible. You can include a clause in your contract like:

Seller will contribute up to $_____ toward buyer's closing costs, title insurance, settlement fees, attorney fees, hazard insurance, points, prepaids, home warranty, home repairs, etc.

Buyers generally can choose whomever they like to act as their settlement agent. Sometimes banks require the buyer to close with the bank's designated settlement agent but will give a special credit toward buyer title fees, etc. It again depends on the offer. If an offer comes in highest and best among all and the buyer is requesting that the bank designate the buyer's specific title company to close the transaction, the bank usually complies because it wants to maximize the sale price.

SUBMITTING THE CLEAN COPY

The offer packet that you place on the MLS for selling agents to fill out and the actual offer you submit into the bank once it is the winning offer are two different phases. The latter is what I call the "clean copy." It is the winning offer in its pristine form combined into one PDF for the bank's asset manager to sign off on.

- **Step 1:** Streamline the offer packet placed on MLS.
- **Step 2:** Enter all offers manually into the bank's online platform offer screen using the internal offer checklist.
- **Step 3:** Have the selling agent resubmit the winning or accepted offer to you in perfect form.
- **Step 4:** Review each element to ensure completeness to produce a clean copy for the bank to sign off on.
- **Step 5:** Combine pristine copy into one PDF and email to asset manager for signature.

After you attach your streamlined offer packet with the basic elements into the MLS, you will enter all offers into your bank's platform offer screen. You will use your internal offer checklist to ensure the meat of the offer packet is included. Don't be too concerned with spelling errors or missing initials. Your goal is to get the price, terms, and major elements of the offer, such as seller contribution request, into the bank's hands. Your job is to present all offers, and the bank's job is to maximize its sales price.

Once the bank picks the winning offer, you then email the selling agent to fix any errors or provide any missing documents such as proof of funds of EMD, occupancy certifications, etc. The selling agent should return the clean copy to you within twenty-four hours. Upon receipt of the clean copy, you will combine all pages into one PDF so the asset manager can quickly review the document and sign off. Remember, your job as the listing agent is to ensure everything is perfect *before* emailing the clean copy to the asset manager. The last thing you want is an email or phone call saying an initial is missing from a page or that an entire document is missing.

 **INSIDER TIP**

After the bank picks the winning offer, prepare the clean copy yourself and email to selling agent or buyer to simply sign off on it. It's more efficient and it will ensure you get back the clean copy within twenty-four hours; otherwise, it can take days for the selling agent or buyer to get it right.

Before you submit the clean copy, pay particular attention to details. If you are using the REO Plus Model (see Chapter 3) make sure you provide your transaction coordinator with step-by-step instructions to producing a clean copy (see Appendix G). Have them email it to you when they think it is perfect so you can be the final eyes glancing over it before submitting it to your asset manager.

THE MULTIPLE OFFER MONSTER (MOM)

I remember when I received my first offer on my first REO. It was exciting. I couldn't believe I had received an offer within five days from the time I listed the home on the market. It was thrilling but nerve-wracking dealing with countering the offer, reviewing the addendum, negotiating the price and terms, picking title companies, etc. After about ten offers, I finally had a good handle on the process—until I ran into the MOM (Multiple Offer Monster).

The MOM will destroy you. She will put you under the magnifying glass by scrutinizing your procedures, scream at you by filing complaints, reprimand you by calling you into her corporate office, and will always sleep with one eye open to make sure you are kept on your toes.

Multiple offers are when you have more than one offer on a property. This can be from the time you listed it, from the time the bank accepted an offer, or from the time you put your yard sign on the front lawn.

Unlike multiple offers, single offers are easy. You present it to the bank and it gets accepted, rejected, or countered. You go back to the selling agent or buyer and relay the information until you have a meeting of the minds. When you are dealing with a multiple offer situation things get sticky, especially when a seasoned MOM is constantly looking over your shoulder.

MULTIPLE OFFER MONSTER (MOM) = MORE THAN ONE OFFER ON A PROPERTY

Your job as an REO listing agent is to present all offers. The bank's job is to maximize the value of the asset. Therefore, the bank wants every single offer in for review. The following are the steps you take when dealing with the MOM.

1. Email all selling agents or buyers (if you represent both sides) that there is a multiple offer situation.
2. Email or fax all selling agents/buyers a multiple offer notification provided to you by your bank.
3. Set and email a deadline (usually forty-eight hours) for all selling agents or buyers to re-submit their highest and best (H&B) offer on the bank's form. The deadline will be determined by your bank's guidelines. Example:
   - Highest and best offer must be received in writing to the listing agent no later than _____ (Date/Time).
4. Update your online bank platform and notify the asset manager there is a multiple offer situation. Provide them with the MLS

ID along with the date the property was listed to make it easier for them to make a decision. Example:

- Multiple offer situations exist for REO XYZ. The MLS ID is x123456. List date was xx/xx/xxxx. Deadline for all H&B offers is _____(Date/Time).

5. Update the MLS and clearly state in the comments section there is a multiple offer situation and when the deadline is to submit all H&B offers.

6. Email your asset manager immediately and await their response if the following occurs:

- Offer comes in after the deadline passed.
- Offer comes in after the bank already picked or is negotiating with the H&B offer.
- Selling agent or buyer is threatening you with "filing a complaint."

 **INSIDER TIP**

Set up a special email to handle all your offers, along with an auto-responder (offers@xyzrealty.com, see Appendix F for sample). This will enable you to search any offer by property address or name instantly in case MOM gives you the third degree.

So, the winner is . . . ? Whatever you do, do not inform the selling agent or buyer their offer is accepted until you get in writing from your asset manager who has presented the winning offer. Many times, asset managers will go into their system and reject all offers because of upper management discretion.

Imagine informing a potential winner their offer was accepted and then calling them the next day informing them they now have to rebid. Those are shoes you do not want to fill.

THE FIVE OFFER STATUSES

To make matters more confusing, sometimes banks will have "verbally accepted" and "accepted" as different categories internally on their bank platform. Usually there are five offer statuses:

1. Pending Offer
2. Verbally Accepted Offer
3. Accepted Offer
4. Awaiting Approval
5. Rejected

If you submit the offer into the bank and the asset manager has not looked at it yet, the offer status is pending. They have not taken any action. If there was a tug-of-war situation (offer-counter-offer) and the bank decided to accept an offer, the status usually goes first to "verbally accepted." This is, the bank verbally accepted it but still needs management approval to sign off. It is not formalized yet.

On the other hand, "accepted" means the bank chose the winning bidder. Once you see the words "accepted" in your online platform or receive an email from your asset manager, you are safe to inform all parties who has the winning offer. You can also change the status in the MLS to "pending sale."

Sometimes before the offer can be fully accepted, it may fall into an "awaiting approval" state. This is when the bank has chosen to approve it, but may need a special signature from someone else in management to sign off, possibly because there is something missing or the offer is substantially lower than the listing price. Finally, "rejected" status is when all negotiations between buyers and sellers are ceased.

Sometimes buyers tend to play hardball and submit low offers, which get rejected immediately. These investor-type offerers usually come back if they really want the property and submit a new offer. Also, some banks will automatically reject properties if the offer falls within the first three days of the no-offer-accepted period or if an investor submits an offer during the first fifteen-day FHB protection period.

Usually the MOM comes into play when a property was priced too low or is in an incredibly hot area. This is the time when the pressure is on. Not following the multiple offer process is crossing the invisible line into the three shady offer tactics that selling agents use. This is playing with fire, as we shall discuss below.

The Busted Offer

Even when MOM situations exist, there are many times that the offer that is ultimately accepted ends up busting out or falling through (i.e., the buyer backs out and terminates the contract agreement). In these cases, it is necessary that you reach out to all the other agents/buyers who were interested in the property. Tell them it's their lucky day and have them resubmit their offer. In most cases, they will be delighted to do so. Many banks also allow backup offers, in which case the next highest and best offer will be accepted without the listing agent having to relist the property.

Don't fret if a buyer or selling agent backs out. This happens. Don't take it personally. Just be thankful that you have multiple offers so that you can reach out to the others and get a solid contract executed. In cases where banks do not have a backup offer policy, be sure to follow these seven steps as soon as the buyer or selling agent tells you they want to cancel.

1. Call up the selling agent and buyer to find out the reason for their cancellation.
2. Send them the termination agreement (an addendum to cancel the contract) and give them a deadline by which to return it.
3. Inform your asset manager that the deal has fallen through, but you are still waiting for the signed termination agreement from the buyer/selling agent. Inform the asset manager that you will change the status in MLS from "pending sale" to "active" and that you will reach out to any other offers that are in the system.
4. Change status from "pending sale" to "active."
5. Email each party who made an offer for the property to see if they are still interested. Call and confirm that they received the

email and that they will reach out to the respective buyer to determine if an offer should be re-presented.

6. If a new MOM situation exists, inform each party when their highest and best offer is due by.
7. Input all highest and best offers.

THREE SHADY OFFER TACTICS

I have seen a lot of offers. I have seen the same listing agents continue to sell hot properties to the same buyers without even a chance of those properties hitting the market to give a fair shot to the general public.

We strongly advise against using the following methods. They are unfair, immoral, and unethical. We can almost guarantee that if you do get away with such tactics once or twice, your behavior will come back to haunt you and will cost you your bank contract (and possibly a lot more).

Shady Offer Tactic #1: High-Low Method

When a property is in demand, you will know. You will get multiple calls a day on the property. The key will get stolen from the lockbox. You will get threatened by a consumer. It's a multiple offer monster situation, and the bank will soon inform all parties to resubmit their H&B within a certain time period.

MOM SITUATION = H&B OFFERS NEEDED

Many co-operating agents who have been seasoned selling REOs have learned how to master the MOM process by implementing the high-low method. Basically, when the bank requests the H&B offer from all parties, a co-operating agent will exaggerate the offer to ensure the bank picks it.

If the property is listed at $200,000 and the property is in an MOM situation, a typical H&B offer will come in around 30 to 50 percent higher—$260,000 to $300,000. They will also put on the offer "first-time home buyer and FHA financing." Remember, most banks want to promote homeownership since they are receiving government subsidies (bail-out funds), so they usually give preferential treatment to first-time home buyers.

Then, after the co-operating agent's customer is the winning bidder, they will obtain an FHA appraisal during the thirty-day closing period as a tool to drop the price back down to the current market value. For example:

Listing Price: $200,000 on 1/1/2012
Offer 1: $205,000; cash; investor
Offer 2: $225,000; conventional financing; homeowner
Offer 3: $245,000; FHA financing; second home; homeowner
Offer 4: $285,000; FHA financing; first-time homebuyer (**High-low method winner**)
- High-low method buyer wins contract and orders required FHA appraisal
- FHA appraisal comes in at $201,000; ordered on 1/15/2012
- Bank reduces home from $285,000 to $201,000 on 1/20/2012

Most banks usually pick the highest dollar amount of the offer presented regardless of the type of financing the buyer chooses. To the seller (bank), there is not much difference between a cash offer and a financing offer because either way they will receive cash at closing. Therefore, most banks would rather entertain a higher financing offer than any other offer because it is most likely to yield the highest sales dollar to the bank.

Even though Offer 4 (high-low method winner) was clearly over listing price and possibly market value, the bank will pick it because it maximizes their value or pocketbook. Plus, the offer is from a homeowner and the bank thus meets its initiative of stabilizing neighborhoods throughout the country.

High-Low Method with Seller Contribution

Sometimes offers will come in requesting the seller to contribute a certain percentage (e.g., 6 percent) from the sales price to cover the buyer's closing costs. However, this request is used as a tool for negotiation to sway the asset manager's decision in agreeing to the high-low method request. For example, the selling agent will explain to the listing agent (you) that the buyer really wants the house and is even willing to forego the seller contribution it initially requested due to the buyer's strong desire to buy the home.

High-Low Method with Inspection Report

In addition, even when most banks sell their property as-is, the selling agent will order an inspection report (separate from appraisal) to further support their high-low method request. The goal of the inspection report is to itemize as many flaws in the home as possible that can be used to obtain repair credit. The selling agent will not necessarily count on the repair credit being issued, but they will use the inspection as another tool to boost their negotiation efforts.

They will make the case that the buyer is willing to make all of the repairs out of pocket and even waive a seller contribution, only if the seller complies with the state-certified appraisal to reduce the purchase price. Nine times out of ten, if the selling agent is good and makes a good case using the seller contribution and repair credit tactic, the bank will grant the purchase price reduction.

 **INSIDER TIP**

Many banks require homeowners to sign an occupancy certificate verifying they are a bona-fide homeowner and do not intend to resell the home for up to twelve months. Search local county records to make sure the winning buyer does not own a home currently, and inform your asset manager if they do to prevent the high-low method.

High-Low Method Summary

1. Buyer submits exaggerated H&B offer with seller contribution to secure contract.
2. Buyer orders inspection and point out damages to home.
3. Buyer offers to pay for inspection damages out of pocket and even waives any seller contribution to show sincerity in purchasing home.
4. Seller complies and reduces home to state certified appraisal amount.

Shady Offer Tactic #2: The Proxy Offer

This next tactic is dirty; a low blow. A co-operating agent creates a proxy offer with a fraudulent pre-approval letter and submits the H&B offer to the bank during the MOM deadline. After they win the bid (as in the high-low method above) and all other competing offers are rejected, the following steps occur:

1. Co-operating agent informs bank during the inspection period (usually ten days) that their customer is no longer interested during their inspection period.
2. Bank informs listing agent (you) to re-list the property bank on the MLS (usually within twenty-four hours).
3. Same co-operating agent submits another offer (this time a real customer) at full list price.
4. Same co-operating agent removes key from lockbox so previous buyers and their co-operating agents (or new ones) cannot gain access to show the home while it is re-listed.
5. Same co-operating agent wins property at the retail list price.
6. Same co-operating agent uses appraisal and repair credits to negotiate purchase price down even further.

Because there is a lead time between when the property is pending sale and active on the MLS (due to the speed of the listing agent), the original co-operating agent has a narrow window of time to slip in his second offer while all other co-operating agents and buyers are left in the dark thinking the property is off the market.

Shady Offer Tactic #3: Straw Offer

The final tactic is for selling agents to go around the first-time home buyer protection period—the period of time that a property is on the market whereby investors are not allowed to win a contract on a property. This allows the investor to purchase a property when only a homeowner is allowed to do so. Most banks do not allow for second home purchasers to win a contract during the homeowner period.

The following steps have been used to make straw offers:

1. Selling agent puts in an offer for a fictitious buyer (in a relative's name) who does not appear in tax records as owning a residence.
2. When this offer gets accepted, and after the contract is executed (i.e., signed by both seller and buyer), the selling agent then requests to add a name to the contract (name of investor).
3. Ten days prior to closing, selling agent will inform the listing agent that the fictitious buyer's name needs to be removed from the contract (due to financing and/or other reasons).

Thus, the investor will be the only party on the contract and the selling agent will keep the investor's name under the radar during the first-time homeowner protection period. Even better, the investor will not need to sign a homeowner occupancy certification since his or her name was added after the contract was executed and onto a separate addendum.

THE FIVE BIGGEST ROOKIE OFFER MISTAKES

When starting in the business, you may feel that sense of euphoria when you get one, two, or a few offers within seven days of listing your property. Unfortunately, the offer process in the REO cycle is the most analyzed and critical process. There is zero room for error and zero tolerance for excuses. Below are the five biggest rookie mistakes new agents make when presenting offers:

1. Disclosing what the highest offer is to other agents.
2. Not presenting every offer regardless of if the offer is missing pages or addendums, or if the MOM expiration period has expired.
3. Not sending back an MOM notification to each buyer or co-operating agent.
4. Not placing listings into the MLS properly and within twenty-four hours.
5. Making it cumbersome for others to present an offer.

Your name and your word is all you have in this business. It can take years to build a reputation. but one complaint to put you out of business. Your goal is to protect your name, your company, and your reputation at all times. Avoid shady tactics and basic mistakes, and you are well on your way to becoming a respected REO expert in your area.

Rookie Mistake #1: Disclosing the Highest Offer

Banks are very smart and loaded with cash. With cash comes leverage to recruit top talent. They will send mystery shoppers or proxy buyers to call your office, your cell, your assistants, whatever it takes to see if you can walk the talk. Are you ethical? Will you follow their guidelines? Can they count on you to handle volume during busy REO boom times? This is what they want to find out—if your word is your bond.

I was once coaching a fairly new REO broker, Michelle in Georgia. She was quite ambitious and had the business down to a science. Around August one year she had an incredible month. Her in-house sales ratio (where she represented both sides of the commission) was over 60 percent. She was double-dipping and leaving no cream in the Oreo cookie.

She called me one Saturday morning at maybe 8 or 9 A.M. When I said hello, she was frantic; talking fast, nervous, and scared, as if she was about to have a breakdown. She told me there was a $400,000 home she had listed and for which she had lined up a couple of in-house buyers. Three out of five offers came in a little over list price, another came in at list price, and one customer told her he would do whatever it took to get the home.

He went on stating he was an all cash buyer, he would use her as his agent exclusively, and he even would sign a buyer-broker agreement. He would come into her office within one hour to sign a contract, and he really wanted the house for his new family. To top it off, he said he was a cash buyer who had just sold his house in Arizona and needed to buy something within thirty days because of his new job relocation.

As soon as she started off with the buyer's rhetoric I immediately knew what was going to happen. Either he really wanted to purchase the home or it was a set up by a mystery shopper. Judging by the call coming in on early Saturday morning, I had a feeling it was the latter. He had the bait hooked and he was fishing for answers.

As he had her thinking about the nice vacation she was going to take with the $24,000 commission ($400,000 × 6 percent), he said, "Look I'm about twenty minutes away from your office. I will leave shortly, but before I go just want to make sure I have a chance to win this home. I want to offer $435,000 cash. That shouldn't be a problem, right?" Such a convincing and innocent remark, or so it seemed. She said with all trust, "Yes, you'll be fine; the highest offer we have is $412,000, and that's financing anyways."

You know what happened next? The gentleman said, "Thank you very much. I'll see you shortly" and hung up. After about thirty minutes when he didn't show, Michelle quickly looked into her iPhone to check recent calls and noticed the number was blocked. She attempted to redial the number, but nothing.

Immediately her stomach fell to the floor with guilt and embarrassment. A month later she was called into the bank's corporate office for a meeting with the REO management disposition team, where they gave her a performance review. She was given one last opportunity before a final termination. Unfortunately, she never received the same level of inventory from her supplier again because she had tarnished her name, her ethics, and her reputation.

Therefore, no matter how clever the question sounds ("Is it above XYZ amount? Is it south of XYZ price? I don't want to waste your time or mine with this offer—will I have a chance?") do not answer. Simply state, "Please present your offer and I will submit it into the bank." In addition, make sure you email that buyer or selling agent in writing that their offer has been submitted.

Rookie Mistake #2: Failing to Present Every Offer

We cannot belabor enough the point of presenting every offer. It is the single most important item in this chapter. Some banks may automatically give you authority to tell the selling agent or buyer their offer is rejected if it falls within the three-day rule (or the fifteen-day rule for investor offers). This does not mean you do not enter the offer. You still enter the offer letting the asset manager know the exact circumstance.

Each bank is different and has its own policy; however they all usually shadow around the three-day and fifteen-day rules. Below are the scenarios and recommended templates you should use when presenting offers in the bank's platform. Always provide the type of offer, the date it was placed in the MLS, the MLS ID number, days left in protection period, items you have received or are missing from the offer packet, and finally whether you recommend or reject the offer.

1. Offer is received from an investor during first fifteen days of listing on MLS:

   Investor offer received. Property was listed on __/__/__. The MLS ID is: X123456. The days left in FHB protection period are XYZ DAYS. We received proof of funds via bank statements. We are missing copy of EMD. We recommend rejecting this offer as per page ___ of our sales policy manual guidelines as offer falls within the first fifteen days of the home buyer protection period.

Normally, if you receive a bona-fide first-time home buyer offer and an investor offer during the first fifteen-day protection period (between days four and fifteen), a MOM situation does not exist, because an investor offer is usually automatically rejected. However, each bank is different; therefore, submit all offers and wait for instructions from your asset manager.

2. Offer is received from a first-time home buyer or investor during first three days of listing on MLS:

   First-time home buyer/investor offer received. Property was listed on __/__/___. The MLS ID is: A123456. The days left in FHB protection period are XYZ DAYS. We received pre-approval letter from buyer's financial institution. We are missing copy of EMD. We recommend rejecting this offer as per page ___ of our sales policy manual guidelines as offer falls within the first three days of the no-offers acceptance period.

Giving your recommendation is a good thing. It shows you can follow the bank's guidelines and shows you are looking out to save the asset manager's time. Of course, back up your recommendations with facts (your bank's guidelines). Once the bank follows your recommendation and does in fact reject the offer (in this example), then send an email to the selling agent (or buyer if you are representing your in-house buyer) and inform them why the offer was rejected (because of the three-day rule) and encourage them to resubmit it during the appropriate time.

 **INSIDER TIP**

Time is money for asset managers. The more things you can provide them without them having to dig around, the more efficient you will be and the more inventory you will receive.

Rookie Mistake #3: Not Sending a MOM
Notification to Every Party

Next, do not forget to send a MOM notification to all parties. Your supplier will provide you with their form to use. Even if the offers that come in during the first round state they are already "highest and best," you still must send to each selling agent and/or buyer a MOM notification.

What constitutes a MOM situation? By definition a Multiple Offer Monster situation is when more than one offer is placed on a property. However, some banks consider only multiple first-time home buyer offers as a MOM situation.

So if a homeowner offer comes in on day five and an investor offer comes in on day fourteen, the property would not fall under a MOM situation because the investor offer would automatically be rejected for falling within the fifteen-day bank rule. Other banks have a catch-all phrase where a MOM is more than one offer regardless of the intent of the buyer (to occupy the home or to invest). When in doubt, email your asset manager immediately and wait for direction.

Never evade a multiple offer situation. For example, if you have a first-time home buyer offer come in on day four and the bank counters it, and meanwhile another first-time home buyer offer comes in on day five, do not tell the other selling agent it's too late and the bank is negotiating with an offer already. You must notify your asset manager so they can reject all offers and you can present an MOM notice to all parties. Remember, the goal is to provide the most bang for the buck to the bank; maximize its sales price; and provide it the most value.

Another scenario is if a first-time home buyer offer comes in on day four—let's say for $100,000—and the bank decides to accept the offer. However, it falls under "awaiting approval" status (meaning it's not officially accepted) and you receive another offer on day fourteen for a substantially greater price, such as $150,000. Expect the asset manager to reject all offers and request a MOM situation.

Even though the original offer might have been your own customer and the second offer is from a cooperating agent, you must always maximize the bank's value. This means not talking the second offer's selling agent or buyer out of buying the property, answering your phones, and of course presenting the second offer.

Do not wait an extra day to see if the original offer becomes fully accepted. You may rationalize it to yourself by thinking the second offer came in after office hours or they called on a non-working day (Saturday/Sunday). However, the banks will not follow your questionable logic, especially if they find out you did not present a $50,000 higher offer. In that case, the selling agent or the buyer for the higher offer will file a complaint to the bank (banks usually have toll-free hotlines) and the heat will be on you. Do not walk over dollars to pick up pennies. It's not worth it. Present every offer and present every MOM notice promptly.

Rookie Mistake #4: Not Placing the Property in MLS Properly

The next biggest rookie mistake is not placing the property in the MLS entirely, because you may have an in-house buyer you are working with already. During a conference I attended in 2009, I met an REO agent from Tampa, Florida, who was quite pretentious; we'll call him Hubris.

I believe he was working in real estate part-time and at a packaging facility similar to UPS part-time, and he was bragging about the big $20,000 commission checks that he would make. He was gloating about how he was "strategically missing in action" when it came time to putting the property on the MLS. He would get his leads from his yard signs or his online marketing, get his buyers pre-approved, and keep them waiting until he received his list price from the bank.

As soon as he received his list price, he would write up an offer with his customer and present it to the bank after the first three days. As soon as the single offer was accepted, he would then enter the listing into the MLS and backdate the listing date field by three days.

- Bank gives List Price 12/1/12
- Hubris waits until 12/4/12 to enter his customer's sole offer (usually at list price)
- Customer offer fully accepted by 12/5/12

- Hubris enters the listing as "active" into MLS on 12/5/12 at 6:00 A.M. Eastern with a back date of 12/2/12 in the listing date field
- Hubris changes status of property on 12/5/12 at 6:05 A.M. Eastern to pending sale.

Therefore, before a soul is awake, he has entered the listing and immediately placed it under contract or "pending sale" five minutes later. Because he backdates the listing by three days, he still falls within his bank guidelines of entering listings into the MLS within twenty-four hours. He gets rich from both sides of the commission and he puts his competition out of business.

As everyone piled up around the water cooler listening to his shady tactics, I knew it would be a matter of time before he would get caught and fired. Sure enough, a couple of months later I heard his license had been revoked and he was back at the packaging facility, this time working full-time.

Moral of the story: place your listings in the MLS ethically and on time. You may cheat the system for a while, but it will catch up to you in the end and perhaps even put you out of business permanently.

Rookie Mistake #5: Making It Difficult
for Buyers to Place an Offer

Finally, I have seen agents make it extremely difficult for selling agents and/or consumers to place offers by having thirty- to forty-page offer packets filled with disclosures and requirements so stringent it is as if someone was applying to work for the IRS. The offer packet needs to be as simple as possible. Remember, banks want to promote homeowner-ship and give everyone a fair shot at owning a home. Never put any rules in your offer packet such as "no offers will be submitted without XYZ."

Also, do not require offers to have a pre-approval by a certain bank unless it's in your bank's policies. I have seen many MLS listings that state "pre-approval required by XYZ lender" or "must be approved by XYZ bank for offer to be submitted." In addition, I have seen many offer packets that have an instruction sheet on how to properly fill out

offers. Although this may be helpful for you, it deters buyers from placing offers and selling agents from showing your REO listing. Keep your
offer packets pristine and user friendly.

The REO business is about volume. In order to receive it, you must
perform ethically. If you hinder offer submissions or violate any of the
five biggest rookie mistakes, it will be only a matter of time before you,
too, will be looking for employment elsewhere. Only by playing by the
rules and working hard will you achieve long-term success. Remember,
REOs are not a race—they're a marathon.

THE DREADED PERFORMANCE REVIEW

There may come a point where you have done everything right, worked
24/7 nonstop to keep your asset manager happy, and gone the extra mile
when you had the opportunity to. Even after all this, you can get the
dreaded call from the asset manager regarding your performance. This is
how it will sound: "Good afternoon, I'm calling about REO AXXXXXX,
there were several issues brought up regarding your performance and I
think it's best for you to come into our office to discuss."

Don't worry. It happens to the best of us. First, do not panic. Next,
never admit guilt! Ever! Don't give anyone a reason to terminate you;
if an asset manager wants you terminated, let them work and prove it.
Don't make it easy for them by admitting guilt (assuming of course
you were not guilty).

If they request that you come in, make sure you have at least five
days before going in to their office. The first two days will be for you to
internalize what just happened, and then the next three days will be for
preparing. You will need to prepare for two outcomes:

- Prepare an explanation or apology for your performance issue
  and say that it will never happen again.
- Gather hard facts and statistics that show how good of an REO
  listing agent you are and then fight to show that this performance was out of the ordinary.

The latter option will always be better. You want to prove your dedication and drive to be successful, and you will let actions speak louder than words by writing up a detailed report to prevent the occurrence from happening again. In the report, highlight your success with handling their inventory, discuss your eight successful measurement tools (Chapter 11), and discuss how your team or company's goals are aligned with the bank's. Try to get two weeks to create this.

Believe it or not, when asset managers call you in for a performance review, they don't care about how good you once were or how well other asset managers like you; they simply want you to know that your performance was an issue and that they will either suspend you or terminate you. If you have proven your case and have hard facts that show the actual performance issue was out of your control, you can further validate your case by asking for voluntary suspension.

This is when you ask them for time to restructure and minimize errors (whether you had them or not) so you will avoid having them put you on involuntary suspension. You are putting yourself on the offensive. It makes you look good, highlights your work ethic, and shows that you are sincere.

Once you master offers, you will be ready to receive the next biggest document that will leave you one step closer in cashing in on your ATM: the executed contract.

 SHARE YOUR STORY

Do you have a success story you would like to share about offers? How about how you spotted one of the three shady offer tactics and how you handled it? How about dealing with mystery shoppers or the dreaded performance review? Please log on and submit it for your chance to be featured in the next revised edition of *REO Boom*:

www.reoboom.com/story

POINTS TO REMEMBER

- Never admit guilt in a performance review committee. State your case with hard facts and further validate it by requesting a voluntary suspension.
- Encourage all offers to be submitted, enter listing into the MLS within twenty-four hours, email MOM notices to all parties, present every offer to the bank regardless of time, and keep every offer you receive entirely confidential.
- Avoid the three shady offer tactics (the straw offer, the proxy offer, and the high-low method) at all times and double check county records to make sure first-time home buyers are not investors.
- Call all selling agents and buyers and inform them of their lucky day if the original offer busts.
- Multiple Offer Monster (MOM) is when there is more than one offer on a property and highest and best (H&Bs) offers are needed.
- Use the internal offer checklist to review and submit all offers.
- Prepare the clean copy yourself and email to the selling agent or buyer to sign off on to ensure a twenty-four-hour turnaround time.
- Keep a very short and concise offer package with only the state contract, bank addendum, and any occupancy certifications to sign. Avoid rules and cover pages. If an offer is missing any element, submit it and state what is missing.
- Banks want to maximize their sales price within the shortest period of time.
- The bank's three-day rule rejects all offers submitted, and the bank's fifteen-day rule rejects all investor offers submitted.

Closings: The Finish Line!

"I do not think there is any other quality so essential to success of any kind as the quality of perseverance. It overcomes almost everything, even nature."

—John D. Rockefeller

CLOSING YOUR FIRST DEAL

Closing the deal is what counts. In the REO business, there is no "E" for effort; there is only "R" for results. It's all about results. You must persevere until you get results; results mean closings. You can be the best marketer, have the best listing, have the best at BPOs, but if you can't close it doesn't mean squat. Remember: Always Be Closing!

In most REO closings, there are two sides to the transaction: one side that represents the buyer and one side that represents the seller. Accordingly, closings rely on more than one party to perform, and it will require a team effort in order to close on time. Your job as an REO agent is to manage the six moving parts:

- Buyer
- Buyer's title company
- Selling agent
- REO agent's team (listing specialist or staff)
- Seller's title company/foreclosing attorney
- Seller

THE TWO REO CLOSING RULES

When it comes to closing your first deal or even your hundredth deal, it is very important to under-promise and over-deliver. You must maximize the chances of closing on or before the closing date. To do this you need to follow the two golden REO closing rules:

Rule #1: Set the contracted closing date on the executed contract for thirty to forty-five days out according to the REO closing timelines to leave more than ample time for all closing conditions to be met.

Rule #2: Close as early as possible within fifteen to thirty days.

 **INSIDER TIP**

> Avoid having executed contracts (contracts that are signed by both bank and buyer) that are set to close in fifteen days. This typically does not provide enough time to complete a closing, and as stated earlier, it is much better to set the closing date out in the future and to end up closing before.

There is one big closing misconception. Selling agents are under the impression that if they put in an offer that has a closing date within fifteen days, the seller will see that as a positive thing and will accept their offer. To the contrary, what ends up happening is the seller accepts an offer because it is the highest offer, regardless of when the property will close.

Banks know that every REO closes. They also know there is no big difference between financing and cash. At the end of the day, a financing transaction is cash in their pocket just like a cash transaction. Will they wait an extra fifteen to thirty days for a high-purchase price from a buyer that has a 700-plus credit score? Absolutely.

If a contract is accepted within fifteen days that also happens to be the highest offer out of all the competing offers, and the deal doesn't close, it will reflect badly upon you as the REO agent as well as upon the selling agent. Because a short fifteen-day window leads to havoc and chaos on the week of closing (due to closing delays), an extension will be needed, and sometimes the bank will not approve one. To avoid this vicious cycle, follow the two golden rules of closings.

THE CLOSING CYCLE

Closing early can be difficult. There are so many parties involved in the transaction, so many bureaucratic processes that must be followed, and so many hiccups that often come along with closing an REO. Below is the typical REO closing cycle.

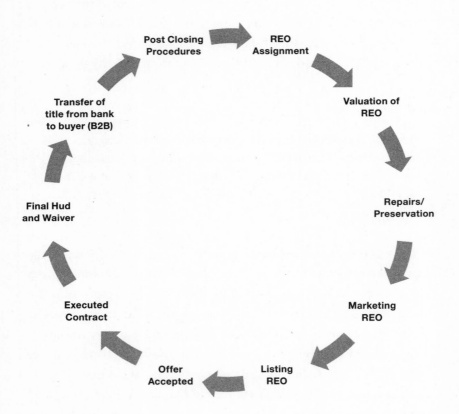

Remember from Chapter 1 the length of time from receiving your first REO assignment to closing is, on average, ninety days. Once the offer gets accepted and the contract gets executed, you have a waiting game anywhere between fourteen days to forty-five days. It is your responsibility to influence the REO closing cycle to close on time.

The recommended minimum closing timelines based on type of payment and type of property are discussed on the next page.

REO CLOSING TIMELINES: CASH VERSUS FINANCING

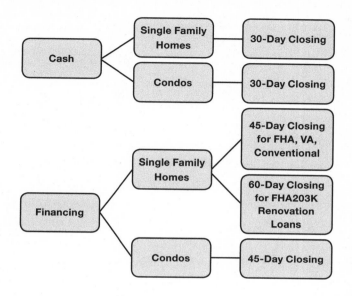

So, how do you get the buyer and seller to agree on meeting the minimum closing date guidelines above? Well, as the listing agent, you know the details of transaction better than all parties and can explain to either party what closing date should be set and why. Both the buyer and seller may want to close quickly, but only you can gauge the realistic closing date. It is in your best interest to set the closing date out to the minimum guidelines above. If closing dates do not follow the above guidelines and instead are set too early, extensions will be needed. Every time you request an extension, there is some chance the asset manager may ask, "Why is this agent asking for an extension, why couldn't the buyer close on time?" To avoid this completely, set closing dates out from the beginning and avoid a meltdown later.

CHOOSING A TITLE COMPANY

If the buyer is choosing their own title company to insure title, then you have an opportunity to start the closing process even before the contract is executed. Remember, before a contract is executed by both parties, there is the REO countering process:

Offer > counteroffer > verbal acceptance > management approval > full approval > buyer signs contract > contract sent to seller > seller signs contract.

This process can take up to a week. As soon as the counteroffer is verbally accepted, it is a smart idea to find out who the buyer's title company is. Then, call the buyer's title company and ask them to order the title.

Explain to them that the executed contract will be sent by the end of the week but that you need them to order title right away in order for the buyer to meet the contracted closing date. Most likely, they will be more than glad to order the title because they want to close just as much as you do. Having the buyer's title company order the title in advance, particularly in advance of getting the contract executed, is a great strategy to save an extra week of time in the closing process.

TEN STEPS TO CLOSE IN THIRTY DAYS

In order to accomplish the two golden REO closing rules, there are ten steps that need to be followed to close your transaction in thirty days or less:

Step One: Email Executed Contract

First, contact all parties in a closing and include the following:

1. Executed contract
2. Transaction summary
3. Contact information for all parties
4. Deadlines

The first email you send will include the executed contract. This first impression will last for the remainder of the time the parties are under contract. Be detailed, set deadlines, and make sure everyone is working toward a common goal.

Below is an example of the initial email content:

Please find executed sales contract attached. Property must close by XX/XX/XXXX. Please make sure loan commitment is provided to us via email by XX/XX/XXXX, all conditions are met 72 hours prior to closing to properly obtain a "clear to close," and title is ordered in advance so we can clear any title issues. Below is a summary of our transaction.

Transaction Summary:
- Address
- REO ID
- Purchase price
- EMD (Earnest Money Deposit)
- Buyer's name(s)
- Marital status
- Cash or financing (type)
- Commission (include any processing fees)

Contact Information (name, phone number, fax number, email, and address):
- Buyer
- Selling agent (co-operating agent)
- Buyer's attorney
    - If buyer's attorney is insuring title?
- Buyer's closing agent (if different from above)
- Lender
- Seller's closing agent
- Listing agent or closing coordinator for listing office
- Homeowners Association or Condo Association

Who should be included in your initial email? Everyone except the asset manager; asset managers will always sign the contract last, making it executed. Therefore, they already have a copy. You don't want to burden them with unnecessary emails. Always be efficient and respect-ful of their time, as they see hundreds of emails a day.

 **INSIDER TIP**

Have a buyer's information sheet (see Appendix C) submitted to the selling agent to complete. The sheet will have accurate contact infor-mation for the lender/processor, buyer's title company, buyer, inspec-tion company, appraiser, and attorney. Be sure to include all these parties in your initial email.

Along with the executed contract, you will need to ensure the title company or your broker is holding the earnest money deposit. Many banks are opposed to the buyer's title companies holding the EMD. If the buyer knows the title company that they have a relationship with is holding their money, they may have an edge to get it back if it comes down to it.

Even if the buyer's title company has the original EMD, make sure you have them wire it to the seller's title company within twenty-four hours. Also, we do not recommend giving your brokerage company the power to hold the EMD. It's not worth the liability issue and head-aches in case there is a dispute. The best case scenario is to follow up on the executed contract along with a confirmation that the seller's title company is in receipt of the EMD.

Step Two: Follow Up with the Title Company

Each email should be accompanied by a follow-up phone call. Many times when parties to the transaction have more files that they can handle, some will end up at the bottom of the barrel. It is your duty to set the upfront agreement and let everyone know you mean business. Every time you follow up with a phone call after sending an email, it sets the norm. The parties will know the next time that you will follow up, and therefore they will do their job.

Oftentimes what happens is that closings get delayed because title companies or lenders are short staffed and they fall behind on their work. Do not let this happen. Be aggressive from the beginning, follow up, and gain the momentum of closing on time from the very beginning.

Using Double Ds (DDs): A Closing Secret

You want to know a little secret? I use delay deliveries (Double Ds) to get closings done and title companies to respond. Double Ds are what separate good REO agents from excellent REO agents. If you remember from Chapter 3, we discussed how using basic technology can cut your response time and increase your performance. Well, Double Ds are technology on steroids.

How does it work? Every time you get a response from a title company or a vendor who says "they will get back to you on XYZ date," I want you to go into your Outlook email or your web-based email and send an outgoing message that is scheduled to go out on a later date (the date they told you they will get back to you).

You can reply to their original email or compose a new message, such as, "Just following up on your timeline; today is XYZ and waiting for your answer."

After you compose your email message, go to "options" on the top of Microsoft Outlook and click on "delay delivery." Set your time for two or three days out or whatever the date was they promised to answer your question, and hit send. That's it. Simple.

I have used this countless times for loan approvals, HUD approval requests, title commitments, homeowner association letters pending, etc. Once you make the other party accountable, they create action. How many times have you said you will follow up or get back to a person and never did so? You might have simply forgotten to or got caught up and lost track of time.

Imagine now someone working at a title company on salary with hundreds of files and hundreds of brokers asking them for things. The only way they will put your name and number to the top of their list is by you being on the top of their minds. This is accomplished by delay deliveries. Besides, by the time they see another email from you they are going to want to get rid of you, so you will be forcing them to respond.

Step Three: Apply to HOA or Condo in Forty-Eight Hours

If the purchase is for a single-family home (SFH) governed by an HOA or for a condo that requires approval from a condo association, then a certificate of approval will be needed. To obtain this approval, the buyer must apply and pay a fee to the appropriate party governing the SFH or condo.

Ensure that the buyer applies within the first two days of the executed contract. To do this, provide the buyer and selling agent with the application and/or contact information for the condo. Let them know that failure to apply within forty-eight hours of the executed contract will cause a delay in closing.

Follow up after forty-eight hours and ask for confirmation that the buyer has applied. Find out who took the application and how long it typically takes to obtain a certificate of approval. Post notes in your online platform informing the seller about the buyer's application process as well as the pertinent HOA information (name of management company, phone number, email, etc.).

Step Four: Order the Estoppel Within Forty-Eight Hours

Estoppels are required for all HOAs and condo associations. As we discussed in previous chapters, the estoppel is an approval from the governing entity that states what past-due balance needs to be paid. We have included an estoppel request sheet for you to see in Appendix Q. The estoppel is usually ordered by the buyer's title company, but more recently the seller's closing agent has begun to order estoppels themselves. As mentioned in Chapter 4, the best practice is for you to get the estoppel ordered as quickly as possible, preferably even before the property goes under contract.

Estoppels should be ordered within the first two days of the executed contract. To do this, provide the buyer's title company with detailed instructions on how to order the estoppel and follow up to make sure that the estoppel has been ordered and received.

Many times there will be more than one estoppel that needs to be ordered; as such, the buyer's title company may be reluctant to pay for this fee upfront. The estoppel fee is customarily paid for by the buyer and charged on the HUD-1 Settlement Statement at closing.

 **INSIDER TIP**

> Ask the company/attorney who prepares the estoppel to add the fee to the actual estoppel pay-off. Some will comply and others will require the fee to be paid up front.

If the estoppel fee needs to be paid up front and the buyer's title company is not willing to pay for it, then the buyer should pay the up front cost. Sometimes, the seller's title company has already ordered the estoppel, which ends up saving the buyer time and money. Make sure the buyer's title company always asks the seller's title company first to see if the estoppel has already been ordered.

It is becoming more common for condos and HOAs to not provide a certificate of approval until the past-due estoppel has been paid. If this is the case, inform your asset manager so they can help you by getting the seller's title company to make the payment. Otherwise, this will cause an unnecessary delay in closing.

Managing Loan Servicers

In some cases, the property that has been assigned to you is not necessarily assigned by the bank who will be the seller on the HUD-1 Settlement Statement. Many times, the mortgage servicer will be the actual party who initiated and completes the foreclosure. Then, the mortgage servicer will assign the property to another party who will be responsible for marketing and selling the foreclosed property.

This is because the mortgage servicer, the party who serviced the loan (collected payments from consumer, filed foreclosures, worked with borrowers to cure late payments, etc.), most likely packaged the mortgage into a pool and sold it to a major institution.

Even though the loan was sold, the mortgage servicer still has many responsibilities from the time the property gets foreclosed on to the time that REO is resold. These responsibilities include:

- Ensuring the subject property is secure and registered as vacant (if applicable).
- Ensuring that liens and code violations are brought into compliance and paid.
- Ensuring that any past-due condo association fees or HOA fees are paid.
- Ensuring that all back taxes, municipality utilities/liens, and other past-due payments on the property are paid for and brought into compliance to ensure a clean title.

Oftentimes, the past-due amounts are so substantial that the servicer will go to court for a "reduction hearing." However, it is most important that you communicate with the servicer at all times when it is discovered that past due payments will be required. Depending on your MLA, some banks require servicers to pay bills and expect you to manage the process.

In this situation, after you request the servicer to pay the past-due amounts, you should follow up and make sure you receive an updated statement reflecting these payments. If after two attempts you still can't get the servicer to make the payment, contact your asset manager and request that the seller make payments directly from the HUD-1 Settlement Statement.

By showing that you have tried twice to make the servicer pay, you are providing your asset manager with good reason to try and get the past-due amount approved to be paid from the HUD-1 Settlement Statement. Remember, your performance ratios are directly tied to this; the longer you wait for the servicer to make payment, the worse your performance measures are.

Therefore, always stay on top of your servicer. Make note of the date, time, and proof of emails to servicers with payment requests.

With these best practices, you can be assured that your closings will not be uncontrollably delayed.

 **INSIDER TIP**

> The best way of staying on top of servicers is obtaining a servicers list with emails, names, and phones numbers for main contacts. Not many people have it. Register online with reoboom.com to download your free copy.

Step Five: Notify All Parties that Inspection Period Is Over

Most contracts will have an inspection period that gives the buyer the right to terminate the contract if their inspection reveals unwelcome results. During this inspection period (usually ten days), which is done at the buyer's sole expense, the buyer can get out of a contract without losing their EMD. The only other contingency period that allows the buyer to walk away from the deal without losing their EMD is the financing contingency period.

After the inspection period is over, inform all parties that the inspection period has ended and that if for any reason the deal does not close (due to no fault of the seller), the seller has the right to retain the buyer's EMD.

Why? Oftentimes when buyers are in a contract they end up noticing another property that just came on the market for a lower price than what they are currently under contract for. To minimize the chance of a buyer changing their mind, let them know right away that it is not an option. Your performance is rated by the amount closings you have, and if deals fall through then your rating goes down.

Step Six: Follow Up with Lender/Processor

Lenders have various contingencies that they have to clear in order for them to get a final loan approval or "clear to close." For example:

1. Verifying borrower's income
2. Verifying borrower's employment
3. Verifying borrower's legal residency

4. Verifying borrower's signed disclosures
5. Verifying borrower's tax transcripts
6. Receiving borrower's pay stubs
7. Receiving borrower's last two year tax returns
8. Receiving a copy of the hazard insurance policy
9. Reviewing the preliminary title commitment
10. Making sure seller on contract is legal title holder of record.
11. Receiving answers to any discrepancies in borrower's credit report
12. Preliminary HUD-1 having correct figures for loan amounts, commissions, earnest money deposits, etc.

Sometimes, lenders do not have the sense of urgency that you are expecting. Other times, they are working with a difficult buyer who is on the borderline of approval. Either way, emailing and calling the lender or their processor is very important to ensure that you are meeting your timelines.

 **INSIDER TIP**

Try to get the lender's processor's contact information. After the lender takes the loan application, the file gets handed off to their processor. This is the key to closing a financing deal fast. Push the processor!

Email and call the lender once a week asking for the stage of financing. What conditions are left to be cleared? Has the appraisal been ordered? Is a final inspection required? Obtain the progress every week from the lender. Always follow up with a phone call and an email. Let them know to put your file above the priority line and ahead of others.

Setting expectations is very important. I email the various lenders I use a list of critical expectations before awarding them my business:

Dear XYZ lender,
Below is a list of my expectations from my mortgage partners. Please respond in writing that you agree and will comply with these expectations before commencing business.

1. All loan commitments delivered by email by deadline (as stated on executed contract).
2. Seven-day advance notice in writing via email if a delay is to occur prior to closing.
3. If we need an extension to close the file, provide reasoning with evidence (i.e., plead your case so we can present this to the bank).
4. All phone calls missed must be returned by end of the same business day. This includes anyone from our office, our customers, co-operating agents, or prospective buyers we refer.
5. If loan program is changed from original pre-approval letter (e.g., FHA to conventional loan) a seven-day advance notice must be emailed to us so we can prepare an addendum for the bank to sign off on.
6. Email is first choice of communication method. This way everything is kept in writing and we are time efficient.

Step Seven: Clearing Title

Even though you already contacted all parties regarding the estoppel and certificate of approval, it is now time to get confirmation that the past-due amount of the estoppel has been paid and that the buyers were indeed approved to purchase the property from the HOA or condo association. Without these two items, the deal cannot close.

Title conditions need to be cleared; often times there are partial releases that need to be obtained by the seller's title company. Even though this is not your department, do not become disinterested. Instead, make sure the buyer's title company is on top of following up with the seller's title company to clear the condition. Empower them. Let them know that sometimes the seller's title company can take a long time. Let them know that you are counting on them to be aggressive with the seller's title company. This is the only way to ensure that the title issues will be cleared.

Payment of outstanding violations is usually the responsibility of the listing agent for all expenses under a certain amount (e.g., $1,000).

Don't worry, you will get reimbursed by the bank; just take care of this early. You don't want to have to ask for approval from your asset manager the same day of closing. Ask the buyer's title company if there are any past due utility bills and/or violations that need to be paid. Get documentation and forward to your asset manager. Request reimbursement approval and make the payment. Don't forget to send proof of payment to the seller's title company so they can clear that condition.

If you show the seller's title company that you are working diligently to help them clear title impediments and provide an insurable title, they will keep the pace. If you are lax and don't respond to their request to make payment, they will be lax too. Get it taken care of right away. You will end up having to pay anyway, so get it approved early and make the payment.

Finally, make sure you empower the buyer, selling agent, and buyer's title company to follow up with the lender. The more pressure all parties put on the lender, the more likely it is that the lender will want to work on your file first. Sometimes it takes the persistence of entire parties for the lender to realize that they will have to spend more time responding to your follow up calls/email than it would take for them to just do the work.

Your goal is to hear the three magic words: "Clear to close." Then you can shout: "I GOT IT!" However, before that magical moment, you have to get past two more obstacles.

Step Eight: Get Preliminary HUD-1 Approved

Once the lender delivers the closing package to the buyer's title company, the buyer's title company will request the seller's fees so they can draft a preliminary HUD-1 Settlement Statement (see Appendix D). The HUD-1 Settlement Statement will usually need to be approved by the lender and the seller.

 **INSIDER TIP**

Do not submit any invoices for repairs, utilities, or property maintenance items to the title company, as they are not paid on the HUD-1.

Generally big ticket items ($1,000 or more) and recurring expenses are taken care of outside of closing. This includes repair bills, termite treatment, lawn care, roofing, utilities, HOA dues, etc. Either you as the listing agent have requested reimbursement from the bank and ordered your vendor to perform the work, which you will pay for at a later date (see Chapter 3), or the bank has coordinated with the servicer for payment (e.g., inflated tax and HOA liens).

During this time, depending on which bank you are working with, you want to have your rekey vendor send an invoice to the buyer's title company to change the locks. You will need one final lock change ordered; after a successful closing, the locksmith vendor will arrange a time with the customer to have a new set of locks created for their new home. Also send any commission instructions, changes, and incentives.

With all the fees, the buyer's title company will send the preliminary HUD-1 Settlement Statement to the seller's title company at least forty-eight hours prior to the closing date stated on the HUD-1 Settlement Statement. The seller's title company will often require the buyer's title company to make changes to the HUD-1 Settlement Statement. Because of these revisions, it is a good idea to ask seller's title company to review the HUD-1 Settlement Statement prior to the forty-eight hour window that banks typically require to approve all HUDs.

 **INSIDER TIP**

Most banks will allow for a twenty-four hour HUD-1 Settlement Statement approval during the last two days of any given month.

During the last two days of the month, the seller's title company will usually work extended hours to help meet the mutual goal of getting as many files as possible closed during that month. Asset managers are also available for you, as the listing agent, to request assistance with HUD-1 Settlement Statement approval.

Remember that asset managers earn bonuses on how many files they close per month. To make sure your asset manager is satisfied with your performance, push as many closings as you can in the month. Better yet, bring closings that are scheduled for the subsequent month back to the current month so they close early. Show your asset manager that you are allocating resources and are serious about closing early.

Ideally, your goal is to obtain a twenty-four hour HUD-1 Settlement Statement approval. If everyone in the process follows up and is persistent with the seller's title company, a twenty-four hour or even same-day closing will occur. Once a final HUD-1 Settlement Statement has been approved, the closing will be scheduled.

The Three Steps to Twenty-Four Hour HUD Approvals

1. Ask the buyer's title company to confirm that all changes have been made to the HUD-1 Settlement Statement and that there are no errors or omissions.
2. Call the seller's title company and ask them to request permission from the seller or bank to submit the HUD-1 Settlement Statement for same-day approval. Be brave. Ask for a same-day approval and you'll get a twenty-four hour approval (sometimes you may be lucky and get it approved the same day).
   a. Remind them that banks allow for twenty-four hour approval during the last two days of the month.
   b. Remind them that the buyer must close and will not be able to close at any other time.
   c. Tell the buyer, buyer's title company, lender (if applicable), and any other party to call the seller's title company and follow up with the status of the HUD-1 Settlement Statement approval.

3. Verify the HUD-1 approval by logging into your bank's platform. Usually, all comments and notes are posted for every file. Comments will say something like "HUD Approved for XYZ amount." Thank the seller's title company for assisting with closing on such short notice.

Don't forget the most important part: your commission. Make sure you turn to page two on the HUD-1 and verify that your commission is correct (see Appendix D). One oversight can cost you an extra percent or two, especially during end-of-quarter time periods when heavy incentives are rolled out to meet closing quotas.

Step Nine: Obtain Final HUD-1 Settlement Statement and Waiver (If Applicable)

Once the HUD-1 Settlement Statement is approved by the seller and lender, the buyer will bring their remaining cash as indicated on the HUD-1 to the buyer's title company. The buyer will then sign all closing documents to finalize their transaction, including a waiver (depending on the bank).

A waiver is sometimes used by banks as a blanket cover your assets (CYA) addendum telling the buyers that they are buying the home as-is. What they see is what they get and they cannot hold the bank responsible for anything that goes wrong in the home after the transaction materializes.

On the day of closing, be sure to do the following:

1. Request Executed HUD-1 Settlement Statement and waiver (if applicable).
   a. Tell the title company you will not release keys to the buyer unless you are provided with a signed copy.
2. Make sure you tell the buyer to transfer utilities to their name.
3. Thank all parties for a successful transaction and welcome the opportunity to do business again.
4. Email executed (signed by all parties) HUD-1 Settlement Statement and waiver to the asset manager and servicer (if any).

Finally, let your accounting clerk know that the property has closed, to turn off all utilities, and to submit all final bills for reimbursement.

 **INSIDER TIP**

Make sure you verify the buyer(s) signed every document at closing and ask if the file is ready to disburse. If one signature or initial is missing, your commission check will be delayed for a week or more.

Step Ten: Highlight Your Performance

So you did it, even better—you closed another one before the contracted closing date. You think you are the only one who's happy? Think again. Most asset managers get bonuses based on their closings, so when you close ahead of time, they get paid more. Asset managers like money, so if you make money, they like you—bottom line.

CLOSING EARLY = HAPPY ASSET MANAGERS = MORE PROPERTIES

After you send the final HUD-1 Settlement Statement and waiver to the asset manager to let them know the deal has closed, it is important to highlight the fact that you closed early. Do this by emailing your asset manager and posting comments in the general platform system. Always do both. You will want a pristine log in case you will be evaluated for additional territories.

Finally, show off. Let your asset manager know that you closed ahead of schedule and that you're proud of it; if the deal was financing, even better. Highlight it. Prove to them that they can count on you. Results speak for themselves, so let them speak for you.

Dear Asset Manager,
Please find final executed HUD and waiver attached for REO XXXXX, address: XXXXXX.
Summary:

Executed contract date	12/20/2012
Closing date	12/28/2012
Turnaround time	5 business days
Subject type	Condo
Financing type	N/A
# of extensions	No extensions needed
Contracted sales price	Above list price

POST-CLOSING PROCEDURES

After the file is officially closed, make sure you remove the lockbox from the property, change the status on your MLS from "pending" to "closed sale," and flag that closing until your commission check arrives. All sales proceeds are usually disbursed (to the seller, brokers, etc.) within twenty-four hours of settlement. If a delay prevents a file from being disbursed, you will not be receiving your commission early.

With the high volume of closings, I guarantee if you do not keep track of your accounts receivables, sooner or later one commission check will fall through the cracks. Some title companies will hold it in their escrow account, but if a claim is not made within twelve months, they will keep it. Be careful. Be prudent. Make sure you get your commission check within seventy-two hours of closing.

Finally, if the buyer was your own customer (i.e., an "in-house" customer) it's a good idea to get them a small closing gift. Something from Home Depot or Lowes is usually a good idea. Stay away from anything that is liquid. The last thing you want is a law suit because you gave a customer a bottle of Blue Label and they went to the hospital for alcohol poisoning.

 **INSIDER TIP**

After a successful closing, enter your customer's contact information on a database so you can send them holiday cards, newsletters, etc. By subtly communicating with them, the next time they want to sell, rent, or refinance their REO, you will be the first person they will call.

Delinquent HOA Dues

HOA groups have smartened up. They now think, "If banks can get bailed out, why can't we?"

Knowing that past-due payments must be made prior to the title being transferred from the bank to the new owner, they have enlisted attorneys to charge special assessments, legal fees, and many other miscellaneous charges. They have begun to realize that they have nothing to lose by posing large special assessments that banks must pay off prior to selling the foreclosed property to the new owner. Some states impose caps in the amount of past-due payments an HOA or condo association can collect.

 **INSIDER TIP**

Just because a state regulates the amount of past-due payments that can be collected doesn't mean that HOAs won't try to collect as much as they can. In fact, some HOAs will wait for the seller's title company to send an official "dispute" letter before they even think of revising any estoppel amount to conform to state statues.

If the HOA does not have a "reserve study," which is a thirty-year plan for anticipated major repairs, then most likely special assessments will be levied. Make all parties clear on this from the beginning; there is nothing worse than putting time, energy, and effort into a deal that would have never happened had all parties had complete information from the very beginning.

This negotiation between the HOAs and the banks ultimately causes a delay in closing. Banks will not pay outlandish past-due fees. Buyers will not assume any fees, as they want free and clear title to the property. What's more, some associations are placing future assessments (assessments that are paid in advance for future years) and will not provide a certificate of approval until those assessments are paid.

To ensure that the past-due payments are made in time for closing, it is crucial that when requesting the estoppel, you inform the association that the property you are requesting an estoppel for is a foreclosure. Also specify any and all state statutes that limit the amount of past-due payments the association can collect. Otherwise, they will attempt to collect as much as they can without placing any type of cap.

Some associations will be nearly impossible to work with. In cases where you can't find these associations, inform the seller. Do not let the seller expect to close if you know there is an issue with the association. It is necessary to ask the association the following questions.

The Five Must-Ask HOA Questions

1. Are there any special future assessments that must be made prior to closing? (This can change everything and be a deal disaster—look out for it!)
2. Will the certificate of approval for the buyer be contingent upon payment of past-due estoppels? (If this is the case, then maybe payments have to be made before the HOA will approve the buyer.)
3. Is it acceptable to make the past-due estoppel payments directly at closing as a charged line item on the HUD-1 Settlement Statement? (Many banks will pay from the buyer's proceeds at closing.)
4. What are the rental restrictions and/or restrictions for investors purchasing the property? (Make sure if investors are under contract, they know what the restrictions are and have accepted the restrictions.)
5. Is there a master insurance policy, and when does it expire? (Important for financing—no insurance, no financing—i.e., cash only.)

With the above questions answered, you will know exactly where to guide the seller. If there are future special assessments that must be made, inform the seller—most likely they will be willing to pay a portion of the special assessment, but it is doubtful that they will pay the entire amount. However, you don't want to inform the seller on the day of closing, as typically this will cause a large delay.

Some banks will require the servicer of the loan to make the past-due payments, as these payments were due prior to the foreclosure sale date. In this case, it is important to follow up with seller's title company to ensure that such payments have been requested from the servicer, and further, that such payments were actually made. Otherwise, there will be a request for payment to be made on the HUD-1 Settlement Statement, which in most cases will not be approved unless multiple attempts have been made to have the servicer pay.

CODE COMPLIANCE MANAGEMENT

Most REOs are sold as-is. Sometimes, bank-owned properties will even have the purchaser assume responsibility of evicting the former owner or tenant from the property. However, just as HOA and condo associations try to milk every penny from the banks, so do counties and cities.

Many counties are imposing violations on these abandoned and foreclosed homes simply because they know the violations must be paid prior to the bank selling the home to the purchaser. The amount of violations sometimes accrue at over $250 per day, thereby resulting in the bank's attorney having to "file motions" in court for a "court-reduction hearing" so the amount of the violation can be reduced to an agreed-upon amount. I have seen violations on properties amount to $70,000 when the property is only worth $35,000.

There are only three ways around the violations:

1. Complete the repairs and schedule an inspection. Then the seller's attorney will schedule a reduction hearing so the amount of violation will be reduced and paid. This process can take anywhere between two to six months.

2. Have the buyer sign a HHA (Hold Harmless Agreement) whereby the buyer will hold the seller harmless for the past-due violation and the buyer will assume responsibility of correcting and paying said violation(s). This will most likely have to be negotiated by offering the buyer an additional seller contribution or a purchase price reduction.

3. Obtain an invoice for the amount and forward it to the servicer (if any) for payment. Many times, if the amount is substantial, the servicer takes care of the payment or negotiations.

WHEN YOUR LISTING GOES TO AUCTION

In rare occasions, many REOs that do not end up selling through an REO listing agent will end up at an auction. Many auctions have no cost to the seller as they require the buyer to pay the premium (usually 3 to 5 percent of the purchase price) if their bid is accepted. In addition, these auction companies sell properties subject to the bank's final decision (i.e., even if a bidder wins the highest bid, the bank can still say no and reject the winning bid). This could happen for many reasons:

1. The bank has reduced the price every month for three months, and the property still will not sell. Rather than reducing it again, they open the market up and see what bidders are willing to pay.

2. The property has significant code violations and has not attracted any investors/buyers in your local area but may attract buyers from out-of-state or out-of-country.

3. The property is occupied by a tenant/owner, and the bank does not want to undertake the responsibility of evicting the occupant and so transfers that responsibility to the new buyer.

If you listed a property for the bank and it ended up at auction, then it is important that you take the following steps to ensure that you earn a portion of the commission you are entitled to.

1. Complete an updated broker's price opinion (BPO) for the asset manager, so they can review the winning bid compared to the most updated BPO to determine whether or not they will accept the bid.
2. Keep utilities on.
3. Conduct open houses. (Some auction companies conduct the open houses themselves.)
4. Upload all information pertaining to the property to the auction website, including HOA information, condo documents, certificates, violations, etc.

SUBMITTING REIMBURSEMENTS

You can have the best REO offense by closing on time. However, if you neglect reimbursements, your defense, you will lose money and a lot of it. I have personally seen real estate agents' entire profits eaten away because they neglected the reimbursement process. When managing the six steps of the REO cycle, you tend to put the paperwork (reimbursements) last on your priority list because you value closings, offers, or BPOs more. Even though this may be true in the short-term, if you don't have your systems in place, you will be forced to shut down.

Most banks have a cut-off in which the listing agent can request a reimbursement for expenses that are reimbursable. The final cut-off for most banks is anywhere between ten and thirty days after the property closes. If you don't submit your bills by then, you will not get reimbursed. Yes, you will eat the costs.

As such, it is important to develop an accounting system that enables you to request reimbursement immediately after closing the property. In addition to the time cut-off, many banks have a minimum amount (usually $250) that needs to be accumulated before you can request a reimbursement (unless the property was sold, sent to auction, or reassigned to another listing agent).

As a listing agent, you want to keep track of your expenses and submit them for reimbursement as soon as possible. When submitting a reimbursement, always follow your bank's rules. Always include the REO ID, loan number, and property address on all documents pertaining to the reimbursement and adhere to the following rules:

1. Itemize each expense;
2. Attach copy of invoice; or
3. Attach proof of payment (check copy or credit card statement);
4. Do not include security deposits (they are not reimbursable since they are refunded to you from the utility company after property changes owners).

Some asset management companies, however, will charge you per reimbursement request, which may make it better for you to submit reimbursements all at once after closing—to minimize the transaction cost. You should value what's most important for you, quicker cash flow or less transaction costs, and then communicate this strategy with your accounting clerk (if using the REO Plus Model).

Make sure that your accounting clerk has a database with all the utility deposits made so that after the accounts are closed, you can keep track of and confirm that the checks have been refunded.

Finally, make sure that you have a system of checks-and-balances for accounting. Each week your accounting clerk should prepare a report of what items were reimbursed, requested, paid, and shorted for the week. The goal is to monitor all reimbursement requests so by the time the file closes, most, if not all, reimbursement requests have already been approved and paid. When the property does close, there should be two persons allocated to signing off on reimbursements for the property (see Appendix E).

The final steps to mastering the REO closing cycle are managing title companies and co-operating agents. You can do everything right, but if you neglect supervision of these two roles then you can miss a big closing deadline.

MANAGING TITLE COMPANIES

First and foremost, make sure the buyer has enlisted a separate company or attorney to insure title to expedite the closing. Unless there is an issue with the title insurance whereby a buyer's title company can't insure the title and only the seller's title can insure, then buyer should have their own representation.

Next, inform the buyer's title company that this will not be an ordinary closing. Let them know that the seller's title has over two desk-piled-high files of paperwork daily and that they should not expect anything near an ordinary closing. Set their expectations by stating the following will occur:

1. Numerous unreturned emails, phone calls, voicemails, requests
2. Excuses (i.e., file is still in "processing" and has not been assigned to a closer)
3. Runarounds (i.e., file has been transferred to X who can be reached at X)
4. Ignores (i.e., after you try to call, email, and otherwise contact, you write a complaint to the supervisor, which then leads to the closer ignoring all of your emails)
5. Mistakes (i.e., informing buyer's title company of last-minute requests/fulfillments that need to be made before the file can close)

Then, explain to the buyer's title company that it is in their best interest to call the seller's title company relentlessly until the seller's title company realizes that it takes more of their time to respond to the phones calls, emails, and messages than it does to actually do their job.

Also explain to the buyer's title company that they should not expect the seller's title company to order anything. The buyer's title company should order all title work in advance of receiving the final executed contract. They should order the estoppel, title, and lien search, preferably in advance of getting the executed contract signed by both the bank and the buyer.

Inform the buyer's title company of the bank's requirement or time-line needed for them to approve the HUD-1 Settlement Statement. From that date, work backwards to ensure that there is enough time needed to meet the closing date.

THE BUYER'S TITLE COMPANY SHOULD ORDER ALL TITLE WORK IN ADVANCE OF RECEIVING THE EXECUTED CONRACT

MANAGING SELLING AGENTS

Selling agents or co-operating agents will not do much for you in clos-ing. Do not expect anything more than receiving an email from them stating where to mail their commission check. Why? Because they know that you as the listing agent for the bank will have to close on time; otherwise you will have to explain why you couldn't to your asset manager. Because the selling agent knows that you are required by the bank to close, they will leave it up to you to handle the process. Once they send you the contract signed by the buyers, do not expect any-thing else from them at all.

Once in a while, you will encounter selling agents who are proactive and results-oriented. Take the opportunity to convince them that you need their help to push the title companies to close on time. Let them know that if you are the only one following up, the closing will not occur on time and hence no one will get paid.

If you let them know that all they have to do is follow up once in a while with the buyer's title company, they most likely will not have an issue putting forth the extra effort. But remember to remind them through Double Ds, phone calls, and text messages.

Empower the selling agent to tell the same to the buyer. Have them tell their buyers to call the title company and follow up. Ultimately, the more pressure everyone puts on the title company, the more likely they will be to put your file at the top of their priority list and close on time.

Ultimately, there are going to be two types of REO listings agents. The first type is the type who is not going to close on time and as an excuse, will blame another party. The second type will find a way to make it happen and close ahead of schedule, to then show off their performance. Asset managers love listing agents who can close—that's the bottom line.

If you are going to let an asset manager know that you can't close on time, it should be the last thing that comes to your mind after you exhaust every other possible solution to close the deal. Asset managers allocate new properties based on how many deals you have closed. It's plain and simple: the more you close, the more you get. They reward you based on performance.

Remember, there is no "E" for effort in the REO business. You have two options: you close on time and receive more properties, or you don't close and make more excuses. At the end of the day, closings are going to fuel your business, keep your asset managers happy, and keep your pipeline of properties flowing in. So, remember: Always Be Closing!

 SHARE YOUR STORY

Do you have a success story you would like to share about closing your REO transaction? Any difficult hurdles you faced when dealing with title companies, loan companies, selling agents? How about using Double Ds and getting results? Please log on and submit it for your chance to be featured in the next revised edition of *REO Boom*:

www.reoboom.com/story

POINTS TO REMEMBER

- Use a buyer's title company and empower them to follow up with seller's title company.
- Manage selling agents by asking for their help to push the title companies to close on time; otherwise they may lose out on a big commission.
- Close all utilities and submit all final reimbursements in fifteen days. Submitting after thirty days = no reimbursement!

- Send final HUD-1 Settlement Statement in time for seller's approval.
- Do not let lenders take their time. Make them put your file on the top of their priority list by pressing their processors.
- Get past-due HOA fees within state statutes, and confirm that the seller agrees to pay well in advance of closing date.
- Stay on top of loan servicers, as they are usually responsible for paying for large outstanding bills.
- Double Ds. Anytime you receive an email with a date mentioned, reply with a delayed delivery using that date to follow up.
- Follow up. Email, call, confirm. Always call to let parties know you emailed them, and then email them back to confirm that they have received your email.
- Closing early = happy asset managers = more properties. Follow the ten steps to closing within thirty days.
- Follow the two REO rules of closing: Set the closing date out as far as you can (thirty to forty-five days) and close early (fifteen to thirty days).
- Always Be Closing. There is no "E" for effort; there is only "R" for results.

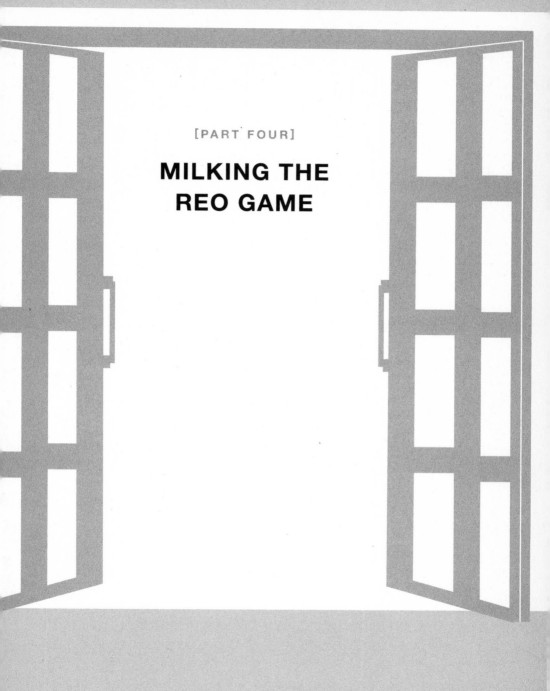

[PART FOUR]

MILKING THE REO GAME

Double/Triple/Quadruple Dipping!

THE SIX HIDDEN INCOME STREAMS

So you learned how to land the million-dollar REO contract and mastered the six steps in the REO cycle. Now we want to tell you how the seasoned agents make it happen. This is the icing on the cake.

There are seven different streams of income in the REO business. You know the first one. We will now uncover the hidden six.

1. Listing commission
2. Selling commission
3. Financing
4. Buyer processing fees
5. Home warranty
6. Flipping
7. Property preservation

When you first start in the business, you will primarily focus on satisfying the seller. You will only care about making sure everything goes perfectly as planned and you will be content with only making the listing side of the commission. It's natural to feel overwhelmed at first. However, after a couple of months (six to twelve months) you will start seeing hidden opportunities to make additional cash. This chapter is going to shave at least six months off the learning curve for you!

Hidden Stream #1: Selling Commission

If the bread is the listing commissions, then the butter is the selling commissions. It's the flavor, the 93 octane, the premium gas. In Chapter 2, we discussed how with little to no marketing effort you will, on average, achieve a 35 percent in-house buyer's ratio. To refresh your memory, this is when you have your own buyer as opposed to a cooperating agent bringing a customer for your listing. To increase this 35 percent ratio to let's say 50 percent, you need to direct your focus and energy on becoming the selling agent.

Remember, the selling agent is whoever sells the property and brings a buyer. Therefore, start showing properties. Show the potential buyer the property they called you about and other REOs that you have in inventory. If you are set up on the REO Plus Model, then you should be the one focusing on selling to maximize both sides of the commission.

Alternatively, instead of only showing your properties, you can cross-sell other REO listing agent's properties. If you can't beat them, join them. Here is how it works. Every buyer who calls in for one of your properties is a potential customer. If they call you for a home that you may have under contract, then your job is to invite them to your office and find them something else in the area on another listing agent's REO. In essence, you now become the selling agent for another listed REO.

Remember, customers want to work directly with listing agents (you) for two reasons. First, they assume that by working with a listing agent, they are more likely to get their offer accepted, and second, they know that listing agents have experience from the inside so they will be better able to advise them. They are already sold on you.

Instead of saying, "Sorry, there is a contract already on the property you called about but if it falls through I'll let you know," jot down their contact information and sell them another listing agent's REO. Stop throwing away leads; keep a log of customers who call in and cross-sell them.

There are many REOs on the market. Being that you know exactly what to do to get the customer's offer completed in its entirety in a prompt manner, the chances of you getting your customer's offer accepted are very large. In fact, many agents still don't know how to fill out an offer properly, nor do they understand why their offers never get accepted. Remember, you are the listing agent. You are in control. You have the power. Turn those callers into customers. Always be closing.

The Three Lead Buckets: Hot, Warm, and Cold

Unfortunately, out of everyone who calls in, not all of the leads will be ready, willing, and able to actually buy. Therefore, you need to identify the ones who are and act upon them immediately. What I tell my REO agents that I coach is to put leads into three buckets. The first bucket or physical file folder should be labeled "HOT." The next bucket should be labeled "WARM," and the final should be labeled "COLD."

Each lead who calls in should be placed in the respective folders. Some leads may be on the borderline and that is OK, as these folders are not mutually exclusive. The key to increasing your selling side commission (SC) is identifying who the "HOT" leads are and focusing in on them.

Hot Leads

Hot Leads (Ready/Willing/Able)

1. Been on the market for more than four months.
2. Seen over twenty listings.
3. Made at least five offers, all of which have been rejected.
4. Need (not want) to purchase by a certain date. E.g., they are relocating or they sold their current home and must find something.
5. Has relatives or friends in a certain area who validate where they are looking to buy.
6. Does not have an attorney who can destroy the deal. Remember, bank contracts are as-is, so when an attorney looks at it they will find at least five things "wrong" with the contract.
7. Has proof of funds to purchase with all cash or to cover the down payment.
8. Has a bona-fide pre-approval letter reflecting credit-worthiness.

I would say other than them being able to buy (i.e., #7 or #8), the hot lead having been on the market for more than four months is critical. When buyers first get on the market, their expectations are through the roof. They think because they are financeable or have cash it's their way or the highway. However, after a couple of months, reality sinks in, especially after they see five or six dream homes slip away because they were too late in presenting an offer or did not want to offer full price for the REO. I have buyers call me and say, "I want this house and I will do whatever it takes. Please help me." This is a HOT lead!

Warm Leads

Warm leads may not possess all eight criteria of hot leads but are pretty close. They already are pre-approved and have shown you proof of funds for the down payment or the entire purchase price amount if paying cash. However, they are just beginning their house hunting search. They are relatively new to bank-owned properties and are still in the learning phase. They are price sensitive and are reluctant to offer full price for an REO.

What I advise my agents to do is work with these leads but give them homework. For example, ask them to email back exactly what they are looking for and most importantly, why. Remember Chapter 2 when we discussed the REO FARM Play? You always build motivation before talking about the money. I actually say things to discourage them from purchasing to gauge their motivation. For example, "Why this house and not the one next door that's cheaper?"

The more you say NO to them, the more they will say YES if they are motivated. It's kind of like dealing with children. If you say no, they want it even more. Many times, I have buyers tell me "Oh, I don't know we just started looking." This is music to my ears. The best thing a home buyer can tell you is what bucket they are in—hot, warm, or cold.

Warm Leads

1. Has proof of funds to purchase with all cash or to cover the down payment.
2. Has a bona-fide pre-approval letter reflecting credit-worthiness.

3. They "want" to buy versus "need" to buy.
4. They provide you with a long window of time to purchase (six months or greater).
5. They are price sensitive.

Cold Leads

Cold leads are the ones who just saw a sign while driving, and maybe the wife or the husband told the other, "Hey, call that home and let's see how much it's going for." They had an idea pop into their minds about purchasing and started the curiosity stage. They may still be renting or living with family. They usually have not even begun online research (realtor.com, etc.). They most likely don't have a pre-approval letter or proof of funds. Some buyers who call me have good reasons, such as "I'm getting married and need to start planning for a house." Their time frames may be much longer into the future (one year or longer).

So do you turn them down? No. Everyone buys eventually, just like every REO sells. It's a matter of massaging them into becoming a home buyer. You need to become their trusted advisor. Help them by referring them first to a good mortgage lender who can let you know if they qualify for a home loan or not. If they don't, you want to make sure the lender can put them into a game plan to eventually purchase. Everyone should own their home. It's a great feeling. It's the American way.

Cold Leads
1. Just started the curiosity phase.
2. Has a time frame of about a year or greater to purchase.
3. Has not been pre-approved for a loan yet.
4. Looking for a guide/coach to hold their hands.

Whether the leads you get are hot, warm, or cold, you must follow up with them consistently. Put them on an email list and send them weekly newsletters, personal emails, and up-to-date property information. If a lead wants something in a specific neighborhood, make sure you tell them that as soon as a home becomes active and available, they will be the first to know.

One thing that I advise my REO agents to do is set up an exclusive weekly property list. Since they will have two hundred to three hundred properties in inventory but only 10 percent actually "active" with a list price (Chapter 3), the buyers can know what's coming on the market ahead of time. They can start their due diligence by checking out a home is an area they could see themselves living in. One last thing—make sure you answer every phone call and handle every lead as if they were a hot lead. Everyone eventually buys. It's just a matter of when. It's better you close the lead and find them a home than someone else.

 **INSIDER TIP**

By taking advantage of streams #2, #3, and #4, you can make an extra $100,000 a year.

Hidden Stream #2: Financing

Once you are comfortable in the business and you have your dream team ready to go, you need to think about automation and standardization. Remember, we discussed how the REO Plus Model is like an assembly line. The belt is constantly moving into a rainbow with a pot of gold at the end of it. However, if there is nothing on the belt, then your pot will be empty.

So, the first thing you need to do is get your mortgage loan originator license to receive referrals. It's an incredible return for your investment of time. Take a course, pass the state test, and you will have a license to make money and the skills to sell to your customers.

How many times have you relied on a mortgage professional only to watch your deal fall apart? Well, imagine now quickly explaining to your customer the difference between an FHA, VA, or conventional loan with minimum down payments and what seller contributions can apply.

One of the fastest ways to boost your in-house buyer ratio to exceed 35 percent is to know your mortgage products. You can quickly qualify someone on the phone and know exactly which financing to place them in. Either you can originate the mortgage loan yourself (take the loan application, negotiate, etc.) or you can outsource the lead to a mortgage specialist and receive a referral fee.

Once you receive a buyer lead, assign it to a mortgage specialist, and sit back and let them go to work. Make sure your mortgage specialist is well versed in the business so you don't get taken for a ride. Remember, you will not be doing the mortgage applications, gathering, documents, etc., for the borrower. You just need the knowledge and the license to legally get a referral fee (if your state allows it).

If you don't have the time or energy for it, I understand. Handling REOs for banks is very demanding. Your second alternative is to bring someone on to your team who has a mortgage loan originator license. Ask your broker. Maybe someone in your office is recommended that is trustworthy. Once you're legally allowed to make commission, you want that person to focus on pre-qualifying all of your leads.

Since you are holding all of the cards by being a direct REO agent, you control the work flow. Therefore, a common and customary split is fifty-fifty. Any mortgage professional who is ambitious and diligent will be more than glad to make this arrangement because they will know the value of leads. By offering 50 percent of their pay, they are treating that as an advertising expense for a "warm lead." It's a true win-win and easily done. Just make sure you choose someone who has years of experience and is not a fly-by-night affair. This commission split applies to a non-affiliated mortgage partner or someone you bring on your team with a license.

🏠 INSIDER TIP

When interviewing your mortgage partner, ask them what they would do if they got a lead that had a credit score of 600 or less. If they say they cannot work with them, move on to the next mortgage partner. You want someone who has the ability to place any lead into a home. Maybe not now, but if they can create a custom work-out plan to follow, eventually that lead will bear fruit.

Once you find your mortgage partner, your job is to have them qualify every single inquiry. Every lead is money. Instruct them to never reject a lead. Have them put the customer on a game plan and help them with their credit. Guide them, and within six months you might have turned a definite no into a yes.

In the REO game, the amount of cash closings and financing closings are pretty even. Sometimes one can outweigh another by 60 percent/40 percent, but usually you're dead even. From the financed transactions, expect about 30 percent to successfully close per direct bank contract.

PER BANK CONTRACT
50% CASH CLOSINGS
50% FINANCING CLOSINGS
30% WITH YOUR MORTGAGE SPECIALIST
50% REFERRAL FEE

So if you are closing thirty transactions a month per direct bank contract, fifteen will be with financing and four or five of the fifteen (30 percent) should be generating you referral fees. How much is the fee? Usually you can expect about 1 percent of the loan amount. Using the national median home price of $158,800 and assuming a buyer puts 10 percent down, the potential referral fee commission is:

$158,800 × 90% = $142,920 × 1% = $ 1,429
$1,429.00 × 4 closings/mo. × 12mo.
$68,592.00 in Mortgage Referral Fees!

This is just for one direct bank contract. Multiply this by three to five and now you are talking about some serious cash. Even if you only do half of that, it's still a nice chunk of change and a great return on your mortgage loan originator license. Remember, if you want to make even more money, you can always originate the loans yourself, and instead of receiving only 50 percent of the referral fee, you can keep all of it. Don't forget to get licensed and check with your state's laws on whether referral fees are legal or not.

Hidden Stream #3: Buyer Bonus Fees

Many times when you sign your Master Listing Agreement, your contract will have a provision that will prevent you as an REO listing agent from charging your customer a buyer processing fee. It will say something like this: "Under no circumstances shall XYZ Company/Agent/Broker be entitled to any compensation which exceeds the net commission due . . . Seller shall not be obligated for any additional commissions arising out of co-broker or multiple listing agreements."

In short, all they will pay you is the standard listing commission of 2.5 percent or 3 percent. If you put a standard "processing fee, storage fee, transaction fee, etc." like many real estate companies do on the HUD-1 Settlement Statement, the seller will not approve the HUD and will request you to remove the clause.

Therefore, the trick is to have your buyer sign a special clause in your local state or promulgated as-is contract stating they will pay a standard processing fee or "additional commission fee" out of their own pocket to your brokerage company. With this clause, the title company will put the processing fee of $295, $395, $495, etc., on the buyer's side of the HUD-1.

The clause should read something like: **"A standard additional commission fee of $295.00 shall be applied at closing paid for by buyer."**

Every time you have a buyer, you need to make sure you have them agree to the additional commission fee. However, first make sure this is not in violation of the Real Estate Settlement Procedures Act Section (RESPA), or local or state laws.

 **INSIDER TIP**

Make sure you label your processing fee as "commission" instead of "processing" because of a recent judge ruling in the U.S. District Court, Northern District of Alabama, Southern Division (Vicky Busby v. RealtySouth). Also disclose it on the buyer/broker agreement, GFE, and buyer proceeds costs on the HUD-1. Finally, have the title company disclose it on the same line item as the commission on the HUD-1. For example: real estate commission X % and $395.

Here are some fun and realistic numbers to expect within your first twelve to twenty-four months of hidden buyer's processing fees per direct bank contract:

250 closings × 35% (where you represent your own buyer) × $395.00 = **$34,562 in Buyer Bonus Fees!**

Hidden Stream #4: Home Warranties

Next is the home warranty plan; every new closing should have a home warranty plan. A standard referral fee is around $75, depending on which company you are working with. Make sure you invest in obtaining your state home warranty license so you can receive referral fees.

Usually, this is run through your state's department of financial services and allows you to legally receive commissions from companies that provide plans to new home buyers. After you obtain your license, you will want to sign the marketing service agreement with each new home warranty company so you can offer your customers some variety. Per direct bank contract, you can make an additional $6,562 in buyer home warranty fees:

250 closings × 35% (where you represent your own buyer) × $75 = **$6,562 in Home Warranty Fees!**

Hidden Stream 5: Flipping Your Own Listings

Real Estate Arbitrage

The best thing about being an REO agent is that you get to be involved in the transaction from the initial foreclosure of the original borrower, back to the bank, then to the end buyer. Once you get a good handle of the business (within six months) you will know immediately which deals are bad, which deals are good, and which deals are a steal.

One of the big ways you can make money as an REO agent is by purchasing your own listings. Of course, check your contracts and make sure it is not a conflict of interest with your suppliers. If all signs are a go, a good goal to have is to purchase and resell (i.e., flip) twelve homes in your first year as an REO agent.

If you recall from the REO cycle, after a listing comes into your inventory, your job is to market it and sell it for your bank within ninety days. After ninety days, the listing becomes old or "aged" and that's when the bank usually sends it to a big auction house company to sell.

Banks have funny ways of accepting offers. Assume you had a listed property and your list price came in at $125,000. You can present an offer to the bank at $105,000 and the bank will most likely reject it. However, 120 days from now you find the same exact property sold for $85,000 at auction. Why? It's an internal bank guideline. They cannot sell a property for a certain percentage within a certain timeframe, otherwise all the bank asset managers would use a slash and burn mentality just to meet their bonuses.

 **INSIDER TIP**

Banks usually drop the list price 5 to 10 percent every thirty days if they see no movement.

This is excellent news for you. During your ninety-day listing period, you might even have received offers close to full asking price that were rejected by the bank. Usually the buyers who placed offers forget about the home when their offer is rejected and go shopping for another property.

As soon as the listing goes to auction, you have a golden opportunity to purchase the aged property, close on it, and turn around and sell it to any buyers who might have shown interest at a higher price from when you first listed it. For example:

- You listed a property on 6/1/12 at $100,000.
- You received five offers between $80,000 and $96,000, all of which were rejected by your asset manager.
- Property was assigned to an auction company on 9/15/12.
- You buy property at auction for $75,000 on 10/1/12.
- You contact all previous buyers who were interested but had their offers rejected.
- You relist on MLS for $90,000 on 10/15/12.
- You find a new buyer for $87,000 and close by 11/15/12.
- You make a $12,000 profit over 60 days (not including closing costs).

 **INSIDER TIP**

Buy your own listings at auctions after they are aged for a deeper discount.

You tested the demand, you know all the ins and outs of the property, now you just have to go to the auction and purchase it yourself. The best thing about it is that you as an REO listing agent still make money from the listing commission. Usually, they discount all commissions paid to real estate agents to roughly 1 to 2 percent from both the listing side and selling side, but it's still better than nothing. So you now have an opportunity to bid on a home, pick it up 20 to 30 percent cheaper than when you listed it, and still earn commission from both sides of the transaction.

Sometimes, auction companies will not pay you a selling commission if you represent yourself as a buyer. It's always a good idea to put your broker at your office, as the broker representing you or another agent, and compensate them with a referral fee of 20 to 30 percent. It's better than not receiving anything. Also, if you have any family members you will be partnering with and buying the home under, they usually will not pay you a commission. Be wary of this. Auction companies look at relatives and last names closely.

In auctions, some offer a minimum reserve, some allow you to see the highest bid current (like eBay), and some are anonymous. It all depends. The point is, you have an opportunity to participate in some real estate arbitrage by filling the void in the market. The six biggest auction houses where you will be purchasing your homes are:

www.auction.com
www.gohoming.com
www.altisourcehomes.com
www.lpsauctions.com
www.realtybid.com
www.hudsonandmarshall.com

Visit each one of them and check out the rules and regulations. Since you are already a listing agent for the bank, you will be facilitating the auction company to earn your discounted commission by doing some open houses or whatever else they require (e.g., upload documents, etc.) so you will already be familiar with the process.

STEALING PROPERTIES AT AUCTIONS

I went to a live auction once. It was hosted in a five-star hotel. If you have never attended one, I highly recommend doing so. Think of an auction in a movie or television show, and it is exactly like that. The room was packed with stadium-style seating. It was 7:30 A.M. open registration and the auction started around 8:15 A.M. Upon registering you need to bring your checkbook, proof of funds (i.e., a bank statement show-ing you have enough funds to purchase), and a cashier's check for the minimum amount the auction company requires (around $2,500).

If you don't have time to print out your statements or you didn't bring them with you, they have work stations in the back with internet connection to facilitate you. Their main goal is nothing more than to sell, sell, and sell. Their business model works like this:

BANKS/DISTRESSED SELLERS

(No charge to banks to list)

AUCTION COMPANIES

BUYERS

(Buyer pays 5% of PP)

Auction companies solicit different large institutions and offer them a completely free service. Their sales pitch is that they will bring a room full of buyers and sell the bank's homes. If the properties don't sell, the banks have nothing to lose. Auction companies make their money from the buyers (you and I). They charge around 5 percent of the winning bid or a minimum amount (e.g., $2,500), whichever is greater.

Therefore, if you win a home for $200,000 your total purchase price will be $210,000. Alternatively, if you are buying a condo and win a bid for $30,000 they will charge you $2,500, making your total purchase price $32,500.

At the auction I attended, the minimum fee was $2,500. After regis-tering, I received a property auction flyer list and an auction number; it looked like a bib number that you attach on your shirt when enter-ing a marathon race. You raise this number up when you are bidding against other buyers in the room.

As I walked in past the registration booths, there were two rooms. The first room was where everyone sat down to bid; it had water stations and cheap chinaware in the back. The second room was a pit filled with dozens of desks and chairs with different employees waiting for winning bidders to come in and sign their life away.

I scanned the room to find a good area to sit and noticed a couple of things. First, the cash buyers and investors who had been to an auction before sat in the front third of the room. They were confident. They knew what they wanted, they were eager, and they were ready to purchase and get out as soon as possible. In contrast, the first-time home buyers and novice purchasers mingled around the back of the first room. Also, in the first room there was a small section with actual desks for buyers to sit down to place laptops on and work from. These were for buyers who purchased multiple properties and thus got the privilege of using a special area.

As I got my seat (in the front, of course), the auction started. There were three or four gentlemen in black tuxedos in the front. They all had beards and some were eccentrically groomed, with a third of their beards white, done intentionally. Behind them on top of the podium were the auctioneers and staff. Everyone was good looking. Everyone was upbeat, and they created a real buyer frenzy atmosphere with motivational money quotes flickering in the background.

By 8:30 A.M. the auctioneer was off. I had never heard someone talk so fast in such little time before. It was as if he had a motor in his mouth. Each property was numbered from 1 to 100. He went through each property, all of which were projected on the big screen behind the podium. What was interesting was they would list the "previously assessed value" from when the property sold two or three years ago while displaying a starting bid. So a property number one would look something like this:

Auction House Features
- Property #1-XYZ, CA
- 3 bedrooms, 2 baths, 2,400 square feet
- Previously valued at $550,000
- Starting bid $35,000

They would pitch every property that went up for auction as if it was the best buy you could ever make, even if it looked like a tornado had hit it. These people were professionals. Some properties that I did research on went for 10 to 20 percent above the actual market value just because people got emotional in the room.

The bidding process was interesting as well. Depending on the purchase price of the home, the auctioneer would start the bidding either at the minimum amount (e.g., $25,000) or start it at $500. They also increased the bid increments randomly while people were bidding depending on the mood of the audience. Some would increase by $2,500 rapidly until the crowd quieted down, and then bid increment would drop. For example:

- Starting bid: $25,000
- Increment 1: $27,500
- Increment 2: $30,000
- Increment 3: $32,500
- Increment 4: $35,000
- Increment 5: $33,750

The reason they had so much control was that the banks had a hidden reserve that wouldn't be disclosed. Therefore, even if the highest bidder in the room won, they would mumble "subject to seller's confirmation" underneath their breath right before congratulating the winning buyer.

The bank then would have fifteen days to decide whether or not they would accept the winning bidder's offer or take the chance of putting it back on the market (with another REO agent or an outsourcing company) hoping for a buyer willing to pay what they wanted. Therefore, not only would you not win the home, you would spend two or three hours at the auction signing contracts and doing paperwork all for nothing.

 **INSIDER TIP**

You will know when the property hasn't met its reserve when the auctioneer stalls the bidding. He or she may repeat the highest bid (e.g., $33,750) five to ten times and mention how cheap the price per square foot is compared to the replacement costs, or throw out the word "new construction" even if the property was built five years ago. When they throw back-to-back adjectives during the bidding process, you know the property hasn't met the reserve.

Some properties at the auction were clearly marked "cash only." That doesn't mean you need all cash on the spot to purchase, but there was no financing contingency allowed. Because closings are set thirty days out, you would put a deposit and bring the rest to the closing table with the seller's designated title company. Other properties would be labeled "buyer assumes responsibility of occupancy," meaning the bank is most likely selling the property with a tenant inside.

This means you will be responsible for starting or completing the eviction process before you can gain access. Remember, the banks will insure clear title, but they may not guarantee the property is vacant. Because auctions are advertised a minimum of thirty days in advance, you have ample time to do some homework. One thing to check for with properties that may have tenants in them is the court docket. Go to your local clerk of court and see if a writ of possession has been executed or not. If it has, then it will be easy for you to enforce the eviction. If not, then it may take you longer.

Hot Auction Properties
- Cash only
- Buyer assumes responsibility of occupancy

The best deals in auctions are when they limit the buying pool. Just by requiring only cash customers, a third of your competition is gone. Then, when they make you evict the tenant (whether you have to or

not), another third is eliminated. Now you're left with a third to compete with. This is how you pick up steals at auctions.

 **INSIDER TIP**

> If you do win a property that may be occupied, instead of evicting the
> tenant, do what the banks do. Knock on the door and offer them money
> to leave voluntarily. Ask them—would you rather work with me or with a
> sheriff with a badge and a gun? Ninety percent of the time, they will be
> grateful you are helping them with moving expenses.

When my number came up on the auction flyer list, I was ready for
a bidding war. After the bidding process was over and I won my bid,
I was approached by the auction staff and quickly shuffled to the side
of the room. It was an assembly line. One person handed me a folder.
The next person walked me to a place to verify documents. The third
person walked me back to the back room ("the pit"), where I spent
about another thirty to forty-five minutes waiting to sign all the relevant documents. As I was waiting, I took a tally of what properties
sold for versus what they were previously assessed at.

AUCTION PROPERTIES SELL FOR APPROXIMATELY 50 PERCENT OF THEIR PREVIOUSLY ASSESSED VALUE

On average, I discovered, properties sold for approximately 50 percent of their previously assessed value. So if the auctioneer advertised a
property assessed at $550,000 the highest bidder was almost around the
$225,000, mark even if the starting bid was $500 or $25,000. Whatever
you do, make sure you do all of your homework and due diligence in
advance. Auctions are a buying frenzy atmosphere with a lot of emotions in the air. Write down the maximum you are willing to pay and
stick to it. Don't pay a penny more.

As I was wrapping up with the paperwork, one of the staff workers told me two interesting things. First, on average, they sell twenty-
five homes per hour—sometimes less if a winning bidder doesn't have

proof of funds, or cashier's check, or didn't know it was a cash only purchase, because then the property goes back to the auction, slowing down the process.

Second, he said you could participate in the live auction from home on your computer. I sure wished I had known that before going. But even if I had, I still would have attended the live auction. It was quite a show. I highly recommend it.

AUCTIONS VERSUS LISTINGS

Whether you choose to purchase at auction or just purchase your own REO listings is up to you. Sometimes, you may have so much demand for a house (e.g., thirty phone calls within an hour's period) that you buy the house for yourself. Of course, you have to disclose if it's an agent purchase and follow your bank's rules and regulations, but that is the benefit of being an REO listing agent. You are always one tick ahead.

Some other interesting things to point out: when purchasing through auction companies, their contracts are usually non-negotiable (take it or leave it) and force you to close with their own title companies. Also, forget about assigning properties (i.e., assigning your rights to your end buyer for a quick $5,000 flip), as their contracts always state the property is not assignable. Therefore, you will be forced to close on the first transaction, then put the property back on the market the following day and find an end buyer.

Also, because you will not be allowed to buy with your own title company, you most likely will not be able to do a "double close." This is where you buy a property and close with the seller (bank) at 10 A.M., and sell the same property and close with your end buyer at 12 P.M., minimizing closing costs and lag time.

One caveat when thinking about buying at auction is to make sure the seller (bank) will issue a clear title and, if the property is a condo, will pay the entire estoppel amount. The last thing you want is to find yourself with a killer deal and be stuck with a $10,000 back-due homeowner association bill that wasn't paid.

🏠 INSIDER TIP

> Before closing with the seller's title company, you will receive a title commitment. Give a copy of this to your own title company to make sure they have no issues clearing the title for you when you sell the property the next day.

THE THREE EXIT STRATEGIES

Depending on your purchasing goals, you will have various exit strategies. Basically, there are three:

1. Hold and Rent
2. Fix-to-Flip
3. Lease to Own

Option #1: Hold & Rent: Twelve Homes in Twelve Months

Your main goal is to purchase homes extremely cheap. What does that mean? The home you buy must be cash flow positive. This means after all taxes, association fees, insurance, mortgage, etc., your bank account is positive every month. With REOs you will have a variety of options. You can purchase a condo, a high-end home, a duplex, a loft, a townhome, etc. Regardless of what it is, you first need to check the rentals comparable in the area. Look for how long the properties take to rent (average rental days on the market) and what prices the properties rented at.

Next, you need to take the structure into consideration. If the home is old, that is OK. Stay away from wood-frame homes and any roof damage structures. A little cosmetic work is good (paint/carpets/clean, etc.), but anything major such as plumbing or roof work can be detrimental.

 **INSIDER TIP**

> Other than structure, location is key. Try to buy rental properties close to schools and churches. Your vacancy rates are usually lower and the homes are usually in better conditions due to the high demand.

Assuming your goal is to get the friendly tax advantages of owning real estate, building a nest egg for your family, and investing your money in good old-fashioned tangible concrete, then you can turn your twelve homes into a nice retirement safe haven.

In order to purchase one property a month, you will have to either have credit, or some cash. However, by this time you should have saved over $250,000 through your REO listing business, which allows you to leverage your savings.

Remember from Chapter 2 that each bank account, if managed correctly, will produce you $372,120 net. With three to five bank contracts, you have the ability to produce a million dollars net. However, to be conservative, let's stick with the figure of $250,000.

With the market how it is today, if you are buying investment homes, you will need at least a 20 percent down payment and you may be capped off at a certain amount of homes. For example:

$250,000 / 20% = $1,250,000 REO Purchasing Power
$1,250,000 / 12 Homes
$104,166 Max Price per Home

In this example, with your $1,250,000 purchasing power you can buy twelve REOs with a purchase price of no greater than $104,166. This doesn't assume closing costs and other closing fees, but you get the picture.

"I work in Phoenix, Arizona. With the market shot, I took the advantage of buying as many cash-flow properties as I could. I used the one-a-month strategy and accumulated twelve homes. My goal is

to keep each one rented until both of my kids go to college and hopefully double if not triple my money. I cannot believe how many deals are out there. Now is the opportunity to buy real estate. As long as the property cash flow is positive every month, you cannot go wrong."

—George Garcia
Phoenix, AZ
REO listing agent

Sometimes your lender may cut you off after you reach four or five properties. When that happens, you have to be creative and purchase under your spouse's name, your family's name, a living revocable trust, a land trust, etc.

Alternatively, you can use "hard-money," which usually has a higher interest rate than traditional financing and comes with more up-front fees (e.g., 14 percent interest rate and 4 to 5 percent of the purchase price in fees as "points" upfront at closing). Also, they will usually loan you no more than 60 percent of the home's value.

So if you are looking at a $100,000 home, the max they will loan you is $60,000. This means, for you to continue to maintain your goal of twelve homes a year, instead of purchasing twelve homes at $104,166 you would have to find twelve homes at $52,000 or less.

If you do decide to build wealth through real estate while you continue to cash in on your ATM REOs, one very favorable option is to qualify your homes for Public Housing Choice Voucher programs (e.g., Section 8) designed by the U.S. Department of Housing and Urban Development (HUD). This is a subsidized housing program that assists low-income families, the elderly, and the disabled afford decent, safe, and sanitary homes.

Vouchers are administered locally by public housing agencies (PHAs) that receive federal monies from HUD. Many times, an eligible family may qualify for almost all of the rent or close to it, which is directly deposited into your bank account through the local PHA. This is a great way to minimize vacancy and get your rent automatically every month all while promoting the affordable housing initiative.

 **INSIDER TIP**

> When implementing the hold and rent strategy, as soon as any property increases in value by 50 percent, sell it and get your money out. You make money when you buy, not when you sell. Therefore, the faster you can sell your property the better of a deal you got when you purchased.

Is this the bottom?

I get asked this question all the time. The truth is, I will never know if this year or the next couple of years will be the bottom. All I know are the hard facts. If a property with all expenses included costs you $600 a month and you can easily rent the property for $1100 without breaking a sweat, then it doesn't matter if it is the "bottom" or not.

A good rule of thumb to predict when a market is bottoming out is if hypothetically you were buying a home with 100 percent financing (remember those days?) and your principal, interest, taxes, insurance, and association fees (if any) are still less than the market rent.

Option #2: Fix-to-Flip

This is my favorite option. The easiest way to make extra income from REO listings is to follow the REO Fix-to-Flip Rule: Find an REO listing that has aged for more than ninety days, which requires it to be fixed up to meet basic FHA financeable standards, so you can flip it to a hungry first-time home buyer.

"One deal we worked on was a single family home in a good market area. It was a three bedroom, two bath, one car garage that was converted to an efficiency. We knew we couldn't get a first-time

home buyer approved for financing so we spent about $4,500 and converted the efficiency back into a garage. We had the FHA inspector go out and approve the work and immediately we sold the home. Our purchase price was $145,000. We purchased it with 50 percent down and got a hard-money lender to loan us $72,500 at 10 percent interest per year. We sold it for $175,000. After title closing costs (2 percent), co-operating agent commissions (2.5 percent), three months of hard-money interest fees ($1,812.50) and all rehab fees ($4,500), we made $15,812.50 net profit within four months."

—Jason and Kristy Davis
Fort Lauderdale, FL
REO listing agent

If you are buying a condominium or loft, make sure the actual building is FHA approved. Usually FHA approval requires a maximum amount of percentage of foreclosures allowed in the building (e.g., no more than 15 percent), otherwise the building will not qualify for FHA financing. The last thing you want to happen is to get stuck with a property and have 60 percent of your potential buyers eliminated because they rely on financing to purchase your unit.

 **INSIDER TIP**

Slow months of REO inventory are a great time to flip houses. There will be soft supply and strong demand from buyers. Because an REO takes up to ninety days to close, you have a three month gap to find a steal, fix it up, and flip it before you begin competing with new REOs that come on the market.

Option #3: The Lease-to-Own Program

Nationally, credit scores have never been worse. With unemployment rising, jobs being outsourced overseas, and an unstable economic environment, many consumers simply do not have the credit or the cash to buy their own home. However, what they do have is the desire. One great option that serves as a win-win solution for both you and your prospective tenant is a lease-to-own program.

Instead of collecting a first month's rent and security deposit as you would do in a standard hold and rent strategy, here you will be collecting an non-refundable "option deposit" that will apply toward the purchase price (which is set by you) only if they decide to buy. For example, you find a hungry tenant who has a strong will and desire to purchase a home within the next two years by working on his credit. From one of the twelve homes you own, you offer it on a two-year lease-to-own option:

$150,000 purchase price (option to buy; expires in two years)
$7,500 (5% non-refundable option payment)
$142,500 (balance owed to you within two years)

If the tenants exercise their option to purchase, then the $7,500 will be credited against the purchase price. If the tenants fail to buy or cannot buy, the $7,500 is non-refundable and is yours to keep. Of course, your goal is to sell the home so you can cash out, but you can also choose to extend the contract for another twelve months for an additional 5 percent non-refundable option payment if the tenant is unable to purchase.

This benefits the tenant by locking in a purchase price today for two years out. This also benefits you by having a stable, steady renter for two years who would be foolish to walk away from his 5 percent option deposit payment by not paying the rent. You also have your locked-in rental price upfront.

INSIDER TIP

When doing a lease-to-own option, do not accept a potential renter unless they are willing to give you at least 5 percent of the purchase price; otherwise they will walk away from their deposit. Because you are doing them a favor by locking in the price of the home for two to three years from now, they have plenty of time to work on building their credit to buy.

Hidden Stream #6: Property Preservation Goldmine

Property preservation is by far one of the most important aspects of marketing for REO properties. No asset manager wants to be a subject of discussion on why an inspection revealed an REO to be marketed poorly. Yes, there are mystery shoppers who go and inspect homes. Yes, these mystery shoppers grade your assets on various criteria including, but not limited to, cleanliness, safety, marketability, etc. Asset managers want homes to be sold for as much as the market bears. So why not add value with property preservation?

Ten Frequently Used Preservation Needs

1. Landscape package
2. Pressure cleaning of driveway
3. Carpet cleaning
4. Heating, ventilation, and air conditioning (HVAC) inspections
5. Securement of door frames and windows
6. All locks (front/back/gates) changed
7. Sliding doors secured
8. Initial pool cleaning (if applicable)
9. Periodic pool cleaning (if applicable)
10. Removal of damaged material

As you first start in the business, you will be approached by numerous vendors claiming to provide you with the best service and flexible payment terms. Many times companies will offer you an open line of credit. You pay them only after you get reimbursed from the bank.

Remember from Chapter 3 we discussed how to use other vendor's money (OVM) to finance your REO Bootstrap Model. As you scale your business and change structures to the REO Plus Model, you may want to think about starting your own property preservation company. This is assuming it's legal and doesn't violate your bank master listing agreement, as some do not allow you to use affiliated members to handle property preservation.

If other companies are willing to give you 120-day terms and excellent service, there is profit to be made. Why give it away? Other than the money, as a real estate entrepreneur in the REO business, control is key. Because the work is so time sensitive as well as detail sensitive, your name is on the line. Therefore, it is important you control the property preservation and make some money while doing it.

There are six vital steps to starting your own property preservation company:

Step One: Create a property preservation company, similar to industry giants such as Safeguard Properties, Cyprexx Services, or Field Assets.
- For $200 (see Appendix A), you can find someone to create a website for the company you just created, with content that shows you as a reputable property preservation company. It's well worth the upfront investment.
- Create a logo, virtual office, phone number, and email address.
- Open a business checking account.

Step Two: For each of the ten frequently used preservation needs (above), find a reliable low-budget sub-contractor who is in need of business and is results oriented (not effort oriented). Search Craigslist.com and negotiate rates with the promise of high-volume work. Set up a meeting, shake hands, and set your expectations: service within twenty-four hours, before and after pictures, and dependability.

Step Three: Set your margin requirements. Banks value the time you take to ensure the security and marketability of assets. As such, they usually set maximum reimbursement amounts for the services below.

 **INSIDER TIP**

You should require at least a 50 percent return on your investment for each of the ten items below. If you can't find a contractor to give you that margin, look further. They are out there, and they need business.

Preservation Type	Typical Maximum Reimb. Amt. (from bank)	Max Out of Pocket Expense	Profit Margin
Landscape package	$250	$100	40%
Pressure cleaning driveway	$250	$150	60%
Carpet cleaning	$200	$90	45%
HVAC inspections	$400	$250	63%
Securement of door frames/ windows	$500	$300	60%
All locks changed (per unit)	$150	$75	50%
Sliding doors secured	$150	$60	40%
Initial pool cleaning (if applicable)	$500	$300	60%
Periodic pool cleaning (if applicable)	$250	$80	32%
Removal of damaged material	$500	$220	44%
Average	$315	$162.50	49%

Step Four: Make bid proposals for all your properties. The bid should be on a professional document made from QuickBooks or similar accounting software. Be sure to include your logo, address, etc., as discussed in Step One. Email the bid to your brokerage company and submit the bid into the bank for approval.

Step Five: Obtain two bids to send to asset managers (one from an industry giant and second from your preservation company); the one you recommend should be the lowest cost. Your asset manager will want to improve the marketability of the home, so you should not have any hesitation making your request.

 **INSIDER TIP**

Some banks do not require a bid and have automatic approvals for certain items.

Step Six: Once your preservation expense is approved, get your sub-contractor to begin work and to send you before and after pictures. Once complete, update your records to indicate that the preservation/repair has been completed to satisfactory conditions. Finalize the payment by writing a check from your brokerage company to your property preservation company and another check from your property preservation company to your sub-contractor. Always keep clean records and books.

REO BROKERAGE CO. (WAITS FOR REIMBURSEMENT)	EASY PROPERTY PRESERVATION LLC (PAYS OUT IN 30 DAYS)	LOCAL SUB-CONTRACTOR (PAID IN 30 DAYS)

Never delay a payment to the local sub-contractor longer than thirty days, regardless of if you have received reimbursement from the bank or not. Remember, you are trading open credit terms for profit.

This should be repeated for every property and for every expense. Creating a system that performs these steps automatically will yield far more benefits than you probably would imagine.

There are two types of REO agents. The first is one who will lose out on an additional stream of income, lose out on making their asset manager look good by adding marketing improvements, and lose out on the opportunity to continue to get inventory by not maximizing the property preservation expenses above.

The second is one who will find a way to create value-added gains through each of the ten items mentioned! All it takes is some digging around to find cheap suppliers, and that's it! Of course, always make sure you are not in violation of your MLA, as banks or outsourcers may prohibit the listing agent from using a contractor that is affiliated with him/her for repairs or any other type of property preservation.

HOW ABOUT TITLE REFERRALS?

Don't even think about it. There are certain agents in the industry all
across the country who are forcing their buyers to use their "preferred
title company," and in return, title companies are giving cash referral
fees under the table.

If your brokerage company owns a title company and you give
proper affiliated business arrangement disclosures and do not violate
any laws, then by all means promote it. It's good to have a seasoned
title company that is experienced in the REO and foreclosure business.
However, don't even think about getting a referral fee or "kick back"
from anyone else. You might get away with it once or twice, but the
third one will catch up with you, and that is a serious RESPA offense.

 **INSIDER TIP**

> Did you know a title company makes approximately 70 percent com-
> mission off your customer's title policy plus 100 percent off the settle-
> ment or closing fees? If your customer is paying anything above $395
> for "settlement charges" as indicated on the HUD-1 (section 1100), they
> are paying too much.

 SHARE YOUR STORY

> Do you have a success story you would like to share about how you
> milked your REO ATM? Any auction deals, any fix-to-flip opportunities,
> or any hidden income goldmines you took advantage of? Please log
> on and submit it for your chance to be featured in the next edition of
> *REO Boom*:
>
> **www.reoboom.com/story**

POINTS TO REMEMBER

- Title referrals are not hidden income; just say NO!
- Six steps to property preservation: form an LLC, source cheap contractors and set expectations upfront, set your margin requirements for the ten frequently used preservation needs (minimum 50 percent), create a bid, submit two bids to the bank, order work, verify, and pay out in thirty days.
- Auction properties sell for 50 percent of their previously assessed value.
- Real estate arbitrage is buying cash properties at live auction or purchasing your own listing and utilizing the three exit strategies to profit from: hold-to-rent via housing vouchers, fix-to-flip to FHA buyers, or lease-to-own.
- Banks drop their list price 5 to 10 percent every thirty days if they see no movement; after ninety days, property becomes aged and moves to a live auction.
- Obtain a home warranty license to earn an additional $6,500 on warranty plan referrals.
- Buyer bonus fees can earn you an extra $34,000 per direct bank contract. Have the buyer sign a buyer bonus agreement and disclose it on the HUD-1.
- 50 percent of closings are finance buyers; 30 percent of those who close will be with your mortgage specialist, who will pay you 50 percent referral fees (up to $68,000 per direct bank contract).
- Hot leads are those who are willing, able, and ready to buy, which will increase your in-house buyer selling commission ratio up to 50 percent.
- Focusing on the first streams of income is for beginning REO agents. The pros build up and focus on the hidden six: selling commission, financing, buyer processing fees, home warranties, flipping, and property preservation.

Blueprint to a Million in Twenty-Four Months

"Entrepreneurs are simply those who understand that there is little difference between obstacle and opportunity and are able to turn both to their advantage."

—Niccolo Machiavelli

I'VE COACHED MANY real estate agents, and some of them do not want to grow their business. They are happy with what they have. They landed their first direct bank contract and they are content with the substantial income it is generating. I feel, however, that this is a temporary state of mind. The reason they do not want to take their business to the next level is fear. Fear of the unknown. They do not know how. They do not have a framework behind their motivation.

The REO business is new to many; agents have tried and failed by using old methods and tactics while others have succeeded by following a Plan-A blueprint. Anyone who is willing to follow a proven formula can overcome any challenge, capitalize off of every opportunity, and make a lot more than a million dollars. However, a right framework behind a strong desire is necessary in order to make it.

It will not happen overnight, but time is on your side. There are so many REOs on the streets but so few listing agents who are good at managing them. Have you ever dealt with an REO listing agent? Most of them do not know what they are doing, they don't care to change, and they think their way is the only way.

The industry is changing. Banks are opening their doors to new REO agents. There are so many rumors and speculations floating around in the business that its hard to keep track of them all. My favorite is the "REO mafia" stigma, where only a selected few are privileged to participate. This is farthest from the truth.

When I started I knew no one. I didn't have large amounts of capital, connections, or a big franchise name behind me for support. Most importantly, the demand wasn't close to what it is today for REOs. It was a long and tedious up-hill battle. The only thing I had was a burning passion and faith. After painful trial and error sessions, I figured out the formula: first to land a contract then to manage it effectively so I could get more contracts and more REOs. It was a simple step-by-step process.

There is such a large supply of REO properties that banks are desperate for talent. Banks are looking for you. They need an agent who has the ability to grow. They need seasoned agents. If they feel the need to load you up with properties, you need to be able to deliver an exceptional performance, just as if it was not your first REO assignment.

You've already learned how to land your first account and how to manage it effectively to create a pipeline of cash flow. If you have not landed your first direct account yet, don't worry; we have outlined a 90-day action plan for you in this chapter. Now, we want to share with you how to grow your business. This is the advanced REO section. Are you ready?

Some REO agents aren't up for the tasks. They don't have the time, framework, or desire to grow their business, so they only stick to the one or two accounts they have. If this is you, then you can stop reading here. On the other hand, other agents I coach have successfully grown their business to three, four, and five direct bank contracts and made millions. The best part about it was they did it just like everyone else.

They mastered the blueprint outlined here and hit the pavement running. They understood that there was very little difference between an obstacle and an opportunity, as they both require the same passion and diligence. So if this is you, let's get started now.

THE MILLION-DOLLAR REO BLUEPRINT

It takes approximately twenty-four months to make a million dollars in the REO business. The blueprint is simple. In Chapter 2, I discussed how each bank contract can yield you approximately $1,000,000 in gross commission income (GCI), or over $372,000 net. Therefore, to achieve a million dollars net, you would need to land three direct bank contracts.

MILLION-DOLLAR REO BLUEPRINT (3 DIRECT BANK CONTRACTS)
$3 MM GCI / $1,116,000 NET

Input Needed
- 9 new BPO assignments a week
- 90 active listings on MLS
- 300 total properties in inventory
- 35% in-house buyer ratio

Remember from Chapter 2 that working with a direct account is very different from working with an outsourcer. While an outsourcer account will assign you properties sporadically, a direct account will continue to feed you properties. I would say having one direct account is the equivalent of having approximately five outsourcer accounts. Don't get me wrong, both accounts are great. Just the consistency factor is different.

With a direct account, you will be fed properties until you demonstrate you cannot handle any more. Therefore, it's a consistent pipeline of money coming in. Remember, there are five key benefits of working with a direct account that help you produce $372,000 net: you work with the decision maker, you earn full commission, you earn guaranteed commission, you get high volume of inventory, and you employ leverage.

It's leverage that takes you from one direct account to three or more direct accounts. Once you master one, you have a proven track record to go after their competition. Usually what one major bank does, the rest follow. For example, if one bank offers you the ability to scan your checks into your phone without visiting a physical branch to make a deposit, the rest will eventually follow or they will lose customers.

Similarly, if you have what banks want (i.e., a system to maximize value and minimize disposition time for their REOs), then the other banks will want you and your team. In fact, once you perfect the REO Plus Model, you will have created an intangible asset. I say intangible because you're not selling physical inventory or goods. You're selling yourself, your team, your brand, your system, and your expertise. It's all about you.

The rest of the banks will want your intangible asset to ease their pain. Just as you learned about building motivation before talking about business (MOB) when going after your first account, banks are motivated to work with you to help stop the bleeding if you are proven.

BANKS WANT YOUR INTANGBLE ASSET
TO EASE THEIR PAIN

The great thing about working with a direct REO account is that it's performance based. If you close on time, you get a new assignment; you either produce consistently or the bank finds someone who can— bottom line. That's why it is so critical to master Chapters 4 through 9.

Because the REO business is performance based, meaning the better you perform the more inventory you will receive, all you need is three new BPO assignments a week from three different direct bank contracts (nine new assignments a week) to achieve a million dollars within twenty-four months.

9 NEW BPO ASSIGNMENTS A WEEK = $1MM NET IN 24 MONTHS

Of course all of this depends on how well you do at managing your REO business before branching off and going after more accounts. We say it takes twenty-four months because you need time to fine-tune your systems. If you get greedy and go after too many new accounts early while your team is not ready, you will fail.

You may get three direct bank accounts within ninety days, but

when they all start firing away new BPO assignments at you and
you're sitting in front of your dual monitors thinking "there is no way
I can do nine BPOs within twenty-four hours," then you will fall flat
on your face.

I have seen new REO agents receive up to 20 BPO assignments a
week and have watched them go out of business within three months
because they could not execute properly. They were late on all their
tasks, they wouldn't do weekly inspection checks, they wouldn't submit offers from selling agents, etc., which all led to the bank asset manager re-assigning the properties to another team that was proven. You
must be able to anticipate what asset managers want so you can save
them and yourself time. This comes from experience, and experience
takes time.

The first twelve months of your REO business should be focused
on getting your first direct bank account and perfecting the REO
Plus Model. The next twelve months should be spent investing your
cash and leveraging it. In Chapter 2, we discussed how you will make
$372,000 net from one direct REO account. This is a conservative
number estimated at a 35 percent net profit margin.

Net profit is your gross commission income (GCI), minus your
operating costs. Your operating costs are broken up into both variable
costs and fixed costs.

GROSS COMMISSION INCOME (GCI)
-VARIABLE COSTS (VC)
-FIXED COSTS (FC)
_____

NET PROFIT BEFORE TAXES (35% OR MORE)

After the first twelve months, you will have to invest in your business. You cannot be a jack of all trades. You must take a good portion
of the $372,000 and leverage it. In the beginning, you might have been
short on money but had a lot of time on your hands. Now that you
have your systems in place and some cash, you need to leverage that so
you can have a lot of time and tons of money.

Thus, in order to leverage your business from one direct bank contract to three or more direct bank contracts, you must leverage your cash and bring on two key players to your dream team:

- Business Development Role ("closers")
- Account Manager Role ("executioners")

The business development role is finding a key person who can do what you did in the beginning to get your first account, just full-time and non-stop. Their only job is to land bank contracts, going after all the direct bank contracts and as many outsourcers as they can. The more the better; they are your closers.

They need to be able to see your vision, have the same values as you, and take the ball and run with it. They will promote your statistics, maintain your positive track record, and do everything you learned in Chapter 2, fifty to sixty hours a week. This includes fine-tuning your polished proposal and résumé, applying to more accounts, handling phone interviews, networking, and meeting and greeting. Once they land another contract, they will pass the ball off to your account managers.

The account manager role will take the new bank contract that the business development person procured and execute it; they are your executioners. They will supervise the entire REO Plus Model, including your dream team, and make sure every single task from the REO cycle is done accurately, timely, and to the highest quality. They will work hand-in-hand with the business development person and work as a team.

You will motivate both of them with residual income. For every single new account they bring in, you will give them a quarter of one percent (0.25 percent) from the listing commission (LC) on every deal that closes. For example, assuming a conservative 2.5 percent listing commission on a $100,000 home, both the closer and executioner will get a quarter of one point:

$100,000 \times 0.0025 = \$250.00$ (to the closer)
$100,000 \times 0.0025 = \$250.00$ (to the executioner)

It may not seem like a lot, but it adds up in volume. With one direct account you will be closing around twenty deals a month. Imagine three direct accounts (sixty deals a month). Now, multiply $250 × 60 deals a month × 12 months. What do you get? You get a win-win-win situation for both the business development person and the account manager to make great money, and for you to put your business on autopilot.

$250 × 60 deals a month × 12 months = $180,000 residual to both the closer & the executioner.

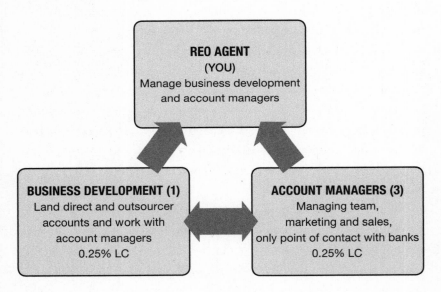

In addition, I would offer them both a base of no more than $2,000 a month to get them rolling until their residual income outweighs their base salary. Therefore, once they start making above $2,000 a month, their base is eliminated. This is usually removed after the first 90 to 120 days because the new contracts are kicking in and the REOs are cranking out cash. Remember, you have to invest in your business if you want it to grow.

Also, you need only one business development person but multiple account managers. I find it works best when you have one person dedicated to landing bank contracts, as different banks have headquarters in different areas. They will be flying around to various conferences and visiting asset managers' sites. Plus, it gives them exclusivity. Meanwhile, you will put each account manager in charge of each bank contract. They will be the bank's main point of contact after the business development person lands the account.

INSIDER TIP

Always set goals with timelines with your business development role. If you are offering exclusivity to them along with residual income, they need to be able to produce results; otherwise you will find someone else who can. A ninety-day trial period is customary.

The best part of the two new roles is that it creates a system of checks and balances for you. Because the closer can only get paid if the executioner manages every task of the REO cycle, they will work hand-in-hand. If the executioner is late on assignments, the closer will be on top of them because it affects their pay. It's one step closer to automation.

The account manager role will be put into place to supervise your REO Plus Model, so you can take a step back from working forty to fifty hours a week and put it all on autopilot. They will step in to your shoes and take over the day-to-day operations. They will be the main point of contact for the bank's asset manager. All the members of your dream team will report to them, and they will report to you. The structure would look something like this:

THE ACCOUNT MANAGER ROLE

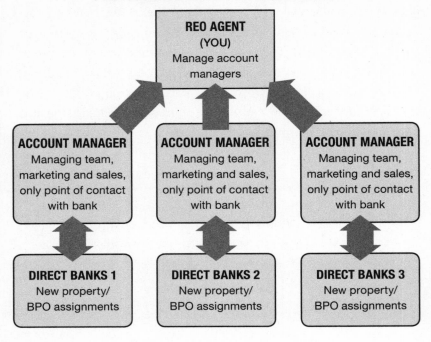

In addition, they will be responsible for selling and increasing your in-house buyer ratio. Remember, without much effort you will have a 35 percent in-house buyer ratio where you represent both sides of the transaction. I have many agents who share the selling side of their commission as well with their account managers as an incentive to them to get this ratio higher. It's all up to you. How hands off do you really want to be?

 **INSIDER TIP**

When bringing on both the business developer and account manager, keep the accounts payable role to yourself. Since they will be focusing on landing new accounts and executing, they may want to incur certain expenses that you may not agree with.

PUTTING IT ALL ON AUTOPILOT

The Million-Dollar REO Blueprint is more than just financial success. It's about being well-balanced so you can have free time. For instance, no matter how much money I make, if it means being stuck in an office sixty hours a week, I am not interested. I would rather spend time at home with my family. Therefore, once you master the REO Plus Model, your job is to put it on cruise control.

In Chapter 3, you learned about standardization. Well, now I want to teach you about automation. That is the reason why bringing on account managers and business developers is so important. They help you work "on" your business instead of "in" your business. They free up your time so you can take a birds-eye view of what's going on. Once you automate your business, you should be working twenty hours a week maximum.

BRING ON ACCOUNT MANAGERS SO YOU CAN FOCUS "ON" YOUR BUSINESS INSTEAD OF "IN" YOUR BUSINESS

Having this structure is critical to the longevity of your business. You want your business development person and account managers to be motivated to get more properties, which in turn will make them and you more money. They will help you achieve your targeted inputs so you can achieve your targeted outputs of $1,000,000 net a year.

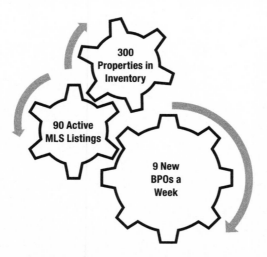

= $1,000,000 NET INCOME (OUTPUT)

While automating your sales-producing activities by bringing on a business development person and account managers, you also want to automate your operations functions with the use of technology so everyone in your dream team is on the same page.

Many large REO agents use software programs online to manage their REOs (see Appendix A), from offer submissions, expense tracking, BPO inputting, sending out automated emails to your team, and communicating with different bank platforms. Some are more expensive than others. Once you scale up to the REO Plus Model and start thinking about taking your business to the next level, you can look into the different software programs in the marketplace.

Technology will help your account managers by giving them resources to efficiently execute their day-to-day tasks and keep everyone organized. It will be the one tool that you can use to maximize the eight success measurement tools that are discussed later in this chapter.

LEVERAGING VIP LEADERS

Once you put your business on autopilot, you will be working less than twenty hours a week but giving away a lot of decision-making power to your team. Therefore, it is critical to find the right account managers, business development people, and members of your dream team. You do this by identifying leaders. Agents leave managers to join leaders. How many times have you encountered a manager in your career who competed with you or didn't listen to your needs? They micromanaged you or played foolish power games to let you know who was "boss". A critical success factor in achieving a million dollars net in the REO business is finding and leading people who are leaders; I call this leveraging leaders.

When you leverage leaders, you gain exponential growth. The REO business is people-driven. You are only good as your team. Would you rather have a team where you are the only leader and the rest are followers, or have a team where you are a leader managing five other leaders under you? Leaders attract other leaders. They usually have a large pool of influence with buyers, investors, and associates. Your goal when growing your team is to identify leaders and quickly offer them an opportunity.

You must also empower them to be successful with you. Provide them with the correct tools to build up a large network for your team. This includes giving them residual income and the proper technology so they can focus on what they do best. Some characteristics I use when identifying leaders is if they are a VIP leader:

1. Vision
2. Influence
3. Passion

A VIP leader has three characteristics: vision, influence, and passion. Do they possess visionary thinking? Are they forward thinking, or past and present thinkers? Do they have a large sphere of influence? They should have good character, act ethically, and know how to build relationships.

Most importantly, they must be trustworthy. You will be outsourcing your entire REO cycle to them when starting (REO Bootstrap Model) in the beginning, and at the end when you bring on your two key roles, so your name will be on the line. After the vicious learning curve period is over (three to six months) you will feel a sense of euphoria as you will have built enough trust with them to know that your work will be turned in on time and it will be done to your standards.

Finally, each person must absolutely love what they do. They must be passionate. No part-timers allowed. You need someone who loves the real estate business and is willing to work 24/7 at it. Passion creates dedication. Passion gives people the extra push to stay up late, work extra hours, make sacrifices, and strive to achieve great results and hit your team goals.

LEVERAGING VIP LEADERS = EXPONENTIAL GROWTH

MEASURING YOUR PERFORMANCE

There's an old management adage that says you cannot manage what you don't measure. You can have the perfect dream team, have five direct bank contracts, and have the REO Plus Model down to a science, but if you don't measure the results, you will not know if you are doing better or worse than before. Chances are if you stop getting your nine BPO assignments a week, you know you are doing something wrong. However, do you want to wait to get to that point?

I had many agents tell me that their asset manager just stopped giving them new assignments for no reason. This happens. Remember, asset managers are people with personalities. Some like to talk and some don't. Some are so time crunched they don't have time to take five minutes out of the day and tell you about your performance. It's up to you to be proactive and highlight your performance to them.

So how do you measure your performance? How do you know if you are doing a good job? Just because you are receiving more properties doesn't necessarily mean you are performing at your peak. Maybe there is just too much supply and you have the fortune of being at the right place and the right time. Maybe your supplier hasn't brought on more agents in your market to spread the REOs.

To fool-proof or validate your growing number of properties, you need to measure and continue to measure your performance by eight key performance indicators or measuring tools. As you recall from Chapter 1, the timeline per property is approximately ninety days:

New BPO → Listed → Offer Accepted → Closed Deal = 90 DAYS
(7–10 days) + (21 days) + (14 days) + (30–45 days)

Depending on your bank, properties are usually "coded" internally to reflect the current status during this timeline as follows:

- *Value*: Property is ready to be valued (new BPO needed)
- *Repairs*: Property is pending repairs to be completed
- *Active or Listed*: Property has a list price and is ready for MLS

- *Accepted*: Bank has accepted offer and is waiting or has executed contract
- *Off the Market*: Property has a lien/code/violation or is occupied by a homeowner or tenant and is off the market temporarily
- *Closed*: Property has sold
- *Eliminated*: Property has switched to another agent or gone to a large auction house

Your job is to go from "valuation" to "closed" as fast as possible. The following benchmarks will determine how well you are performing in a month. Always analyze your performance with the following eight success measuring tools.

THE EIGHT SUCCESS MEASUREMENT TOOLS

Success Tool #1: Closing Ratio Percentage (CRP)

The REO business is about results. Banks want closings. They need you to stop the bleeding as fast as possible. The number of closed transactions indicates how many properties you were able to close in any particular timeframe. The goal is to maximize the number of closed transactions, minimize the days it takes to close those transactions, and maximize the sales price for each transaction. In bank terms, they may refer to this as maximizing execution and minimizing disposition time. Therefore, a very critical tool to measure is your closing ratio.

- Closing Ratio % = Actual Closed/Scheduled to Close
- Example: 35 Closed/50 Scheduled = 70%

The higher your closing ratio, the better. The more closings you produce the more properties you will receive. Your CRP every month should be 70 percent or greater compared to what you have scheduled on the closing calendar. Don't worry, the other 30 percent will still close, just not in that month. They will be extended to the following month usually due to a title or financing delay. Remember, the beauty of being an REO listing agent is that everything closes. It's just a matter of when. On average, your monthly stats per account should look something like this:

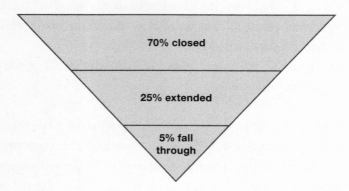

So by the end of January 31, 2012, if you have thirty-five scheduled REO closings, on average expect 70 percent to close, 25 percent to be extended to February or March 2012, and 5 percent to fall through or bust out (not closing). The final 5 percent will have to be remarketed with an updated BPO and new pricing.

Success Tool #2: Days on Market (DOM)

Days on market (DOM) is defined as the difference in time between the date the property is "active" on the MLS to the date the bank accepted the offer and the property is considered "accepted" or "pending sale" from the MLS point of view.

- DOM = Date Accepted from Date Active
- Example: January 1, 2012, to January 15, 2012 = 15 Days

For example, you receive a list price and place the property on the MLS on January 1, 2012, and the bank accepts the offer January 15, 2012. Your DOM would be fifteen days. This is a direct measure of your ability to procure a contract; the faster the better.

The bank will usually price its property high enough to maximize its sales price but not so high as to be priced out of the market. The quicker your DOM, the more likely it is that you are marketing your properties effectively to get the property offer accepted. A DOM of thirty or less is ideal.

One variable that would affect this number would be repairs. If you get a property that is being repaired but the bank still wants you to list it on the market because the repairs are minimal, it may be a deterrent to potential buyers. In this scenario, your DOM may be slightly higher. This is when your management skills with your contracts are tested (see Chapter 8). Every day the repairs are delayed, your DOM will be affected. Be cautious.

From there, the average days to close (see below) measures your performance after the property is under contract.

Success Tool #3: Days to Close (DTC)

After the offer is accepted you need to keep your eye on the number of days it takes to close the REO. Days to close (DTC) has a direct correlation with how well you manage or, in many cases, babysit your buyers. Once the property is under contract, how will you prevent buyer's remorse? Are you following up with all parties? Are you keeping the buyer motivated? Are the buyers' financing cleared? Are the buyers mentally prepared for the new move?

DTC is the difference between the time the property is "accepted" to the time the property is "closed" or the transaction is closed. In the MLS, this would be labeled as "closed sale."

DTC = Date Closed from Date Accepted
Example: January 15, 2012, to February 15, 2012 = 30 Days

This number should be as low as possible to ensure that you are not keeping a contract that has no potential for closing active on the market. If the buyer is not qualified, is uncertain, or is unlikely to close the deal, inform your asset manager so they can decide whether or not they want to grant an extension or move on to another buyer.

🏠 INSIDER TIP

> Disclose, disclose, disclose. If you feel the buyer cannot close (e.g., buyer loses a job, buyer loses communication with you for days, etc.) for whatever reason, contact your asset manager immediately. Time is crucial in this business. It's better to put the property back on the market and find an ironclad buyer than dance with lukewarm buyers who delay the closing for months. The faster you can get a qualified buyer to purchase the home, the better it is for all parties.

Success Tool #4: Resources Ratio (RR)

The resources ratio (RR) compares both the number of days the property is on the market (DOM) over the number of days it takes to close an REO (DTC). RR ratio measures how efficiently you are allocating your resources (your dream team's attention). Are you pushing your staff to focus on selling and marketing, or are you pressuring title companies and mortgage lenders to execute?

RR Ratio = DOM / DTC
Example = 15 Days on Market / 30 Days to Close = 50%

There should be a clear balance between the two important functions (marketing and closing). This ratio should not be greater than two. If resources are all allocated to marketing but not closing, you will notice that your marketing efforts become futile; buyers back out because the contract expires and the title is not ready to close.

If resources are all allocated to closing, then you will notice that some properties will stay on the market for longer than average, and thus you will ultimately be biting off more than you can chew. Make sure your marketing efforts are perfected so that you can perfect your closing efforts. Both functions are critical, and there should be a balance between the two.

Success Tool #5: Gross Execution Percentage (GEP)

Gross Execution Percentage is the list price of an REO divided into the sales price.

Gross Execution % = SP/LP
Example: $126,000 /$130,000 = 97%

It measures your ability to execute. Anything above a 95 percent GEP is good; above 100 percent GEP is excellent. Did you provide a good-quality BPO? Did you recommend the correct marketing strategy (repaired versus as-is)? These are factors that will affect your GEP percentage. Days on market and GEP percentage have an inverse relationship. The lower the days on market, the more likely the property sells at or above the list price and the higher the gross execution percentage.

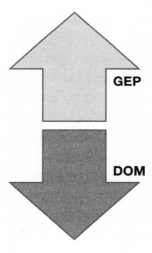

This can occur when there is strong demand for a property and you have multiple offers above list price. Chapter 8 discusses the three shady tactics agents use to get offers accepted—avoid those! Remember, it's not quantity but quality that you are looking for.

Success Tool #6: Price Accuracy Percentage (PAP)

If you think you can produce a low-ball BPO and submit it to an asset manager and get a low listing price, think again. Banks hate low-ball BPO. It speaks of carelessness and sloppiness from an REO agent. Mastering your BPO is important; if it pinpoints at the perfect market price, it will produce price accuracy. Each function of the REO business has checks and balances. Your BPO is checked by the bank's appraiser to arrive at a final list price (see Chapter 5). The closer you are to the list price, the more you appear to be taking care of the bank's interest—not your own pockets.

> Price Accuracy % = BPO Value / List Price
> Example: $120,000 / $130,000 = 92%

Because you will not know the list price until after the BPO and repairs (if any) are completed, price accuracy percentage is a post-measurement success tool. Your goal is to maintain a 90 percent or higher accuracy.

Success Tool #7: Aged Inventory Percentage (AIP)

Aging can feel depressing at times. No one likes it. Not even asset managers. If you see a little REO sitting on the market longer than ninety days, you will have your first aged property. It's like your first white hair. You want to pluck it as soon as possible before anyone notices. The only reasons an REO hasn't produced any offers is either it's priced too high or you recommended the wrong marketing strategy (e.g., as-is versus all repairs).

Any active listing on the MLS for longer than ninety days that has not sold is considered aged. Comparing your aged listings to your total active listings tells you how good of a job you are doing procuring a buyer; the smaller the AIP the better. A good barometer to success would be keeping this number under 10 percent.

Aged Inventory % = Number of Listed > 90 days / Total Number Listed

Example: 3 Aged / 30 Total Active = 10%

AIP ≤ 10%

Success Tool #8: Run-Off Ratio (ROR)

A major part of your success will be based on closed sales. This is what counts. You can think that you did a great job by getting an offer accepted that is much higher than the listing price. But does it count? Did it close? Remember, always be closing!

RESULTS = CLOSINGS

Run-off ratio is based on the theory that you will get more inventories based on your performance in closings. The more you close, the more you get. The ratio should be as close as possible to 100 percent.

ROR = # of closed transactions in any time period / # of properties you have listed + # of properties you have accepted or under contract

Example: You closed 20 properties from January 1 to February 1. On February 1, you had 10 properties listed, and 10 properties under contract. Your run-off ratio would be: (20 / (10 + 10)) = 100%.

The premise is that your performance is based on what you close. You can be the best at listing and marketing, but if you can't close, then your ROR will show it. Many asset managers use the ROR to determine who will get new assignments.

Think about it from their perspective, how can they justify giving new assignments if your ROR is low? If they do that, they will be contributing to make your ROR even lower (i.e., when they give you a new property to list, it will make the denominator bigger, and if your closings aren't increasing, then they will be most likely think twice).

AGENT'S SCORECARD:
MAKING THE BANK'S "A" LIST

It is critical to stay proactive in your REO business. Your first step is to continuously measure the eight key indicators. Just as you measure, some banks may also send you a report once a year, twice a year, or quarterly giving you a comparison among your competition. This is called an agent's scorecard.

Why does it matter? Because if a bank has two agents in the same area, one with a very high scorecard and one with a very low scorecard, they will most likely give new assignments to the better agent. Although you can have all the internal measures based on the eight key metrics above, whereby you measure yourself and set goals to improve, you must also note how you are performing compared to others. Without a comparison to how other agents are performing, you have no benchmark other than what your past performance has been.

SAMPLE AGENT SCORECARD

XYZ REALTY			VENDOR NUMBER: XXXXXXXXX	
1ST QUARTER YEAR XXXX				
RUN OFF	3 MO INVENTORY	CLOSINGS	ROR	PEER RATING
	33	25	75.76%	A
AGING	3 MO ENDING INV	AGED INV>90 DAYS	AIP	PEER RATING
	42	0	0.00%	A
GROSS EXECUTION	3 MO. AVG SP	3 MO. AVG LP	GEP	PEER RATING
	120000	100000	120.00%	A

Why Do Ratios Matter?

You want to make the bank's "A" list. The agent's scorecard gives you exclusive information on how other agents are performing. You can use this information in a variety of ways, most importantly to focus your improvement initiatives in the right areas.

For example, if you have a run-off ratio of 75 percent and your peer rating is an "A," then you should realize that even though you are not at the ideal 100 percent mark, you are still performing better than your competition (i.e., other agents).

Since your grade is an "A," you may choose to focus on other key metrics instead of this one. However, had you not received an agent's scorecard, you would never have known your true performance, as you would only have been able to see your performance at face value versus in comparison to others.

SHOWING OFF:
TOTAL GROSS SALES VOLUME

I love to show off on semi-annual conference calls. Instead of gloating about my statistics, I will pose a question: I ask the group of competing listing agents or asset managers, "What is the average gross execution percentage or gross sales volume in the past quarter?" When you do this, half of the agents in the call will have no idea what you are talking about. The only ones who do will be you and the asset managers, their managers, or their director.

The best "show me off" number will be your gross sales volume. It is a broader measure of the number of closed transactions you did in a given month.

GROSS SALES VOLUME = # OF CLOSED TRANSACTIONS TIMES THE AVERAGE SALES PRICE OF ALL YOUR CLOSINGS

For example, closing thirty-five homes in January 2012 with an average sales price of $200,000 is closing $7,000,000 for one account ($200,000 × 35); not too bad. Two caveats. First, numbers are deceiving. For example, closing ten condominiums with an average sales price of $30,000 is equivalent in sales volume to closing one single-family home at a sales price of $300,000.

It costs the same for you (in time and money) as the REO listing agent to sell a $10,000 property versus a $300,000 property. Ideally, receiving all high-priced REOs is great, but unfortunately this is market specific. Expect 20 to 30 percent of your inventory to be low priced (under $75,000).

Second, you want to pay attention to your average monthly sales prices. Summing the gross sales volume for all thirty-five closings (e.g., $7,000,000) and then dividing it by the actual number of closings will give you your average sales price of $200,000. Watch this number compared to previous months or quarters.

If you notice your average selling price of a home in January 2012 ($200,000) is less than the average selling price a year ago in January 2011 ($300,000), you can infer that you are still in a down market. More supply is on the market than there are buyers, driving down prices; great for you as an REO agent but not so great for first-time home buyers or investors. This is valuable information you can share with your team and investor database.

MANAGING CASH FLOW

As your business picks up I want to caution you to carefully watch your cash flow; you need to monitor the amount of cash you have in the bank to make sure it's not running out. Remember OVM from Chapter 3? The reason why the REO Bootstrap Model works so well is because it relies on OVM. If you don't have the cash to pay for minor expenses under $1,000, your vendor is paying for it and you are reimbursing them within 120 days (or more). They are bank-rolling your operations. Nothing down!

Cash flow is more important to look at than your bottom line profits. Would you rather see a statement from your accountant that says you made $1,000,000 and have $100,000 in the bank or would you rather have $1,000,000 in the bank and have a statement that says you only made $100,000?

REOs are all about the bankroll. If you run out of cash to operate your business, you will be forced to shut down regardless of how much profit you make. Think about this. If you have a Ferrari Enzo that does zero to sixty miles per hour in 3.4 seconds racing against a Honda Accord EX, will you win? Sure, if you have gas.

In the REO business, cash flow is gas. If you can't pay your utilities or hourly wages on the first and fifteenth of every month, then no matter what you say, your dream team will leave on the spot. No one works for free. That's why when you have fewer than thirty active listings you must start with the REO Bootstrap Model, even if it means turning down additional accounts in the beginning.

I have seen a lot of companies in other industries hire the best sales force that goes and gets five to ten new accounts within a month's time and then cannot service the customers because the company ran out of bankroll. This makes them look bad and non-credible. Don't let this happen to your REO business.

TRIMMING THE FAT

Measuring your performance and monitoring your cash flow are necessary steps. If you can perform and have enough of a bankroll you will not have to worry about too much. However, if you notice your expenses rising while your sales are staying constant, or your sales decreasing while your expenses are staying constant, you have an expense problem; you're spending too much money.

There are only 100 pennies in a dollar. Every penny you allow to leave your business that is unnecessary means the fewer dollars you will have. Pennies are your expenses, and the dollar is your profit.

I like to travel. I have visited many places outside the United States. One thing I noticed that was shocking while outside of the United States was no matter which country I visited, I did not find one penny (or equivalent currency) on the floor. In the United States, in almost any street you will find a penny, a nickel, and even dollars.

The secret to achieving a $1 million dollar net in this business is to watch your fixed expenses. Every penny you spend should be allocated with caution. If you are still printing documents in hard copy, signing in blue ink, or faxing via a traditional fax, you are throwing away pennies from your dollar. The more pennies that go out, the less you keep.

In your business there are two areas of fixed expenses or pennies you need to watch before they sneak away from you:

- Advertising
- Rent

Advertising, specifically print advertising, will kill your profits. Don't even think about making a healthy bottom line if you are planning to do print ads. As an REO agent, you will rarely use print ads. With the advent of technology and the move to social media marketing, print ads are extinct. Plus, they are a rip-off.

The only exception is if you are in a small rural area with a local flyer that circulates for free around town and is what everyone reads—that might be the exception. Regardless, your annual advertising expense should not be greater than 1 percent of your gross commission income, and all of it should be spent online or for items outlined in Chapter 2.

$1,000,000 (GCI)
$\times$ **1%**

$10,000 (Max Advertising Allowance)

Remember from Chapter 7 that you want to showcase as many of your REOs online as possible. The good news as an REO agent is that your banks will have all of your listings on their preferred marketing sites, which will provide approximately 60 percent of your leads. Since you are the REO listing agent, you will be the name and face on the listings on every preferred website. The 40 to 50 percent will have to come from you maximizing the magnet marketing plan and building relationships with consumers.

Sometimes it's a hard thing to do, and the learning curve may be steep, but you must implement and use technology. It is your best friend. It makes you extremely efficient both with your time and your money. For example, some agents I have coached have eliminated printing entirely by using Adobe Professional to handle their printing needs.

Instead of printing out hard copies, they "print" and save the document to their computers. They even use Adobe to sign signatures digitally. It cuts about 50 percent of their time dealing with other cooperating selling agents, customers, and banks.

Rent is the next necessary evil. Although you will need it when transitioning to the REO Plus Model, you must keep a lid on it. Some of the REO agents I coach willingly choose not to transition from the REO Bootstrap Model. They know they will make less but they simply do not want to deal with a live office and the intricacies involved with it. The choice is yours.

However, remember that to achieve a million dollars within twenty-four months you must make the leap to the REO Plus Model as it ensures you achieving 35 to 50 percent net profit margins and high-quality work; sticking with the Bootstrap Model means you will be leaving big money on the table (see Chapter 3).

In the REO Bootstrap Model, your listing specialist works from home and either meets you at a title company, a local coffee shop, or at a virtual office to finalize a transaction. You then gather weekly conference calls and set up a physical meeting once a month with your team. If you do not feel comfortable transitioning, just remember you're trading off your net income.

In the beginning, I had signed up for virtual offices. It ran less than $200 a month and allowed for six free hours a month to utilize a conference room on the fiftieth floor (out of sixty) of a high-rise overlooking the city and bay. It was in the best location possible. If I had physically leased a space there, I would have been bankrupt the next day, as the lease rates were $40 to $50 a square foot triple net.

Once you leverage your REO listing capacity above thirty active listings, you will want to transition into the REO Plus Model, and then you will physically need an office. Depending on which part of the country you are in, you will not need more than 1,500 square feet and should not pay more than $15 a square foot gross lease (meaning it includes utilities and taxes).

Finally, make sure your lease terms are flexible. Commercial landlords are hurting now as well. Get flexible terms such as "options to renew" at your below-market rent or get an escape clause allowing you to back out without penalty with a sixty-day notice.

 **INSIDER TIP**

If the landlord is hesitant, offer to sign a confidentiality agreement where you will not disclose a below-market rent to other tenants in the office building.

Whatever you do, resist the urge of splurging on your office, especially after you land a big account or two. The times of incentivizing agents and staff with plush leather sofas and big offices are over. Everyone is on the road, working from home and out of coffee shops.

In my office, I have nothing but IKEA furniture. I assembled it myself. It looks good and is very inexpensive. Technology has changed the game. Lavish offices are an unnecessary expense and should be avoided.

SECRET TO MAKING A MILLION: STAY LEAN BY CUTTING ADVERTISING AND RENT EXPENSES

A couple of years ago, during the "easy" real estate days, I met this estate agent who we'll call Brody. He probably had one of the best marketing campaigns money could buy. In addition, he was sharp as a tack and was pretty charming in person as well. Every time I would drive down the highway I would see his picture. It was him and his puppy. He was living on billboards.

If I had to guess, his marketing budget must have been at least $30,000 a month. Every other billboard within a three to five mile radius was him. I remember saying to myself, "Either this agent is really smart, or has a very high risk tolerance." It was clear he was implementing the "old school method" of selling real estate; throw a whole bunch of mud on the wall via advertising and see what sticks.

During spring of 2007, I attempted to call him since I had some customers who were looking to list their home in his market, and his number was disconnected; I Googled him and nothing. No Facebook, no Twitter, no LinkedIn, it was as if he had disappeared. I called his old brokerage office, and they said he had left the real estate business. Turns out he did have a very high risk tolerance.

The biggest difference between today's real estate markets, dealing with REOs, versus the old school conventional method of obtaining listings is how you control and manage your expenses. Before, in order to make a million dollars, you basically needed to mortgage your house, car, boat, and your kid's college tuition plans.

This is exactly what Brody did. He was used to the good old days of average sales prices being $250,000 and earning a quick 3 percent listing side commission. Since financing was easy to obtain and the market was hot, he figured he could sell 453 homes a year; piece of cake.

453 HOMES A YEAR × $250,000 AVERAGE PRICE × 0.03 LISTING COMMISSION × 30% CONSERVATIVE PROFIT MARGIN = $1,019,250

Unfortunately the market shifted, homeowners became upside down on their mortgages, average home prices were brutally slashed in half, banks tightened their lending guidelines, and Brody went from living on billboards to possibly on park benches (I hope not).

The lesson is that the old days of aggressive prospecting and marketing are over. Old-school methods of spending big money do not work today. Remember, whoever controls the listings controls the cash. Therefore, the golden geese in today's market are banks; the new-school method of real estate is going after the REO golden goose–bank contracts.

If you focus on spending your 1 percent advertising budget on revenue generating activities such as procuring new bank contracts (yielding you $1 million in GCI per contract) or online marketing of your

REOs, while keeping your advertising and rent expenses low, you will increase your bottom line profits.

90-DAY ACTION PLAN

Becoming an REO listing agent is not something that will happen overnight. It takes time. The good news, however, is that everyone gets in. It's just a matter of when. But it's not going to happen by chance. It is your job to take action. The more passionate and disciplined you are, the shorter the time it will take you to land your first contract (in case you haven't already).

In Chapter 2, I talked about all the strategies for you to get your foot in the door. Please re-read that chapter. It is very important. Whether it is your first contract or your tenth, the tools and strategies remain the same.

We have itemized a 90-day action plan for you to get started in the business immediately. Therefore, take action today. You have two options. The first one is that after you finish reading the next and final chapter, you close this book, store it in your collection, freeze, and say "you will get to it later," or you take action today.

Commit to yourself today that you want change in your real estate career. You want to add an abundance of wealth to your life and your family's. In the next chapter, we talk about the difference between wealth and money. They are two very different things. I also discuss my personal struggle and how the REO business literally changed my life. Review the 90-day action plan below, photocopy and print it out from Appendix L (or visit reoboom.com for a free download), and get started today.

90-DAY ACTION PLAN
DAYS 1 THROUGH 30 (PREPARE AND PLAN)
Week One:

- Obtain all of your REO certifications. Research the REO listing agents in your area. Go to their websites. What certifications do they have? You must have at minimum these certifications.

- Create your polished résumé (see Chapter 2) including the ten key tools. See Appendix O for a sample résumé.
- Create the polished proposal (see Chapter 2). Print fifty portfolios, as these are necessary for you to obtain your first account.
- Do mock BPOs on your own house and family and friends' houses. Offer a free valuation. Watch how fast you will gain experience.
- Use the Reach Around Method from Chapter 2 and join a real estate office that is a "direct" listing agent. Offer to work for free. Ask to hang your real estate license with the company. Tell them that you have what it takes, that you will do it for free, and that you just need a couple of weeks to prove that you are the agent they have been looking for. Be the first one in the office and the last one to leave.
- Gain experience. Handle calls, go to properties, and look at different REO listings. Use the information in this book and hands-on experience in the field to see what type of results that direct listing office is producing and how you can improve performance.

Week Two:

- Start networking. Go to networking events, REO conventions, and local board meetings. Start spreading the word that you work with a direct REO listing office. Even though you may not have any listings, focus on the fact that you are the best REO listing agent on the market. It will come. It's not a matter of "if" but "when." Keep in the back of your mind, preparation + plug = first bank contract.
- Print out business cards, show houses, follow listing agents at the office, and absorb as much information as you can. Learn. Learn. Learn.
- Ask for one; just one listing. Even if you don't make commission, you want to learn. Once you get it, use our systems to impress everyone. Make them believe in you.
- Implement the REO Lunch Method. Find "aged" REO properties that have been on the market for greater than ninety days.

Identify who the asset manager is. Contact the asset manager
(remember MOB—motivation over business) and tell them that
you work as a direct listing agent for XYZ and that you would
like to do a FREE second opinion BPO. Continue doing this—
you will see that the behavior is reciprocated by the asset manager giving you a listing.

- Find a mentor who has done it. Ask them to give you some
pointers. Take them out to lunch. Tell them once you get rolling
and knee-deep in the business you will hire them on a consulting basis. However, if you have the money, invest it with your
mentor. It's worth every penny.

Week Three:

- Start building your buyer network. Order one hundred yard
signs and wire stands (one color, double-sided) and place them
out in your farm area on Friday afternoon through Sunday
evening. Use yard signs combined with landing pages and drip
campaigns to build a large database; the larger your network, the
more value you will add to the banks.

- Start your REO Bus Tour (see Chapter 2). Gather investors and
home buyers to go on a bus tour with you to visit REO properties for sale. Take them to the property that you are doing a second opinion BPO on. You shouldn't be surprised if a passenger
says, "Wow, I would buy that right now." It works. Just make sure
your co-op partner is pre-qualifying all the leads.

Week Four:

- Network. Network. Network. Go to all REO conventions. Meet
asset managers.
- Use the REO FARM Play (see Chapter 2) when you get in front
of asset managers.
- Listen first. Draw out their motivation. What are they motivated
to find from a listing agent? What are they lacking? What problems are they having in their local market? Build their motivation

before getting into business. Remember, motivation before business (MOB).

- Show them that you have what it takes to solve their problems, that you know how to stop the bleeding, and that you are different than the typical listing agent. It's important to show them, not tell them. Give them an example, a story, a situation. Make them believe that what you have done before, you can do for them.
- At the end of your fourth week, you should know all the items that are required of a listing agent. Now it's time to apply.

DAYS 31 THROUGH 60 (PERSEVERE)

Week Five:

- Apply. Apply Apply. Apply everywhere (see Appendix B).
- Spend time with the application questions. Don't just respond the same for each application. Each bank is different. Each has different needs. Research their needs before completing the application.
- Think through each response, re-read Chapter 2, and then complete the responses.
- If you are applying online, be sure to include a print-out of your application along with your polished résumé and a polished proposal, and mail it to the bank that you are applying to.

Week Six:

- Focus on the one. Just one asset manager, one bank, or one institution.
- Go through your progress from weeks one through five. Which asset manager responded best to your REO FARM Play? Who was the most motivated? Who do you have the most likely chance of getting in with?
- Once you choose the one you will most likely have success with, follow through. Go back to the REO Lunch Method. Bring out their motivation again and show them that you can solve their problems by using the REO Lunch Method and doing FREE

BPOs. You can even find an aged property that they are managing that has been listed for more than ninety days. Either way, give them the free lunch and watch how they reciprocate with a listing!

■ Ask for the business. Tell them about your guarantee (from your résumé). Remember, they have nothing to lose.

Week Seven:

■ Re-read Chapter 5 and then perfect the second opinion BPO. You have to show your asset manager that you know what it takes to get the property sold.

Week Eight:

■ Submit your second opinion BPO and follow up with your asset manager using Double Ds (Chapter 9). Remind them about your large buyer network. Let them know that you took home buyers on a bus tour. Show them the pictures. Let them know the feedback from the buyers. Show them that you know what it takes to get the property sold.

DAYS 61 THROUGH 90 (CLOSE)

Week Nine:

■ Send a handwritten thank-you card to the asset manager you are targeting. Thank them for allowing you to do a second opinion BPO.

■ Follow through with your proposed magnet marketing plan (Chapter 7) for that property.

■ Strike when the iron is hot. Ask for the listing. Ask them to reassign the listing you did a second opinion BPO on. Show the asset manager that you can execute. Ask them for the opportunity and then prove your worth.

Week Ten:

■ Re-read Chapters 4 through 9 from this book.

■ Master the six steps of the REO cycle and execute. You need to know exactly what the banks are looking for. Remember, banks will test you out on one. You have one shot to shine.

Week Eleven:

- Take the re-assigned property from "active" to "pending sale" on the MLS by the end of the week by sending the reassigned REO to your large buyers list. Implement the magnet marketing plan.
- Follow up with Double Ds and manage the title company and lender (if any) until the transaction closes.
- Show off your performance to the asset manager and let them know that you have what it takes and that you are dedicated to making sure that they meet their own goals.
- Remind them again about your magnet marketing plan and go back to the REO Lunch Method. The asset manager has nothing to lose by you performing a second opinion BPO. In fact, if you are successful with the first one, you may end up with a new assignment without having to implement the REO Lunch Method again.

Week Twelve:

- Follow up with your asset manager and show them that you are hungry and ready for more. Highlight your performance by showcasing your stats (the eight successful measurement tools).
- Once you have successfully closed ten REOs (90/10 Rule), transition into the REO Bootstrap Model and begin forming your dream team.
- Grow your business. Re-read this entire book to learn how to maximize your income using the REO Bootstrap Model and prepare to expand to the REO Plus Model.

Congratulations!

POINTS TO REMEMBER

**Download your free 90-day action plan from
reoboom.com, print it out, and take action today.**

- Trim the fat by keeping an eye on your fixed expenses: advertising and rent. Never exceed 1 percent of your GCI on advertising and always make sure your lease is flexible with a sixty-day escape clause; sign a confidentiality agreement if you have to.

- Cash flow is more important to look at than your bottom line profits. If you run out of bankroll, then you will be out of business. Without gas in your car you will not win the race no matter how fast your car is.

- An agent's scorecard is a chance for you to make the bank's "A" list, as it compares you to your competition.

- You cannot manage what you do not measure. Use the eight critical success tools to show off with your asset manager, but also to stay proactive with your business rather than reactive.

- The eight critical success tool benchmarks are: CRP and DTC greater than 70 percent, DOM less than 30 percent, RR less than or equal to two, GEP 95 percent or higher, PAP greater than 90 percent, and AIP less than or equal to 10 percent.

- You are only as good as your team. Find VIP leaders—leaders who demonstrate vision, influence, and passion. After you find them, empower them.

- Put your business on autopilot by focusing "on" your business instead of "in" your business. Do this by bringing on your closer (business development role) and your executioner (account manager role). Remember, only one closer and multiple account managers. Motivate them by offering a quarter of one percent (0.25 percent) from the listing commission residually on each REO transaction that closes.

- Grow your REO Plus Model by following the Million-Dollar REO Blueprint. All it takes is three direct accounts to make a million dollars net; only nine new BPO assignments a week.

- Banks need you. They need your expertise, systems, and team (intangible assets) to help solve their pain. The demand is overwhelming. REO mafias are a myth. Banks are opening up the doors for those who truly want it. The time to seize the opportunity is now.

- Growing your business and making a million in twenty-four months is easy. All you need to do is follow a formula, a blueprint. As long as you have passion, dedication, and faith you will be unstoppable. Remember, it's a science, but not rocket science.

Printing Money!

BUILDING YOUR MOJO

2006 was a bad year for me. I can still remember driving home one afternoon and having a mental breakdown in the car before pulling into the driveway. I think Murphy's Law was in full effect. Everything that possibly could go wrong actually had gone wrong. I went from selling $50,000,0000 a year to $20,000,000. My income was cut in half.

Real estate was all I knew. Why was it slowing down? What was happening? These were the questions I was asking myself. I mean, how could I go from making $1.5 million in GCI to $700,000? Forget about net. My expenses were through the roof. First the business expenses with marketing, advertising, it was a mess. Then personal expenses—mortgage, taxes, medical, investment properties, the list was endless.

I had gotten to the point where I needed help. How could I go home and tell my wife we were in financial trouble? It was a very tough moment for me. So, I did what any other aggressive and smart real estate agent would do. Fight. I tried many things. First, I went digging through a box in the back of my closet trying to find my health insurance policy. I remember tip-toeing in the night when everyone in the house was asleep so my wife wouldn't find out.

Like a typical man I needed to figure this out for myself. I had remembered someone telling me about health insurance covering shrink bills. I figured, hey it was worth a try. Maybe I could get some mental health counseling. In fact, I did, but to no surprise my wife did find out about it. Staying up many late nights on a couple hours of sleep, being jittery all day on caffeine, and coming home earlier and earlier might have given it away. It didn't help that she was a licensed family and marriage therapist either.

So, I went and it lasted three sessions. For one, that's all what my health insurance covered, and two, it slapped me in the face. It woke me up. I had this master plan my whole life to becoming successful, from writing goals every year to creating a game plan, working backwards with checks and balance systems placed in between.

From April to October 2006, I reflected on my real estate career. I internalized everything. All my life I read how real estate was the path to wealth, to success. You name the author or seminar and I read it or attended it; from Mike Ferry to Robert T. Kiyosaki, I followed everything I learned to the tee.

During the six months I was in this meditative state, I came to the realization that there was nothing wrong with me. I had the entrepreneurial mind, the discipline, the faith, and the courage to fight. I had the tools of self-educating (constantly reading books, listening to audio tapes, attending seminars) and a proven prior success record. It was actually the timing.

To further validate my belief, I went and studied some of the most successful real estate and business figures in our times who achieved success in their careers. I studied Donald Trump, George Soros, Bill Gates, John D. Rockefeller, Warren Buffett, and several other successful role models. That's where I came to the realization of three things:

1. Success is about timing.
2. History repeats itself.
3. Successful people seek mentors.

You see, the tools and methods I was using to sell houses did not work anymore, not because they were bad, but because the market had changed. The real estate bubble had finally popped. The timing had changed. The real estate bubble money was gone and I had a choice.

I could live in the past like the character Al Bundy on *Married with Children*, or choose to find the next real estate "hot" market.

It wasn't new construction. It wasn't rentals. It wasn't commercial. I had to look further into the future. So far into the future, I had to round the globe and come back to the past. I needed Superman speed. In *CashFlow Quadrant*, author Robert T. Kiyosaki talks about how massive wealth was transferred from employees and self-employed individuals to business owners and investors due to the Tax Reform Act of 1986.

After the tax loopholes were taken away, the real estate market had crashed, and as a result the Resolution Trust Corporation (RTC) was formed. Remember Chapter 1?

Kiyosaki states, "The RTC was the agency responsible for taking foreclosures from the real estate crash, and transferring them to people who knew how to handle them. For me and many of my friends, it was like a blessing from financial heaven."

This was the "a-ha" moment I was waiting for. The subprime mortgage market was melting, foreclosures had started to rise, and fear was in the air. These were the same symptoms that had made a lot of people money in the past. History was repeating itself. Money was about to be printed.

My only problem now was I had no clue where to start. I knew nothing about managing the banks' real estate–owned properties. At that time, there might have been a class or two on short sales, but other than that there was nothing on REOs. All I knew was I had a drive, I had faith, and I was ready to take action. I was ready to build my momentum again. I wanted my MOJO back!

Therefore, I went to the basics. I hit the books. I dug up everything I could find on bank-owned properties and I made a list of all the people who might possibly be my mentor. In business there is an unwritten rule of *quid pro quo*, which is Latin for "this for that" or "a favor for a favor."

I was prepared to pay for help. I realized in life you always pay. Either you pay upfront or at the end through the school of hard knocks. Therefore, I maxed out my American Express and paid for my mentor's time. I managed to find someone who had profited from the first savings and loan busts in the late '80s. Within twelve months I learned everything about the bank-owned property game.

No matter how much theory or studying you do, there is nothing like firsthand experience. So, on top of paying for education, I paid an even harder way—by making mistakes. Mistakes are a double-edged sword. You need them to learn, but they can cost you a lot. The key is never making the same mistake twice.

The good news was that between 2007 and 2008 the bank-owned business was just beginning. Therefore, the mistakes I made were not that impactful. If I were to make the same mistakes in today's REO market I probably wouldn't be writing to you today.

What I learned so far in this business is first, you need to treat it like a business. You must implement systems. The next thing you need to know is this business is very easy; it's science, not rocket science. Most importantly, you have to have faith. You have a choice to decide every morning from the moment you wake up to do something or not. Every decision you make is a tradeoff. You are trading one outcome for another. Sometimes you make the right decision and sometimes you don't. That's OK.

REOs helped me build my momentum back. I love waking up in the morning having a lot of things to do. It's exciting. That "mover and shaker" feeling is thrilling; never let that go. When you look back in life on the big screen, you will see yourself driving to the fork in the road and seeing your choices spread out in front of you.

The choice of you pursuing REOs and taking action will be the seeds in the garden you plant. The hundreds of calls you receive a couple of years from now from the customers you sold REOs to, wanting to relist their properties, will be the fruit the garden bears.

On the next page are some common things I reminded myself of when rebuilding my mojo. I wrote the following five points on a sticky note, initialed it, took a picture of the sticky note with my iPhone, and saved it as my wallpaper so that every time I turn my cell phone on, I see this:

Building Your Mojo

1. Choose. Take action.
2. Educate: Books, audio, and seminars.
3. Seek mentors. Pay well.
4. Mistakes OK. Never repeat twice.
5. Have faith. Fight fears.

YOU'RE BURNING WHY?

There are two things in life that will kill you. The first is self-doubt and the second is negativity. Many times I used to wake up and say to myself, "Who am I kidding, I can't do this," or "Who am I? I don't know anyone special or belong to any privileged clubs." When I first started, I used to tell other real estate agents, some of them close friends, about getting into REOs. They used to laugh and say "What makes you think you can do that?" or "That's a fad, it will never work."

By listening to these comments, I was slowly projecting self-doubt and fear. It was like I had a small voice inside of me telling me not to take action. Not to change. No one likes change. You have to readjust your life and circumstances, but in reality, change is the only constant. Nothing lasts forever.

I knew if I did nothing new or didn't quench my thirst to be successful with bank-owned properties then nothing would be different. Not changing is quitting. I never quit anything in my life, and I sure enough was not going to quit then. Besides, if I did nothing, I knew already what the outcome would have been—nothing. And I knew I could always quit, so why start early?

It was very interesting. When things were bad for me, no one wanted to be around me. The criticism and cynicism was through the roof. All I would hear was "No," "Never," "No way." But I knew that the greatest success stories of our nation did the exact opposite of what everyone else was doing.

During the housing bubble, agents were selling to those who were buying. During the stock bubble, they were shorting stock when everyone was buying. And I studied history, so I knew over the next ten years there would be one of the biggest opportunities to become wealthy, just like the thrift busts in the late '80s.

No matter how many times I heard the naysayers, I kept on telling myself "Yes, "REOs are the answer." Instead of thinking "No," I thought, "How can I?" Every time fear crept in, it made me stronger. The small voice in my head was getting smaller and smaller. "No one can tell me no; I will not lose; failure is not an option." I used to repeat this to myself every day either in the shower or when I was driving.

But I realized one thing while examining why I wanted so badly to be successful with REOs. It wasn't the money. Sure, the money has blessed my family and I am grateful for it. But my burning WHY was more than that. One morning I was sleeping, maybe it was five minutes till 7 A.M., the time that I normally get up every morning, and my wife nudged me on the shoulder. She said, "Honey, why do you get up every morning?" Being half asleep with my eyes halfway open, I carefully rose, making sure not to kick our cat, paused for about three seconds, and said, "For you."

The sole purpose of me working was for my wife and my family. I loved her and I wanted her to have the world. This was my burning WHY and the ammunition that put water on the fire of negativity and self-doubt. You see, what I wanted was not money but wealth; two very different concepts. Wealth is having a loving family, being healthy, accomplishing goals, being passionate about life, teaching others, and having peace of mind.

Money is just a scorecard. It keeps track of things. It's a validator. When I set out and got my first REO contract, hired my first listing specialist to eventually transition to the REO Plus Model and started an automated REO machine, the money that came in was the reward. It validated the decisions I made. I always believed in the power of printing money, because money is always in abundance. Think about it. Money comes and goes. Agents have made millions in selling pre-construction homes and agents now will make millions selling REOs. It's never-ending.

That's why you need something deeper than money as your burning WHY. So, now I ask you. Why do you wake up each morning? What is your purpose in life? What is your mission? To guarantee success in your REO career you need a clear indication of what really drives you to succeed.

The reason why I wake up every morning is _____

_____

The purpose of my life is _____

_____

My mission is_____

_____

Here are some questions you can answer to determine your burning WHY:

Top Five Burning WHY Questions

1. What are the top three reasons that make you committed to being successful in your REO career?

2. Who is counting on you to make your REO career successful?

3. What will happen to those who are counting on you if you quit?

4. If you have a tough moment, a near mental breakdown, what one thing is going to help you bounce back and get you back on track to mastering REOs?

5. Once you become successful with REOs, what will you do with the money?

AVOIDING BURNOUT

There will be many times in the REO business you will feel burnt out and exhausted. It's the feeling of wanting to just drop everything, shut your cell phone off, and leave town for two weeks. Too bad you can't, but it's at this breaking point that we can offer you some advice.

This is especially true if you are operating under the REO Bootstrap Model and have your hands on every granular detail of the REO cycle. One piece of advice I can share with you as I do with the agents I consult with is: How do you eat an elephant? Answer: One bite at a time.

I have experienced many burnt-out phases that have made me want to shut down internally. I remember the first time an asset manager reassigned a property from me; it felt like someone ripped my heart out of my chest. You know those rides at amusement parks where you drop down fifty floors at a blazing fast speed?

When I read that email from another listing agent that said, "The property was reassigned to me, please remove your listing," that's how I felt. I felt like I failed. So many thoughts went rushing through my head, but the one thing I always did was keep my cool. From years of coaching others, I've learned how many agents dropped the ball. The worst thing any one agent can do is to complain or argue with an asset manager. Even if the agent is right, the agent has no right to argue or complain to an asset manager. It makes no sense. It shows low class. It's unprofessional. It's a waste of time. Never bite the hand that feeds you.

Another experience that almost made me lose it was when one of my closing coordinators quit and went to work for another REO listing agent. This was a different feeling from what I described above. I was pissed off! After all I taught her, she left to work for another agent, without even approaching me or warning me. What gave her the right? I was angry. I was upset. It took about a month for me to get over it. At first, all I wanted was revenge. But then I realized there was no point. I became humble. I discovered that it's better to teach than to hate. And believe it or not, my choice of keeping my cool is probably one of the reasons why I have become so good at coaching others and sharing my secrets for success.

There have been other times when I have had critical deadlines due that were missed because one of my listing specialists forgot to turn in a BPO or listing packet. Also, I have had buyers at a closing table who just lost their job and tried to conceal it, resulting in the lender backing out of the loan after conducting a final employment check the day before closing.

The worst one is when I have about ten different windows open on my dual monitors, as I'm working on four to five different tasks at once, and I get a phone call from an asset manager wanting to know about a specific property or situation. I'm left scrambling.

It is times like these when all you can do is take a step back, take a deep breath, and go do something else. There are only so many phone calls or texts you can send to your listing team before they will respond. They are busy just like you. They will eventually respond back. Take the time that you are waiting and go do something else; be productive with it.

I love to run. I can go for a six mile run outside on a bright and sunny day and I feel like a new person after. I also love to work out. I put my iTunes playlist on or listen to Pandora and hit the gym for a forty-five minute intense weight lifting workout as I burn out all the stress from the day.

The final thing I love to do is meditate. I turn off all electronic devices and sit in complete silence, in a relaxed and comfortable state, close my eyes, and chant a silent mantra to calm my body. I try doing this fifteen to thirty minutes before starting my day. I find early mornings are the best, right after you have had a full eight-hour rest period so you are alert and don't accidently snooze off.

Also, since everyone else is probably still sleeping, it's easier to concentrate. This is by far the hardest part. Try stilling your mind to produce no thoughts. It's a great challenge. Sant Rajinder Singh, a profound teacher of the science behind meditation to all different religions in the world, states that the time you spend in mediation is equivalent of four times the amount of rest your body receives during sleep. So if you can manage to meditate for fifteen minutes, it's the equivalent of resting for 60 minutes.

The goal is to rejuvenate or restore your body to avoid a burnout stressful situation. Unfortunately, stress has been linked to both high blood pressure and cardiovascular problems. By implementing activities such as meditation or relaxing, you can recharge your batteries to avoid a burn-out session.

A Quick Five-Step Strategy to Relax

1. Lay down somewhere quiet.
2. Think of a calm, serene place you want to be (forest, waterfall, etc.).
3. Close your eyes and tense every muscle in your body. Hold them for five seconds, counting backwards to zero.
4. Focus your energy on your toes. Sense them and relax them. Concentrate on how they feel.
5. Move the concentration from your feet up to your thighs, torso, chest, arms, fingers, neck, head, and scalp, making each body part as relaxed as your toes.

The lesson is to have a strong work-life balance to avoid burning out. In the REO business, especially when starting or growing, it can be challenging. Here are an additional eight things I do regularly to avoid burning-out:

1. Think positive ("I will not lose.").
2. Eat healthy (six small meals a day).
3. Drink protein (1 gram of protein per every 1 pound of body weight).
4. Drink lots of water (up to one gallon a day).
5. Sleep well (eight hours a night).
6. Listen to motivational music (upbeat, inspirational).
7. Play (with my cats—sorry, no dogs!).
8. Teach (my wife or mom about real estate).

What you put in is what you get out. Your body is a temple of God. Therefore, if you treat it well, it will treat you well. This includes eating, resting, exercising, and most of all, having fun. You will make a ton of money with REOs. Now spend time with your family and have fun.

Make a list of the top five things you will do to avoid an REO burn-out session and itemize them below:

1.

2.

3.

4.

5.

MANAGING SUCCESS

Success. Isn't that what it is all about? There are many levels of success in the REO business. The first level of success is choosing to commit and be ready to embrace change by taking action. The second is obtaining your first bank contract. Next is setting up your models and developing your systems.

After that is mastering your trade and being the best you can be in the market by building your mojo, having the right attitude, and following your burning passion. This, combined with hard work, education, and discipline is the formula for success. From OCRs to post-closing, you want to be the fastest, leanest, sharpest team in your marketplace so you can make the bank's "A" list.

The final level is achieving an autopilot, self-sustaining business that can net you a million dollars within twenty-four months. In actuality, it's not making a million dollars that is important but what that money can buy you—time. Free time is the only commodity that you cannot get back. Having a business run by your team with you working less than twenty hours a week and spending the rest of your time with your family is what real success is about. Remember, money will come and go, but memories last a lifetime.

You have been given a unique opportunity. As an REO agent you have an opportunity to capitalize off our depressed real estate market within the next five to eight years. Starting off in this market is like finding a home worth $1,000,000 that you can get under contract for $250,000. You may not have the cash to purchase but if the deal is good enough, the money will come. If you manage to take action and build momentum, you will create motion.

Your broker, associates, friends, and other families will see your success and how it is rewarding you and will want to be a part of your expansion. Being successful and making a million dollars is nothing more than a state of mind. Your mind creates attitudes and beliefs that lead to action. With action you have the wheels of motion moving and linking up your thoughts, feelings, and beliefs and forming an unstoppable dream team that is ready to take your REO business to the next level.

However, with success comes envy. Maybe success is nothing more than a penalty of leadership. Regardless, envy or jealousy is a weak emotion that you will face after you begin building momentum and obtain success. There will be your own colleagues, fellow REO agents, who will be your best friends at conferences and then stab you when you are sleeping.

I have heard countless sad stories where competing REO agents will intentionally hire people to go to all of your listings and remove your signs, lockbox, or keys. Even worse, agents will hire people to file complaints to your supplier alleging they were customers and you did not present their offer. The worst thing I heard of was agents who would break the law.

They would find out which vacant property you have, give out the lockbox codes, and put tenants inside of them as "squatters." They would create a proxy lease, collect the first month's rent and security deposit, and act as if they owned the home since they met them at the door step. Then they would disappear, using fake aliases—all with the motive of you having to deal with a cash for keys situation or eviction so you delay closing on the property and making commission for an additional six months.

People will do whatever it takes to bring you down. If they can eliminate you from their market, they think they will be awarded your new assignments. This is faulty logic. The worst kind of betrayal is from people in your own organization. During the early years of my career, I had implemented the REO Bootstrap Model and had a stellar dream team. I taught my listing specialists everything there was about REOs. I put a lot of money into their pockets and taught them everything I knew about the business.

Unfortunately, the unthinkable happened. One of them got greedy. After a couple of months, I began noticing his quality of work decreasing. He would take an extra couple of hours to get back to me after I called. He would be late on the assignments. He would not visit properties during weekly inspections. He would intentionally violate our company values and ethics by ignoring phone calls from co-operating agents with the motive of placing his own "in-house" customers into homes.

The worst was when I found out he was secretly in talks with other brokerage companies with the intent to "steal" my bank contacts and branch off on his own, completely violating any and all confidentiality and non-compete agreements we had. It was a mess.

The good thing about the REO Bootstrap Model is that you as the REO listing agent are the sole contact for the bank. Therefore, everything your listing specialist does must have your name on it. If you remember the eight successful measurement tools from Chapter 11, you will know right away if your numbers are under par.

As soon as I saw my numbers off, I began tracking my listing specialist patterns and swiftly took action, firing him on the spot and cutting off all communications from our team. I locked him out of his email account, removed his signs and 800 phone numbers, and even entered comments in our bank's platform letting it know that a certain associate was no longer affiliated with our team.

In the book *Good to Great*, author Jim Collins talks about getting the "right people on the bus" but more importantly getting the wrong ones off. One thing I learned, that is critical to managing success, is to be careful who you bring on your team. They must share your core values (e.g., act ethically), be a team player, be disciplined, and be passionate. Real estate is a people-person business.

There is enough room for everyone to be successful. The ones who see only "I" versus "We" are the ones who will have a short spurt of success but then phase out during the long-term. Sometimes you will be forced to charge it to the game when managing success. It's a cost of doing business, so be prepared.

FINAL THOUGHTS

You just finished the most powerful book ever written on REOs. Our best-selling strategies and tactics have been used by thousands of real estate agents and brokers throughout the country, and now they belong to you. You possess what took us years of experience, trials, and errors in the palms of your hands.

You learned how easy it is to get in the REO business. You learned about the 90/10 REO rule, the six steps in the REO cycle, how to build your dream team using the REO Bootstrap Model and the REO Plus Model, how to use OVM and bankroll your business, and how to perfectly execute every function of the REO cycle, from the OCRs to closings. You learned what asset managers need, and the hidden secrets behind making a fortune in the REO business through the different revenue streams.

Your goal now is to hang your shingle up, so to speak, and begin implementing each one of these strategies; if you are already a REO agent, even better. We want you to fine tune your business by implementing a minimum of three to five lessons taught in this book.

We know that at times taking on a new challenge can feel daunting. It is a natural emotion. However, remember the REO boom is here now. You have a short window of opportunity to get in and cash in on the biggest ATM ever—REOs.

There is a reason you are reading this book. It is your calling to add an abundance of income to your life and your family's. Anyone can make money during an up market, but the real professionals make money when things are going bad, in a down market. At the time this book was written, there will be an additional three to five REO booms coming nationally with final default notices, foreclosure filings, and foreclosure auctions tapering off to 2017.

As a real estate entrepreneur, your job is to find opportunities while everyone else is running away from them and getting day jobs. This is your opportunity to step into the market and make a million dollars within the next twenty-four months.

You were built for greatness. No one can do what you can. Be inspirational, be exceptional, and most of all have fun doing it. We want you to take the change out of the game and milk the REO ATM. Print money! We wish you much success and all the best on your journey in the REO business. Please remember to visit:

www.reoboom.com

Gain full access to bank asset manager's lists, newsletters, coaching tips, and our REO podcasts as they are released. We are here to help you on your lucrative venture in the REO business.

Also, we encourage as much feedback as possible in your local REO market. Your feedback will form the basis for future editions of *REO Boom*. Also, if you would like to be featured or share your success story, log on to www.reoboom.com as we will be selecting a handful of REO agents to be featured in our next edition.

Lastly, remember to pay it forward and share a copy of this book with your associates, team, and/or your broker. Show how proactive you are to your broker and offer to teach some of the concepts in this book to other agents in your office at your next meeting. Sometimes, the best way of learning is teaching others.

Remember, the REO business is a team sport. There is nothing better than to be successful with your associates. As they say, "It is lonely at the top." Make history; when you look back ten years, we want you to say to yourself, "I was a part of that." Take action today. We know you can do this. It is your destiny. We wish you an abundance of wealth and long lasting happiness. Carpe diem!

Sincerely,
ARAM SHAH & TIM SHAH

Your REO Resources

The following are resources you will want to refer to weekly or daily to keep track of the REO market. Many services here are the exact ones I use. My criterion were they either had to be free or very cheap. Like any other purchase, always get three estimates before making a purchasing decision. Enjoy.

Auction Sites

www.hudsonandmarshall.com
www.auction.com
www.gohoming.com
www.altisourcehomes.com
www.lpsauctions.com
www.realtybid.com
www.office.microsoft.com
www.sharepoint.microsoft.com

Blogging

www.blogger.com
www.wordpress.com
www.movabletype.com
www.ezinearticles.com

BPO & Forms Software

www.multiform.com
www.amnforms.com
www.reomaestro.com

Condominium Searches

www.condocerts.com

Consulting

www.score.org

Email Marketing

www.aweber.com
www.fabusend.com
www.fastemailflyers.com
www.happygrasshopper.com
www.contact29.com
www.genius.com
www.mailchimp.com
www.netaspects.com
www.surveymonkey.com
www.fontifier.com
www.metisgroup.com
www.thankster.com
www.inkanote.com
www.qrstuff.com
www.istockphoto.com

Housing Vouchers

www.hud.gov

Investor Meetings

www.nationalreia.com

Lockboxes & Signs

www.padlocks4less.com
www.mfssupply.com

www.supraekey.com
www.gotprint.com

Marketing

www.propertynut.com
www.trulia.com
www.listhub.com
www.zillow.com
www.postlets.com
www.foreclosure.com
www.realtytrac.com

Meetings & Conferences

www.go2meeting.com
www.freeconferencecall.com
www.skype.com
www.userplane.com
www.mikogo.com

Mortgage Resources

www.bankrate.com
www.myfico.com
www.mbaa.org
www.nfcc.org
www.homeloanlearningcenter
  .com
www.trepp.com
www.thefivestar.com

Multimedia

www.animoto.com
www.screenr.com
www.youtube.com
www.tubemogul.com
www.vimeo.com
www.turnhere.com

Notes & Doc Sharing

www.slideshare.net
www.box.net
www.logmein.com
www.pbwiki.com

www.scribd.com
www.gotomeeting.com

News

www.dsnews.com
www.inman.com
www.housingwire.com
www.mortgageservicingnews
  .com
www.realtytimes.com
www.rcanalytics.com

Office Setup

www.toktumi.com
www.ooma.com
www.freedomvoice.com
www.grasshopper.com
www.rapidfax.com
www.explore.live.com
www.davincivirtual.com
www.regus.com
www.intelligentoffice.com
www.adobe.com
www.gotomypc.com
www.carbonite.com

Projects (Hiring)

www.odesk.com
www.elance.com
www.craigslist.com
www.angieslist.com

Real Estate Agent Resources

www.realtor.com
www.alamode.com
www.redatum.com
www.terradatum.com
www.act.com
www.yardi.com
www.topproducer.com
www.ebrokerhouse.com

www.nationalreia.com

www.reomaestro.com

www.ebrokerhouse.com

Real Estate Agent Memberships

www.realtor.org

www.nareb.com

www.nahrep.org

www.areaa.org

REO Associations

www.reomac.com

www.nrba.com

www.reobroker.com

www.creoba.com

REO Charities

www.reo4kids.com

REO Training Programs

www.thefivestarinstitute.com

www.cdpe.com

Signs

www.buildasign.com

www.bigdaddyssigns.com

Social Networking

www.activerain.com

www.hootsuite.com

www.linkedin.com

www.facebook.com

www.shortstacklab.com

www.twitter.com

www.twibs.com

www.wefollow.com

www.flippingpad.com

www.homethinking.com

www.yelp.com

www.peekyou.com

www.digg.com

Search Engine Optimization (SEO)

www.noblesamurai.com

www.domainface.com

www.seopowersuite.com

Used Office Furniture

www.arnoldsofficefurniture.com

www.officeguild.com

www.craigslist.com

Website & Email Setup

www.alamode.com

www.godaddy.com

www.domainsbot.com

www.wordoid.com

www.realestatewebmasters.com

REO Bank List

Below is a direct list of outsourcers and direct accounts you can register with. This list is constantly being updated as links companies change. For the latest update, please visit reoboom.com and register for the free download. Turn to Chapter 2 to refresh your memory on what you will need to submit a powerful application.

Make sure your application is complete and accurate before submitting online. Banks are busy. Constantly call, email, jump on conference calls, do whatever you must until you get a response. Do not give up. Persistence wears resistance. Remember the Double D's? Now is the time to use them!

A

Absolute REO Solutions
www.absreo.com/real-estate-signup.php

Acranet
www.acranet.com

Advanced Collateral Solutions
www.acslinks.com

AHMSI
www.ahmsi3india.com/careers/careersbpo.html#BPO

ALLEGIS
www.allegisgroupservices.com

America's InfoMart, Inc.
https://www.aimyourway.com

Appraisal Bank
www.appraisalbank.org

Asset Disposition Solutions
www.assetdispo.com

Asset Disposition Management
http://admreo.com

Asset Valuation and Marketing
www.assetval.com

Asset Management Holdings, LLC
www.AMHusa.com

ASG Mortgage Services Inc.
www.asgbpo.com

Atlas REO Services
https://portal.atlasreo.com/BrokerApplication/

B

BestAssets
www.best-assets.com/test/vendorinstructions.php

Blackhawk Valuation Service
www.blackhawkonline.com

BPO National
www.BPOnational.com

BPOs Online
www.bposonline.com

BPO Pros, LLC
www.bpopros.com

Brighton Real Estate Services
www.brightonreo.com

Broker Price Opinion.com Inc.
www.brokerpriceopinion.com

C

Chrisley Asset Management
www.chrisleyam.com

Clear Capital
www.clearcapital.com/join/
join_broker_terms.cfm

Corporate Asset Management,
LLC
www.camreo.com

Corporate Valuation Services
www.provalu.com

Crest REO
www.crestreo.com

D

Dinwiddle Property Services
Company, Inc.
www.dinproserv.com

Dispo Solutions
www.disposolutions.com

DRI The Default Solution
www.dridefault.com

E

E Mortgage Logic
www.emortgagelogic.com

EMC Mortgage
www.emcmortgagecorp.com

Equator, LLC
www.equator.com

Equi-Trax Asset Solutions
www.equi-trax.com

Equity Pointe Asset Services
www.equitypointe.com

ETC REO Asset Management
www.etcreo.com

Evaluation Solutions
www.evalonline.com

Executive Asset Management
www.executiveam.com

F

Fannie Mae
http://www.fanniemae.com/
aboutfm/procurement/index.
jhtml

Finiti
https://brokerweb.finiti.info

First Choice REO
http://firstchoicereo.com

First Preston
www.firstpreston.com

Five Brothers
http://fiveonline.com

Freddie Mac
www.homesteps.com

G

Go BPO, Inc.
www.gobpo.com

Goodman Dean, Inc.
www.goodmandean.com

Green River Capital
www.greenrivercap.com

H

HMB Inc.
www.hmbiweb.com/brokers_
agents.html

Housing and Urban Development
(HUD)
www.hudhomestore.com

HUD Pemco
www.hudpemco.com/choose_
BReg.htm

I

I Mortgage Services
www.imortgageservices.com

Infinity Group Direct
Management
www.infinitygroupreo.com

Inside Valuation LLC
http://valuator.insidevaluation.
com

Integrated Asset Services
www.iasreo.com

Integrated Property Source
www.iprops.com

I Short Sales
www.ishortsale.com

J

JEM REO Resources, Inc.
www.jemreoresources.com

K

Keystone Asset Management
www.keystonebest.com

Kinnamon Group
www.kinnamon.com

L

LandSafe, Inc.
www.landsafe.com

LB Market Evaluations
www.lbmarketevaluations.com

Lender Processing Services (LPS)
www.lpsvcs.com

Lenders Asset Management Corp
www.lendersreo.com

Lenders Recovery Services
www.lenderrecovery.com/valua-
tion.htm

Lighthouse Real Estate Solutions
www.lrescorp.com

Litton Loan Servicing
www.littonreo.com

M

Main Street Valuations
www.mainstreetval.com

Mark to Market
https://m2m.aspengrove.net

MCB
www.mcbreo.com

MDA Lending Solutions
www.mdasolutions.com

M.D. Webb & Associations
www.mdwebbinc.com

Millenia Recovery Group Inc.
www.2ndlienrecovery.com

N

National Asset Management
www.namg.com

National Default Servicing, LLC
www.defaultservicingllc.com

National Foreclosures.com LLC
www.nationalforeclosures.com

National Foreclosure Service
www.nationalforeclosureser-
vices.com

National Property Acquisition
Consultants, Inc.
www.npacbpo.com

National Real Estate Asset
Management
www.nationalam.com

National REO Services, Inc.
www.nreo.com/content/signup.
aspx

Nations Valuation Services
www.nationsvs.com

National Vendor Management
Service, Inc.
http://nvms.com/Register.aspx

Nationwide BPOs
www.nationwidebpos.com

Nationstar Mortgage
https://www.nationstarmtg.com

Nationwide REO Brokers
www.nreob.com

Network Mortgage Servicing
www.networkmortgageservic-
ing.com

New Vista Asset Management
www.newvistareo.com

North Point Realty & Asset
Management
www.northpointreo.com

O

Old Republic Default Management
Services
www.oldrepublicdefault.com

Olympus Asset Management
www.olympusasset.com

Outsource Field Services
www.outsourcefieldservices.com

Owen REO, LLC
www.owenreollc.com

P

Phoenix Asset Management
www.phnxam.com

Platinum Real Estate
www.platinum-realestate.net

PMH Financial
www.pmhfinancial.com

Precision Asset Management
http://precisionamc.com/frm-
BrokerSignUp.aspx

Promisor Asset Recovery
www.promisorreo.com/default.
asp?fn=realtor.htm

Promisor Asset Recovery Services
www.promisorassetrecovery.com

Pro-Tech Services
www.protk.com

R

Real Estate Management
www.reotech.com

Real Estate Valuation Partners
www.valuationpartners.com

Real Service
www.real-serv.com

REOTrans.com (also Equator)
www.reotrans.com

Recon Trust Co.
www.reconstrustco.com

Rels
www.relsvaluation.info/asp/
home/login.asp

REM Corporation
www.remusa.com

REO Allegiance
www.reoallegiance.com

REO America
www.reoam.com

REO Brokerage Group
www.reobg.com

REO Connection
www.reoconnection.com

REO Nationwide
www.reonationwide.com

REO Network
www.reonetwork.com

REO One
www.reone.com

REO Real Estate
www.reoone.com

REO Solutions
www.reosolutions.net

REOTrans.com
www.reotrans.com

REO World
www.reoworld.com

RES.net
www.res.net

S

Safeguard Properties, Inc.
www.safeguardproperties.com

Safe Harbor Collateral Solutions
www.safeharborus.com/contact.
aspx

Secured Lending Services
www.irepvm.com

Security National Servicing
Corporation
www.snsc.com

Single Source Property Solutions
www.singlesourceproperty.com

Skyhill REO
www.skyhillreo.com

Strategic Asset Solutions
www.reosas.com

T

The National Groups
www.tngroups.com

Transcontinental Valuations
www.transconvalue.com/Home_
Page.php

T.R.E.O.
www.treonet.com

U

United States Real Estate Service
http://valuations.usres.com/
AGENT_LOGIN

USA Valuation Services
www.usavaluationservices.com

V

Valuation Partners
www.valuationpartners.com

Valuation Support Services
www.valuationsupportservices.
com

Vendor Resource Management
www.vrmco.com

W

Wells Fargo Home Mortgage
www.pasreo.com

Misc.

24 Asset Management Corporation
www.24amn.com

Buyer Information Sheet

SELLING AGENT:
PLEASE FILL OUT EVERY FIELD BELOW AND FAX OR EMAIL BACK TO OUR OFFICE

BUYER INFORMATION

Buyer #1(full **legal** name):_____
First   Middle   Last

Circle one: Single   Married – If legally married, spouse's full legal name:_____

Address: _____
Street Address   City   State   Zip
Email Address:_____
Home Phone:_____   Cell Phone:_____
Work Phone:_____   Fax Number:_____

Buyer #2(full **legal** name):_____
First   Middle   Last

Circle one   Single   Married – If married, spouse's full legal name:_____

Address (if different from above):_____
Street Address   City   State   Zip
Email Address:_____
Home Phone:_____   Cell Phone:_____
Work Phone:_____   Fax Number:_____

Address to be **SHOWN ON THE DEED** if different than the property address:

Address: _____
Street Address   City   State   Zip

LENDER INFORMATION

Name of Lending Institution:_____

Contact Person:_____   Email Address:_____

Lender's Address:_____
Street Address   City   State   Zip
Phone:_____   Fax:_____

BUYER'S AGENT INFORMATION

Agent Name:_____   Email Address:_____

Company Name:_____

_____

Cell Phone: _____   Cell Phone:_____
Fax:_____

MLS Fee?   YES   NO   If yes, amount of MLS fee? $_____

Sample HUD-1

B. Type of Loan

1. ☐ FHA	2. ☐ RHS	3. ☐ Conv. Unins.	4. ☐ VA	5. ☐ Conv. Ins.	

6. File Number:	7. Loan Number:	8. Mortgage Insurance Case Number:

C. Note: This form is furnished to give you a statement of actual settlement costs. Amounts paid to and by the settlement agent are shown. Items marked "(p.o.c.)" were paid outside the closing; they are shown here for informational purposes and are not included in the totals.

D. Name & Address of Borrower:	E. Name & Address of Seller:	F. Name & Address of Lender:

G. Property Location:	H. Settlement Agent:	I. Settlement Date:
	Place of Settlement:	

J. Summary of Borrower's Transaction

100. Gross Amount Due from Borrower	
101. Contract sales price	
102. Personal property	
103. Settlement charges to borrower (line 1400)	
104.	
105.	
Adjustment for items paid by seller in advance	
106. City/town taxes to	
107. County taxes to	
108. Assessments to	
109.	
110.	
111.	
112.	
120. Gross Amount Due from Borrower	
200. Amount Paid by or in Behalf of Borrower	
201. Deposit or earnest money	
202. Principal amount of new loan(s)	
203. Existing loan(s) taken subject to	
204.	
205.	
206.	
207.	
208.	
209.	
Adjustments for items unpaid by seller	
210. City/town taxes to	
211. County taxes to	
212. Assessments to	
213.	
214.	
215.	
216.	
217.	
218.	
219.	
220. Total Paid by/for Borrower	
300. Cash at Settlement from/to Borrower	
301. Gross amount due from borrower (line 120)	
302. Less amounts paid by/for borrower (line 220)	( )
303. Cash ☐ From ☐ To Borrower	

K. Summary of Seller's Transaction

400. Gross Amount Due to Seller	
401. Contract sales price	
402. Personal property	
403.	
404.	
405.	
Adjustment for items paid by seller in advance	
406. City/town taxes to	
407. County taxes to	
408. Assessments to	
409.	
410.	
411.	
412.	
420. Gross Amount Due to Seller	
500. Reductions in Amount Due to seller	
501. Excess deposit (see instructions)	
502. Settlement charges to seller (line 1400)	
503. Existing loan(s) taken subject to	
504. Payoff of first mortgage loan	
505. Payoff of second mortgage loan	
506.	
507.	
508.	
509.	
Adjustments for items unpaid by seller	
510. City/town taxes to	
511. County taxes to	
512. Assessments to	
513.	
514.	
515.	
516.	
517.	
518.	
519.	
520. Total Reduction Amount Due Seller	
600. Cash at Settlement to/from Seller	
601. Gross amount due to seller (line 420)	
602. Less reductions in amounts due seller (line 520)	( )
603. Cash ☐ To ☐ From Seller	

The Public Reporting Burden for this collection of information is estimated at 35 minutes per response for collecting, reviewing, and reporting the data. This agency may not collect this information, and you are not required to complete this form, unless it displays a currently valid OMB control number. No confidentiality is assured; this disclosure is mandatory. This is designed to provide the parties to a RESPA covered transaction with information during the settlement process.

L. Settlement Charges			
700. Total Real Estate Broker Fees		Paid From Borrower's Funds at Settlement	Paid From Seller's Funds at Settlement
Division of commission (line 700) as follows :			
701. $ to			
702. $ to			
703. Commission paid at settlement			
704.			
800. Items Payable in Connection with Loan			
801. Our origination charge	$ (from GFE #1)		
802. Your credit or charge (points) for the specific interest rate chosen	$ (from GFE #2)		
803. Your adjusted origination charges	(from GFE #A)		
804. Appraisal fee to	(from GFE #3)		
805. Credit report to	(from GFE #3)		
806. Tax service to	(from GFE #3)		
807. Flood certification to	(from GFE #3)		
808.			
809.			
810.			
811.			
900. Items Required by Lender to be Paid in Advance			
901. Daily interest charges from to @ $ /day	(from GFE #10)		
902. Mortgage insurance premium for months to	(from GFE #3)		
903. Homeowner's insurance for years to	(from GFE #11)		
904.			
1000. Reserves Deposited with Lender			
1001. Initial deposit for your escrow account	(from GFE #9)		
1002. Homeowner's insurance months @ $ per month $			
1003. Mortgage insurance months @ $ per month $			
1004. Property Taxes months @ $ per month $			
1005. months @ $ per month $			
1006. months @ $ per month $			
1007. Aggregate Adjustment -$			
1100. Title Charges			
1101. Title services and lender's title insurance	(from GFE #4)		
1102. Settlement or closing fee	$		
1103. Owner's title insurance	(from GFE #5)		
1104. Lender's title insurance	$		
1105. Lender's title policy limit $			
1106. Owner's title policy limit $			
1107. Agent's portion of the total title insurance premium to	$		
1108. Underwriter's portion of the total title insurance premium to	$		
1109.			
1110.			
1111.			
1200. Government Recording and Transfer Charges			
1201. Government recording charges	(from GFE #7)		
1202. Deed $ Mortgage $ Release $			
1203. Transfer taxes	(from GFE #8)		
1204. City/County tax/stamps Deed $ Mortgage $			
1205. State tax/stamps Deed $ Mortgage $			
1206.			
1300. Additional Settlement Charges			
1301. Required services that you can shop for	(from GFE #6)		
1302. $			
1303. $			
1304.			
1305.			
1400. Total Settlement Charges (enter on lines 103, Section J and 502, Section K)			

Comparison of Good Faith Estimate (GFE) and HUD-1 Charrges		Good Faith Estimate	HUD-1
Charges That Cannot Increase	HUD-1 Line Number		
Our origination charge	# 801		
Your credit or charge (points) for the specific interest rate chosen	# 802		
Your adjusted origination charges	# 803		
Transfer taxes	# 1203		

Charges That In Total Cannot Increase More Than 10%		Good Faith Estimate	HUD-1
Government recording charges	# 1201		
	#		
	#		
	#		
	#		
	#		
	#		
	#		
	Total		
	Increase between GFE and HUD-1 Charges	$ or %	

Charges That Can Change		Good Faith Estimate	HUD-1
Initial deposit for your escrow account	# 1001		
Daily interest charges $ /day	# 901		
Homeowner's insurance	# 903		
	#		
	#		
	#		

Loan Terms

Your initial loan amount is	$
Your loan term is	years
Your initial interest rate is	%
Your initial monthly amount owed for principal, interest, and any mortgage insurance is	$ includes ☐ Principal ☐ Interest ☐ Mortgage Insurance
Can your interest rate rise?	☐ No ☐ Yes, it can rise to a maximum of %. The first change will be on and can change again every after . Every change date, your interest rate can increase or decrease by %. Over the life of the loan, your interest rate is guaranteed to never be **lower** than % or **higher** than %.
Even if you make payments on time, can your loan balance rise?	☐ No ☐ Yes, it can rise to a maximum of $
Even if you make payments on time, can your monthly amount owed for principal, interest, and mortgage insurance rise?	☐ No ☐ Yes, the first increase can be on and the monthly amount owed can rise to $. The maximum it can ever rise to is $
Does your loan have a prepayment penalty?	☐ No ☐ Yes, your maximum prepayment penalty is $
Does your loan have a balloon payment?	☐ No ☐ Yes, you have a balloon payment of $ due in years on
Total monthly amount owed including escrow account payments	☐ You do not have a monthly escrow payment for items, such as property taxes and homeowner's insurance. You must pay these items directly yourself. ☐ You have an additional monthly escrow payment of $ that results in a total initial monthly amount owed of $. This includes principal, interest, any mortagage insurance and any items checked below: ☐ Property taxes ☐ Homeowner's insurance ☐ Flood insurance ☐ ☐

Note: If you have any questions about the Settlement Charges and Loan Terms listed on this form, please contact your lender.

Reimbursement Checklist

Please ensure all reimbursements are submitted accordingly:				
Items submitted for reimbursement	Yes	No	Not Required	NOTES
Rekey	☐	☐	☐	
Electric	☐	☐	☐	
Water	☐	☐	☐	
Pool-initial	☐	☐	☐	
Pool-periodic	☐	☐	☐	
Violations (code)	☐	☐	☐	
Violations (water)	☐	☐	☐	
HVAC Assessment	☐	☐	☐	
Eviction Move Outs	☐	☐	☐	
Carpet Cleaning	☐	☐	☐	
Emergency Repairs	☐	☐	☐	
Emergency Repairs	☐	☐	☐	
Other:	☐	☐	☐	
Other:	☐	☐	☐	
Date water turned off:				
Date electric turned off:				
Closing date:				

Note: Last three (3) items require date to be entered.

After submitting each reimbursement, both accounting clerk and closing coordinator must sign below, verifying that ALL reimbursements have been submitted on the date specified above.

X _____   X _____

Accounting Clerk   Closing Coordinator

The Multiple Offer Monster (MOM) Email

REO ID:_____   DATE:_____

Dear Agents,

We have received multiple offers on this property. Please open the attached Multiple Offer Notification and Acknowledgment form. Please submit your customers' highest and best offer along with the attached form completed and signed. The deadline to submit your highest and best offer is (insert date and time).

Please send the signed multiple offer form by email to: OFFERS@ XYZREALTY.COM or simply reply to this message. If you prefer, you can fax us the form to 1-XXX-XXX-XXXX.

You do not need to submit all pages of the offer. Simply note any changes in your original offer, you may write those changes in your email or on the multiple offer form. However, we must receive the signed multiple offer form by the deadline stated above.

Thank you,

Xyz
REO Agent

Clean Copy Instructions

REO ID:_____   DATE:_____

To: Transaction Coordinator
RE: Preparing the Clean Copy for Bank Signature

As you prepare the Clean Copy, pay particular attention to details. All items in the bank's platform offer screen must match the winning offer Clean Copy in order for it to be submitted into the bank.

Include the following items when submitting the offer package to XYZ, REO Listing Agent:

1. Bank's cover page: Make sure all contact information is filled out accurately and entirely for lender, selling agent, and buyer's title company. It is imperative that this information is accurate and not left blank. In order for all parties to have seamless communication at all times, the information must be readily available.

2. State or local promulgated contract: Make sure all pages are initialed and signed where indicated.

3. Bank addendum: Ensure that there are no cross outs, changes, additional marks in any of the pages of the bank's addendum. Ensure that each page of the bank's addendum is initialed, and that all signatures are present.

4. Proof of the earnest money deposit (EMD): Wire is preferred, but if unable to wire, a copy of the check will suffice.

5. Lead-based paint disclosure: If home was built prior to 1978, insert the lead-based paint disclosure signed by the buyer.

6. Owner occupied certifications (OOC): Insert the OOC signed by selling agent and buyer.

7. Prequalification letter or proof of funds: A prequalification letter from buyers lender and/or proof of funds (if cash buyer) is required.

8. One PDF: Compile all files into one PDF, and email to XYZ, REO Listing Agent. If any additions are made in Adobe PDF, then please fax the document to our e-fax and combine into one file less than 2MB. Send the file to XYZ, REO Listing Agent using the proper naming convention in the subject line of the email (Ex-REO A1234_Clean Copy).

Please double check the accuracy of all eight steps above prior to emailing the Clean Copy.

Sample Listing Letter

REO ID:_____   DATE:_____

05/13/2012
MARY J
XYZ BROKERAGE COMPANY
REO No: A123456

Dear MARY J:
BANK, also known as "Seller," grants you sole right to sell this property during the listing period below subject to the terms and conditions of the current and revised BANK Master Listing Agreement (MLA).

Listed Property:

Address:	1234 MAIN STREET
	ANYTOWN, USA 123456
County:	
Type of Property:	Single Family Home
REO ID:	A123456
Legal Folio Number:	1234567897651
BANK Internal Loan Number:	987654321

Listing Price, Terms, and Conditions

Listing Price:	$155,500.00
List Start Date:	05/13/2012
List End Date:	08/12/2012
Conditions:	Purchase of the property will be by cash at closing or on terms acceptable to the seller.

Commission and Bonus:

Total Commission:	6.00%
Listing	3.00%
Selling	3.00%
Minimum:	$2,000.00

MLS Listing Instructions:

- Enter the listing in your local MLS and retain a copy of the listing in your files. Email within 24 hours this listing letter signed with your signature, a copy of the MLS listing, and a copy of the pictures combined in one PDF document to your asset manager.
- Enter the MLS ID into BANK PLATFORM if available, otherwise note the comment section of the BANK PLATFORM.
- If permitted by your MLS, insert the following language in your listing:
  - XYZ financing available
  - Buy this property for as little as xyz down

Servicing Lender:

Contact:	BROKER CONTACT
Lender Firm:	XYZ BANK SERVICER
Address:	12333 MAIN STREET
	ANYTOWN, USA

Phone Number:	800-XXX-XXXX

Foreclosure Date:	10/19/2011
Lender Loan Number:	12345678

Please sign and return to BANK
REO Agent/Broker signature:

ATTN: ASSET MANAGER
          BANK

Monthly Marketing Report (MMR) Template

REO ID: XX
PROPERTY ADDRESS: XX
XX DAYS FROM LISTING

Quick Summary

There are XX properties actively for sale in the same building (XX) as subject (ranging from XX). Moreover, there are XX other REO comparable listings within one mile of subject property (see addendum A). Of the XX active listings, XX are REOs and XX are short sales. Subject property has been listed for XX days and has difficulty selling because there are short sales in the same building listed for much less than the subject property.

The current listing price is $XX and in our opinion is over-priced relative to comparable as shown below:

Active Listings

Address	List Price	Sq. Feet Differential	Days on Market	REO
1234 MAIN STREET	$70,000	83 SQ FT LARGER THAN SUBJECT	104	Y
1235 MAIN STREET	$79,000	83 SQ FT LARGER THAN SUBJECT	170	N
1236 MAIN STREET	$85,000	83 SQ FT LARGER THAN SUBJECT	443	Y

Closed Sales

Address	Sales Price	Sq. Feet Differential	Closing Date
1237 MAIN STREET	$65,000	90 SQ FT SMALLER THAN SUBJECT	01/28/2012
1238 MAIN STREET	$94,000	58 SQ FT SMALLER THAN SUBJECT	06/15/2012
1239 MAIN STREET	$97,000	58 SQ FT SMALLER THAN SUBJECT	04/23/2012

Note: Closed COMP #1 and #3 were short sales. Closed COMP #2 was an REO.

FEEDBACK FROM BUYERS AND/OR AGENTS

MARKET CONDITIONS IMPACTING PROPERTY VALUE

RECOMMENDATION

Due to competition from other condominiums within a one mile radius of subject, we have only received XX showing requests within the last XX days (see addendum B).

Our initial BPO recommended an "as is" list price for $XX. Current List price is $XX. We strongly recommend reducing the list price by XX% to $XX to successfully sell subject property in the next sixty days.

BPO Recommended List Price	$99,900
Current Listed Price	$109,450
Suggested Revised List Price	**$98,900**

Addendum A: Showing Requests in the last XX Days:

From	Subject	Received	Size
CRYING BROKERAGE	Showing at 1233 MAIN STREET	Tue 7/13	3 KB
LUKEWARM BROKERAGE CO.	Showing at 1233 MAIN STREET	Sun 7/11	3 KB
SO-SO BROKERAGE CO.	Showing at 1233 MAIN STREET	7/9/2010	3 KB
DYING BROKERAGE CO.	Showing at 1233 MAIN STREET	7/9/2010	3 KB

Closing Checklist

Week 1: Executed Contract

Introductory

Email/Contact Info

Condo Application

Estoppel Ordered

Lender Submitted File

CT/Quit Claim Deed

Week 2

Condo Interview/Approval

Inspection Completed/As-Is

Lien Search

Title Clear on Property/Lien

Estoppel Received

Appraisal Completed (If Applied)

Estoppel Paid

Week 3

Follow up with Lender/Financing

Follow up with Estoppel

Follow up with CT

Loan Approval

Clear to Close

Call Buyer's Side of Co.

Prepare HUD

Week 4: To Close

Add Re-Key

Submit HUD to Bank

HUD Approved by Bank

HUD Approved by Lender

Final HUD & Waiver Executed

Real Estate Commission Received

Thank You Call

Thank You Email

Daily

Update Calendar

Follow up with Callers

Check Bank Platform Comments

ABC—ALWAYS BE CLOSING

Extensions/Amendments

Updates

Trip Notes

REO ID #

BUYER:

ADD:

Sample BPO Form

Residential Broker Price Opinion

This BPO is the ☐ Initial ☐ 2nd Opinion ☐ Updated ☐ Exterior Only DATE _____

CLIENT AND GENERAL INFO

PROPERTY ADDRESS:			
REO #:		Bank:	
Most Recent Listing History	From	To	Last Listed at $

GENERAL MARKET CONDITIONS

Current market condition:	☐ Depressed	☐ Slow	☐ Stable	☐ Improving	☐ Excellent

There is a ☐ Normal supply ☐ oversupply ☐ shortage of comparable listings in the neighborhood

Approximate number of comparable units for sale in neighborhood: _____

No. of competing listings in neighborhood that are REO or Corporate owned: _____

SUBJECT PROPERTY

Normal marketing time in the area is:	days.				
Marketability of subject property is	☐ excellent	☐ good	☐ fair	☐ poor.	
Unit Type:	☐ House	☐ Condo	☐ Townhouse	☐ Multi-family (#. of units)	☐ Modular

Range of values in the neighborhood is $ _____ to $ _____

Are all types of financing available for the property? ☐ Yes ☐ No If no, explain _____

Has the property been on the market in the last 12 months? ☐ Yes ☐ No If yes, $ _____

If condo or other association exists: Fee $ _____ ☐monthly ☐ annually Current? ☐ Yes ☐ No Fee delinquent? $ _____

Overall Property Condition: Excellent Good	Fair	Poor
Are there any items that require IMMEDIATE attention/action?	Yes	No
Title/Legal Issues? Yes No		
Do any environmental issues affect the value of the property?	Yes	No
If yes to any of the above, please explain:		

The fee includes: ☐ Insurance ☐ Landscape ☐ Pool ☐ Tennis Other _____

Association Contact: Name: _____ Phone No.: _____

COMPETITIVE CLOSED SALES

ITEM	SUBJECT			COMPARABLE NO. 1				COMPARABLE NO. 2				COMPARABLE NO. 3			
Address															
Proximity to Subj.															
Current Price $															
List Date /DOM															
Lot Size															
Room Count	Total	Bdms	Baths	Total	Bdms	Baths		Total	Bdms	Baths		Total	Bdms	Baths	
Room Count															
Gross Living Area	Sq. Ft.			Sq. Ft.				Sq. Ft.				Sq. Ft.			

COMMENTS: *Please describe the condition of the comparables.*	
COMP #1:	
COMP #2:	
COMP #3:	

COMPETITIVE ACTIVE LISTINGS

ITEM	SUBJECT			COMPARABLE NO. 1				COMPARABLE NO. 2				COMPARABLE NO. 3			
Address															
Proximity to Subj.															
Sales Price $															
Date of Sale /DOM															
Lot Size															
Room Count	Total	Bdms	Baths	Total	Bdms	Baths		Total	Bdms	Baths		Total	Bdms	Baths	
Room Count															
Gross Living Area	Sq. Ft.			Sq. Ft.				Sq. Ft.				Sq. Ft.			

COMMENTS: *Please describe the condition of the comparables.*
COMP #1:
COMP #2:

ESTIMATED REPAIRS NOTED

Gross Estimated Closing Costs	
Gross Amount of Repairs Needed	
List of Repairs (if necessary)	
Continued.....	

Itemize ALL repairs needed to bring property from its present "as is" condition to marketable condition for the neighborhood.

☐ _____ $ _____   ☐ _____ $ _____
☐ _____ $ _____   ☐ _____ $ _____
☐ _____ $ _____   ☐ _____ $ _____
☐ _____ $ _____   ☐ _____ $ _____
☐ _____ $ _____   ☐ _____ $ _____

THE MARKET VALUE (must fall within the indicated value of the sales used above.)

THE VALUE FOR THE SUBJECT PROPERTY BASED ON 90 DAYS LIST TO CONTRACT IS:

	Market Value	Suggested List Price	Available Financing	Broker Recommends Marketing Either	
As Is	$	$	Conv ☐ FHA/VA ☐ Other ☐	As Is ☐	OR
Complete Repairs	$	$	Estimate of Repairs: $	Repairs ☐	

THE MARKETING STRATEGY must fall within the indicated value of the sales used above.

☐ As-is ☐ Repaired   Most Likely Buyer: ☐ Owner occupant ☐ Investor

COMMENTS (including special concerns like apparent structural issues, encroachments, easements, water rights, propane, hazardous waste, flood zone, etc.) Attach addendum if additional space is needed. Describe your marketing strategy and reasons for As Is/As Repaired recommendations)

_____
_____
_____
_____
_____

_____   _____
REO Agent's Signature   Date

RESIDENTIAL BROKER PRICE OPINION
ADDENDUM

Supplementary Info:

1. Describe the property and its condition:

2. Describe the location of the property, include legal description if available:

3. Describe the current and its projected FUTURE use of the property:

Signature: _____   Date: _____

PHOTO ADDENDUM	
REO #	Asset Manager:
Address:	
Copy/paste your digital photos on this form, or insert picture from file	

90-Day Action Plan

DAYS 1–30 (PREPARE AND PLAN)
Week One:

- Obtain all your REO certifications. Research the REO listing agents in your area. Go to their websites. What certifications do they have? You must have these certifications at minimum.
- Create your polished résumé (see Chapter 2) including the ten key tools. See appendix O for a sample résumé.
- Create the polished proposal (see Chapter 2). Print 50 portfolios, as these are necessary for you to obtain your first account.
- Do mock BPO on your own house and family and friends' houses. Offer a free valuation. Watch how fast you will gain experience.
- Use the "Reach-Around Method" from Chapter 2 and join a real estate office that is a "direct" listing agent. Offer to work for free. Ask to hang your real estate license with the company. Tell them that you have what it takes, that you will do it for free, and that you just need a couple of weeks to prove that you are the agent they have been looking for. Be the first one in the office and the last one to leave.
- Gain experience. Handle calls, go to properties, and look at different REO listings. Use the information in this book and the hands-on experience in the field to see what type of results that direct listing office is producing and how you can improve performance.

Week Two:

- Start networking. Go to networking events, REO conventions, and local board meetings. Start spreading the word that you work with a direct REO listing office. Even though you may not have any listings, focus on the fact that you are the best REO listing agent on the market. It will come. It's not a matter of "if" but "when." Keep in the back of your mind, preparation + plug = first bank contract.

- Print out business cards, show houses, follow listing agents with the office, and absorb as much information as you can. Learn. Learn. Learn.
- Ask for one; just one listing. Even if you don't make commission, you want to learn. Once you get it, use our systems to impress everyone. Make them believe in you.
- Implement the REO Lunch Method. Find "aged" REO properties that have been on the market for greater than 90 days. Identify who the asset manager is. Contact the asset manager (remember MOB: motivation over business) and tell them that you work as a direct listing agent for XYZ and that you would like to do a FREE second opinion BPO. Continue doing this-you will see that the behavior is reciprocated by the asset manager giving you a listing.
- Find a mentor who has done it. Offer them to give you some pointers. Take them out to lunch. Tell them once you get rolling and knee deep in the business you will hire them on consulting basis. However if you have the money, invest it with your mentor. It's worth every penny.

Week Three:

- Start building your buyer network. Order 100 yard signs, wire stands (1 color, double sided) and place them out in your farm area on Friday afternoon–Sunday evening. Use yard signs combined with landing pages and drip campaigns to build a large database; the larger your network, the more value you will add to the banks.
- Start your REO Bus Tour (see Chapter 2). Gather investors and homebuyers to go on a bus tour with you to visit REO properties for sale. Take them to the property that you are doing a second opinion BPO on. You shouldn't be surprised if a passenger

says, "Wow, I would buy that right now." It works. Just make sure your co-op partner is pre-qualifying all the leads.

Week Four:

- Network. Network. Network. Go to all REO conventions. Meet asset managers.
- Use the REO FARM play (see Chapter 2) when you get in front of asset managers.
- Listen first. Draw out their motivation. What are they motivated to find from a listing agent. What are they lacking? What problems are they having in their local market? Build their motivation before getting into business. Remember, motivation before business (MOB).
- Show them that you have what it takes to solve their problems, that you know how to stop the bleeding, and that you are different than the typical listing agent. It's important to show them, not tell them. Give them an example, a story, a situation. Make them believe that what you have done before, you can do for them.
- At the end of your fourth week, you should know all the items that are required of a listing agent. Now it's time to apply.

DAYS 31–60 (PERSEVERE)
Week Five:

- Apply. Apply Apply. Apply everywhere (see Appendix B).
- Spend time with the application questions. Don't just respond the same for each application. Each bank is different. Each has different needs. Research their needs before completing the application.
- Think through each response, re-read chapter two, and then complete the responses.
- If you are applying online, be sure to include a print-out of your application along with your polished résumé, a polished proposal, and mail it to the bank that you are applying to.

Week Six:

- Focus on the one. Just one asset manager, one bank, or one institution.
- Go through your progress from weeks one through five. Which asset manager responded best to your REO FARM play? Which was the most motivated? Which do you have the most likely chance of getting in with?
- Once you choose the one you will most likely have success with, follow through. Go back to the REO Lunch Method. Bring out their motivation again and show them that you can solve their problems by using the REO Lunch Method and doing FREE BPOs. You can even find an aged property that they are managing that has been listed for more than 90 days. Either way, give them a free lunch and watch how they reciprocate with a listing!
- Ask for the business. Tell them about your guarantee (from your résumé). Remember, they have nothing to lose.

Week Seven:

- Re-read Chapter 5 and then perfect the second opinion BPO. You have to show your asset manager that you know what it takes to get the property sold.

Week Eight:

- Submit your second opinion BPO, and follow up with your asset manager using Double D's (chapter 9). Remind them about your large buyer network. Let them know that you took home buyers on a bus tour. Show them the pictures. Let them know the feedback from the buyers. Show them that you know what it takes to get the property sold.

DAYS 61–90 (CLOSE)
Week Nine:

- Send a hand-written thank you card to the asset manager you are targeting. Thank them for allowing you to do a second opinion BPO.

- Follow through with your proposed Magnet Marketing Plan (Chapter 7) for that property.
- Now strike when the iron is hot. Ask for the listing. Ask them to reassign the listing you did a second opinion BPO on. Show the asset manager that you can execute. Ask them for the opportunity and then prove it.

Week Ten:

- Re-read Chapters 4–9 from this book.
- Master the 6 steps of the REO cycle and execute. You need to know exactly what the banks are looking for. Remember, banks will test you out on one. You have one shot to shine.

Week Eleven:

- Take the re-assigned property from "active" to "pending sale" on the MLS by the end of the week by sending the reassigned REO to your large buyers list. Implement the Magnet Marketing Plan.
- Follow up with Double D's and manage the title company and lender (if any) until the transaction closes.
- Show off your performance to the asset manager and let them know that you have what it takes and that you are dedicated to making sure that they meet their own goals.
- Remind them again about your Magnet Marketing Plan and go back to the REO Lunch Method. The asset manager has nothing to lose by you performing a second opinion BPO. In fact, if you are successful with the first one, you may end up with a new assignment without having to implement the REO Lunch Method again.

Week Twelve:

- Follow up with your asset manager and show them that you are hungry and ready for more. Highlight your performance by showcasing your stats (the 8 successful measurement tools).
- Once you have successfully closed 10 REOs (90/10 Rule) transition into the REO Bootstrap Model and begin forming your dream team.

- Grow your business. Re-read this entire book to learn how to maximize your income using the REO Bootstrap Model and prepare to expand to the REO Plus Model.

Congratulations!

Market Adjustments and Repair Costs

Market Adjustments Compared to Subject Property

Square Footage Adjustment	$50/sq. ft (Very Good)
	$30/sq. ft (Average)
	$40/sq. ft (Good)
	$25/sq. ft (Poor)
One Extra Bedroom	$1100–$ 2400
One Extra Half Bathrom	$2400–$ 3500
One Extra Full Bathroom	$3300–$ 4400
Additional Extra Rooms (Unfinished)	$10–$ 20/sq.ft.
One Incomplete Basement	$10–$ 15/sq. ft.
One Complete Basement	$20–$ 25/sq. ft.
One Single Garage	$2400–$3300
One Double Garage	$4400–$7000
One Single Carport	$1650–$2400
One Double Carport	$2400–$3300
Centrally Heated vs. Non Centrally Heated	$2400–$ 3300
Central A/C Systm vs. Non Central A/C System	$3300–$ 4400
Major Electric Upgrading	$2,000

Home Equipment	
One Range (Free Standing)	$220
One Built-in Range	$440
One Single Oven	$300
One Trash Compactor	$220
One Disposal	$110
Central Vacuum System	$900
Security Management System	$1,100
Intercom Facility	$660
Sprinkler Management System	$2,200

Special Feature	
Fireplace (Pre-Fab)	$2,200–$3,300
Fireplace (Masonry)	$3,300–$4,400
Fence (Wooden)	$2,200–$ 3,300
Fence (Chain Linked)	$1,100–$ 2,200
One Wet Bar	$550–$ 800
One Swimming Pool	$10,000
Major Refinished Pool	$2,500
One Pool Pump	$660
Outbuldings or Barns	$10–$ 15 /sq. ft.
One Asphalt Shingle	$200/sq.ft.

Gravel and Tar	$250/sq.ft.
Paint/Pressure Clean/Roof	$3,300
Repair of Roof	$10,000
Yard/Land Carpeting	$500
Presure Clean/Exterior Paint	$1.00/sq. ft.
Replacement of Septic	$4,500
One Well	$4,600
Concrete Driveway	$8/sq. ft.
Fence	$5,000
Replacement of Windows	$300 each
Exterior Replacement of Doors	$400 each
Interior Replacement of Doors	$155 each
Replacement of Sliding Glass Doors	$850 each
Drywall	$27.00/4 vertical ft.
Ceiling/Interior Paint	$1.5/sq. ft.
Appliances	$600
Interior and Exterior AC	$3,500

Floor Coverings	Total Sq. Foot / $9 = sq. yard
Carpet	.75 × adj. sq. Ft
Linoleum	$15.00/sq. yd.
Tile	$4.50/sq. yd

Kitchen Cabinets Replacements	$190/lineal ft.
Counter	$200/lineal ft.
Sink	$200 each
Kitchen Faucet	$150 each
Re-Caulk	$2.00 sq. ft.
Replacement of Toilet	$220 each
Replacement of Toilet Seat	$30 each
Flapper and Flush Valve of Toilet	$35 each
Retile Shower (Standard)	$1,200 each
Replacement of Bathtub (including removal)	$2000 each
Replacement of Showerhead	$40 each
Disposal	$110 each
Refrigerator (Used)	$440 each
Dishwahser/Stove (Used)	$300 each
Replacement of Hot Water Heater	$450 each

Bathrooms	
Replacement of Tub	$800 each
Replacement of Sink	$300 each
Replacement of Toilet	$200 each
Replacement of Tile (Walk-in Shower)	$4.15/sq. ft.
Porcelain Tiles	$4.8/sq. ft.
Dumpsters (20 Yard)	$400

Termite Treatment (Ground)	$500 est.
Termite Treatment	$750–$ 1600
Miscellaneous Repair of A/C	$300
One Wall Plate	$30
One Smoke Alarm Device	$60
One Upgrade of Electrical Outlet to GFI	$60
Heating, Ventilation, Air Condition with HVAC	$120/hour
Forced Air Furnace—New (Without Duct Work)	$2,500
Maintenance of Landscape (Edge, trim, mow, blow) 5,000 sq. yd.	$585

Agent Sign-Off Sheet

REO ID:
PROPERTY ADDRESS:
WORK ORDER NUMBER:

Cleaning—Initial (Completed __/___/____):

Entry Way (Circle deficiencies, if any)
    Floor swept and mopped
    Cobwebs removed from corners and ceilings
    Baseboards and walls wiped down
    Light fixtures, switch and outlet covers are wiped down
    Storm door glass is cleaned

Living Room (Circle deficiencies, if any)
    Floor swept and mopped
    Carpet vacuumed (if any)
    Cobwebs removed from corners and ceilings
    Baseboards and walls wiped down
    Light fixtures, switch and outlet covers are wiped down
    Windows are clean (no streaks)
    Window sills are wiped off
    Door frames are free of dust
    Fireplace is cleaned out (if any)
    Ceiling fan blades are clean

Family Room (Circle deficiencies, if any)
    Floor swept and mopped
    Carpet vacuumed (if any)
    Cobwebs removed from corners and ceilings

Baseboards and walls wiped down
Light fixtures, switch and outlet covers are wiped down
Windows are clean (no streaks)
Window sills are wiped off
Door frames are free of dust
Fireplace is cleaned out (if any)
Ceiling fan blades are clean

Master Bedroom (Circle deficiencies, if any)
Floor swept and mopped
Carpet vacuumed (if any)
Cobwebs removed from corners and ceilings
Baseboards and walls wiped down
Light fixtures, switch and outlet covers are wiped down
Windows are clean (no streaks)
Window sills are wiped off
Door frames are free of dust
Fireplace is cleaned out (if any)
Ceiling fan blades are clean

Other Bedrooms: _____ (Circle deficiencies, if any)
Floor swept and mopped
Carpet vacuumed (if any)
Cobwebs removed from corners and ceilings
Baseboards and walls wiped down
Light fixtures, switch and outlet covers are wiped down
Windows are clean (no streaks)
Window sills are wiped off
Door frames are free of dust
Fireplace is cleaned out (if any)
Ceiling fan blades are clean

Kitchen (Circle deficiencies, if any)
Sink is cleaned
Stove and oven are cleaned both inside and out

Microwave is cleaned both inside and out (if any)

Dishwasher is cleaned both inside and out

Refrigerator is cleaned both inside and out

Floor is swept and mopped

Windows are cleaned (no streaks)

Window sills are wiped off

Counters are clean (no grease)

Cobwebs are removed from corners and ceiling

Baseboards and walls are wiped down

Light fixtures, switch and outlet covers are wiped down

Ceiling fan blades are clean

Porch–Enclosed (Circle deficiencies, if any)

Floor swept and mopped

Cobwebs removed from corners and ceilings

Baseboards and walls wiped down

Light fixtures, switch and outlet covers are wiped down

Windows are clean (no streaks)

Window sills are wiped off

Door frames are free of dust

Ceiling fan blades are clean

Master Bathroom (Circle deficiencies, if any)

Floor swept and mopped

Cobwebs removed from corners and ceilings

Baseboards and walls wiped down

Light fixtures, switch and outlet covers are wiped down

Windows are clean (no streaks)

Window sills are wiped off

Door frames are free of dust

Sinks and faucets are clean

Toilet is clean

Tub and shower are clean

Surrounding area is clean and free of dust

Mirrors, cabinets, drawers, and shelves are clean

*Other Bathroom*_____ *(Circle deficiencies, if any)*

    Floor swept and mopped

    Cobwebs removed from corners and ceilings

    Baseboards and walls wiped down

    Light fixtures, switch and outlet covers are wiped down

    Windows are clean (no streaks)

    Window sills are wiped off

    Door frames are free of dust

    Sinks and faucets are clean

    Toilet is clean

    Tub and shower are clean

    Surrounding area is clean and free of dust

    Mirrors, cabinets, drawers, and shelves are clean

Landscaping (Circle deficiencies, if any)

    Flower beds are free of debris

    Grass is cut

    Debris removed from driveway and yard

    Weeds are trimmed around foundation and fence line

    Weeds are removed from driveway and yard

    Walkways, driveways, sidewalks, and yard are edged

    Shrubs are trimmed below window sill

Misc. (Circle deficiencies, if any)

    Handrails are present (if any)

    Exposed wires are capped

    Windows are boarded if cracked

    Broken glass is swept and noted

    Battery operated smoke detectors are installed

    Air fresheners are present

Sample Résumé

COMPANY LOGO

YOUR OFFICE ADDRESS
Lic. # SA123456 Cell: XXX-XXX-XXXX
Office: XXX-XXX-XXXX
jane@xyzrealty.com www.xyzrealty.com

JANE DOE, ABR, CRS, GRI

OUR MISSION: To assist homeowners in purchasing affordable homes in XYZ AREA by partnering with neighborhood stabilization vendors.

RESOURCES

- E&O Insurance with $1,000,000.00 in coverage.
- General Liability Insurance with $2,000.000.00 in coverage.
- Workers compensation with $1,000,000 in coverage.
- $1 Million Dollars in liquid assets available, with $15,000 allocated initially to each property.
- Capable of Managing and Marketing 300+ REO Properties.
- In-House Tracking Technology. (Calls Returned in 1 Hour, Emails Answered in 1 Hour. That Is Our Guarantee).
- Good Neighbor Implementation
- In House i-Phone and Android Marketing Applications
- Quick Response Barcode implementation

OUR TEAM

- Three Offices Servicing XYZ
- 500 Licensed Agents
- Two Full-Time Field Inspectors
- Full-Time REO Branch Manager
- Full-Time Closing Coordinator
- Full-Time Transaction Coordinator
- Full-Time Marketing Coordinator
- Full-Time Accountant Clerk
- Full-Time In-House Counsel
- Full-Time BPO Agent and Appraiser
- Full-Time AMC (Asset Management Coordinator)

Logo of Platform vendors

<u>OUR EXPERIENCE</u>

Full Service REO Broker in XYZ with over 10 years of real estate experience, from occupancy check, cash for keys, BPOs, MMRs, repair bids, maintaining utilities, listings, working with servicers, sellers title, post closings, and reimbursements.

- ○ Closed over $100 Million Dollars in Volume in 2010.
- ○ Over 360 transactions servicing the following clients:
- ○ XYZ BANK Direct, ABC OUTSOURCER, ETC.
  LIST ALL DIRECT AND OUTSOURCER ACCOUNTS YOU
  OR YOUR BROKER HAVE DEALT WITH.

**Logo of
Affiliations**

<u>Certifications, Education, Affiliations and Platforms</u>

- ○ "A" Rating with the XYZ Bureau.
- ○ Member of XYZ Realtor® Association & National Association of Realtors®
- ○ Certified XYZ Professional.
- ○ Member of the XYZ Minority Council. (IF APPLICABLE)
- ○ <u>Platforms:</u> Equator, Res.Net, LPS, Home Tracker, Home Steps Connect, VRMS. A full list is available upon request.
- ○ <u>Education:</u> LIST ALL DEGREES, DESIGNATIONS, ACCREDITATIONS (REOS)

XYZ Realty is a Proud Supporter of XYZ CENTER for Financial Stability.

**Logo of
Charity**

Sample OCR Report

OCR REPORT DUE WITHIN <u>24 HRS</u> OF NEW BPO ORDER. PICTURE OF OCCUPANCY OPTIONS LETTER ATTACHED TO DOOR MUST BE INCLUDED IN PDF OR JPEG FORMAT ONLY.

REO#: _____
PROPERTY ADDRESS: _____
DATE OF INSPECTION: _____

Occupant Info Questions	Occupant Info Answers
1. Property Type (single family, condo, townhouse, villa, duplex, triplex, quadplex, manufactured housing)?	
2. Number of Units (i.e. residential=1 unit, duplex=2 units, triplex=3 units, etc.)	
3. Number of illegal units (e.g. efficiencies)	
4. What is Occupant Status (owner, tenant, unknown occupied, vacant)?	
5. If Occupied, all occupant Names (husband, wife, kids, etc)?	Occupant 1: Occupant 2:
6. If Tenants, are tenants uncooperative (yes or no)?	
7. If Tenants, are they part of Public Housing Voucher Program (e.g. Section 8)?	
8. If Tenants, do they have children under age 6?	
9. If Tenants, are they physically or mentally ill?	
10. If Tenants, do they have a written lease?	
11. If Tenants have lease, lease type?	
12. If Tenants have lease, lease start date?	
13. Date Occupant Options Letter was posted.	
14. If vacant, how did you determine? (Looked through window and no furniture/items present, neighbors'verified vacancy, utilities off, etc.)	
15. If condo, unit number?	
16. If condo, Gated security?	
17. If condo, CT required?	
18. Does property require any special certificates?	
19. If association present, name and phone number of management company	Name: Phone Number:
20. If vehicles present on property, license plate numbers	Vehicle 1: Vehicle 2:
MISC. COMMENTS: (hazardous conditions, emergency liability issues, etc.)	

Condominium Estoppel Sheet

Please complete the following information

DATE:
NAME:
PHONE:
FAX:
EMAIL ADDRESS:
PROPERTY ADDRESS & UNIT NUMBER:

1. MAINTENANCE AMOUNT? $_____

2. PAYMENT INTERVALS: (CIRCLE ONE) ANNUALLY / QUARTERLY / MONTHLY

3. THROUGH WHAT DATE IS MAINTENANCE PAID? _____. 20____

4. THROUGH WHAT DATE IS THIS LETTER GOOD? _____. 20____

5. ACCRUED LATE FEES DUE, IF ANY $_____

   [Late **if** received **after** ___ days after due date]

6. FULL AMOUNT NOW DUE (ATTACH BREAKDOWN & W-9 FORM): $_____

7. IS WATER INCLUDED IN MAINTENANCE?   (CIRCLE ONE)   YES NO

8. ARE ANY SPECIAL ASSESSMENT DUE: (CIRCLE ONE)   YES NO

   If yes, when was the assessment passed?
   Total amount to pay in full? $_____

9. IS WRITTEN CONDO APPROVAL REQUIRED? (CIRCLE ONE)   YES NO

10. HAS BUYER BEEN APPROVED? (CIRCLE ONE) YES   NO

11. ARE THERE ANY OTHER ASSOCIATJONS OR CLUBS IN WHICH THE REFERENCED UNIT HAS MEMBERSHIP OR FINANCIAL OBLIGATIONS? (CIRCLE ONE) YES NO

    IF YES:
    NAME OF ASSOCIATION/CLUB: _____

    CONTACT PERSON: _____

    PHONE: _____   FAX: _____   EMAIL: _____

    NAME OF ASSOCIATION/CLUB: _____

    CONTACT PERSON: _____

    PHONE: _____   FAX: _____   EMAIL: _____

12. MASTER INSURANCE POLICIES INFORMATION:

    HAZARD: NAME OF AGENT: _____

    ADDRESS:_____

    CONTACT PERSON: _____

    PHONE: _____   FAX: _____   EMAIL: _____

FLOOD: NAME OF AGENT: _____

ADDRESS:_____

CONTACT PERSON: _____

PHONE: _____ FAX: _____ EMAIL: _____

13. IS THERE A RECREATION LEASE?   (CIRCLE ONE) YES   NO

IF YES, WHAT IS THE RECREATION PAYMENT? $_____

14. IF A LEASEHOLD INTEREST, TS THERE AN EXISTING LEASE? YES NO

IF YES, WHAT IS THE LEASE PAYMENT? $_____

IS THIS PAYMENT INCLUDED IN THE MAINTENANCE? YES   NO

PLEASE COMPLETE THE FOLLOWING INFORMATION:

YOUR NAME: _____   YOUR TITLE: _____

YOUR PHONE: _____   YOUR FAX: _____

YOUR ADDRESS:
DATE:

Sample Bid Scope of Work
(To be filled out by listing agent)

Dear Contractor, please provide bid per items described below. If any items are unclear, please call me to clarify.

PROPERTY INFORMATION:

Address: _____

Lot: _____

Block: _____

1. FLOORING
1. Carpet Replace
2. Vinyl Replace
3. Tile Replace
4. Wood replace
5. Other (Describe)

TOTAL FLOORING

2. PAINT/INTERIOR   Materials   Labor Only
1. Interior Pain
2. Interior drywall repair
3. Interior construction
4. Wallpaper removal
5. Mirror or medicine cabinet
6. Other (Describe)

TOTAL PAINT/INTERIOR

3. EXTERIOR

1. Complete exterior paint
2. Pressure wash
3. Decks
4. Windows, Screens
5. Exterior Doors, Hardware
6. Siding Only
7. Fence Repairs
8. Other (Describe)

TOTAL EXTERIOR

4. APPLIANCES

1. List and Describe
_____
_____
_____
_____

5. ELECTRICAL REPAIRS
1. Fixtures
_____

2. Breaker Panel
_____

3. Outlets
_____

4. Meter
_____

5. Other (Describe)
_____

6. HEATING & AIR

1. Water Heater
2. External AC
3. Internal AC
4. Furnace
5. Other (Describe)
_____

7. ROOF
1. Inspection
2. Repair
3. Replace
4. Permits
_____

8. PLUMBING AND CARPENTRY
1. Leaks
2. Fixtures
3. Faucets
4. Bathrooms
5. Cabinets
6. Doors
7. Other (Describe)
_____

BPO Photo Checklist

☐ Exterior Front

☐ Rear View

☐ Street view (multiple views)

☐ Picture of the street intersection

☐ Picture of any highways or commercial buildings that are in direct view from subject

☐ Entrance View

☐ At least 2 pictures of every room (bathroom and bedrooms)

☐ At least 2 pictures of every area (dining area, living area, etc.)

☐ At least 2 pictures of the kitchen

☐ Picture of each appliance

☐ Washer & Dryer

☐ Breakfast Nook

☐ Den

☐ Stairs

☐ Picture of Balcony and/or Door leading to Balcony

☐ Picture of balcony view (left, middle, right)

☐ Backyard

☐ Interior AC Handler

☐ External AC Unit

☐ Water Heater

☐ Breaker Panel

☐ Electrical Meter

☐ Any damage to the property

☐ Include a picture for each repair you recommend

☐ Pictures of the warning signs you have placed around the property

☐ Pictures of all three comparable closed sales

☐ Picture of all three competitive listings

☐ Picture of personal property—added to the end—with estimated garage sale value of each item

About the Authors

Aram and Tim are the two top leading REO listing agents in the country. Collectively they have closed over 2,000 REO properties and produced over $5 million a year in gross commission income consistently. Also known as the "REO Brothers," they are both natural entrepreneurs as their talents lay in starting, expanding, and developing business.

Both Aram and Tim share their hot real estate tips at various real estate conferences, conventions, podcasts, real estate radio shows, live seminars, and television debates. You can follow them on Twitter @reobrothers.

ARAM SHAH

Aarambh "Aram" Shah is a bonafide entrepreneur, coach, mentor, and consistent million-dollar producer. Aram is a direct REO listing broker for various banks throughout the United States, a Realtor®, and a member of the Council of Real Estate Brokerage Managers (CRB). In the past seven years, Aram has participated in hundreds of real estate ventures and coached tens of thousands of real estate agents across the country on how to maximize profits in their REO business. Aram holds a Master of Arts in Mass Communication degree and a Master of Science in Entrepreneurship degree from the University of Florida.

TIM SHAH

Antim "Tim" Shah is a licensed real estate agent, coach, investor, and Realtor®. Tim is a direct REO listing agent for various banks throughout the United States. Tim has also participated in over $50 million of real estate ventures and has trained thousands of real estate agents on investing in single family houses, condos, townhomes, and duplexes. Tim holds a Master of Business Administration degree from Florida State University.

Download the
REO BROTHERS'(™) Glossary
and *REO Boom* index at
www.reobook.com